FREEDOM *in* CHRIST

LEADER'S GUIDE

A 10-Week Life-Changing Discipleship Course

NEIL T. ANDERSON & STEVE GOSS

BETHANYHOUSE

a division of Baker Publishing Group
Minneapolis, Minnesota

Published by Bethany House Publishers
11400 Hampshire Avenue South
Bloomington, Minnesota 55438
www.bethanyhouse.com

Bethany House Publishers is a division of
Baker Publishing Group, Grand Rapids, Michigan

Printed in the United States of America

ISBN 978-0-7642-1952-8

Cover design by Rob Williams, InsideOutCreativeArts

Men, women, and middle and high school students have been radically transformed. The prayers of repentance and the experience of God's cleansing and forgiveness have broken the grip of sin and have caused hearts to be healed and restored. Thanks be to God — our church and community are forever changed.

Bob Huisman, Pastor, Immanuel Christian Reformed Church, Hudsonville, MI, USA

One of the most satisfying and rewarding things in running the *Freedom In Christ Course* is the joy of seeing how the life-transforming Spirit-led teaching opened the eyes of participants' hearts to receive the eternal truth of God that sets us free to live the full life in Christ as his disciples. I recommend it highly to anyone serious about discipleship in the church.

Chuah Seong Peng, Senior Pastor, Holy Light Presbyterian Church, Johor Baru, Malaysia

The *Freedom In Christ Course* changed me and put me in a position to minister to people in a much more effective way. It really changes the way Christians think about themselves. God uses it restore people's lives and to deliver them from a lot of baggage, strongholds, and religion. The course is now the main part of our discipleship program and is a requirement for members wanting to become part of any ministry as well as for couples planning to get married.

Frikkie Elstadt, Every Nation Patria, Mossel Bay, South Africa

Increasingly, new Christians are carrying huge amounts of spiritual baggage, hurts, and strongholds. Traditional discipleship material focusing on growth, gifts, and giving was not getting through. We have seen folk suddenly being propelled forward at a rate unseen before. This is a very balanced, Biblically-based, well-presented course that God is powerfully using.

Sam Griffiths, Wellington Baptist Church, Somerset, UK

Our church has changed as a result of this course. Those who come to Christ and who do the course end up with a rock solid start to their faith. We have also seen people come to faith through it and get very well established by knowing their true identity.

Pastor Sam Scott, Eltham Baptist Church, Australia

We have a vision for many small groups in our church and throughout our region. The *Freedom In Christ Course* has proved to be excellent in helping us fulfill that vision. We have been using it for many years and God has used it to start a lot of new groups.

Barnabás Balogh, Baptist Church Pastor, Szeged, Hungary

I stopped teaching and preaching in the church for three months and concentrated totally on the *Freedom In Christ Course*. It lays a foundation as a wise master builder on which others can build. It is the pure milk of the Word that everyone needs to grow.

Korush Partovi, Pastor, Iranian Church, Isparta, Turkey

We've been doing the *Freedom In Christ Course* for several years. It's a great tool that can help people to apply the truths of the Word of God to their own lives in a practical way. We have seen great freedom as a result of realizing and applying these principles, destroying strongholds and negative mindsets that had been there for years. I highly recommend it to every one.

Alessandro Gatti, Pastor, Baptist Church, Casorate Primo, Italy

Our people have been encouraged and motivated to move up a gear. Many shared that they feel somehow "different" and are experiencing a deeper sense of inward freedom. It has brought unity into our church like never before.

Elizabeth Byrne, Hacketstown Christian Centre, Co. Carlow, Ireland

The *Freedom In Christ Course* helps the individual to understand that most of his problems are rooted in the *way he thinks*. Then, it provides him with the tools to renounce the unhealthy thought patterns and the lies of the enemy by applying the Word of God, by the help of the Holy Spirit. It results in overcoming weaknesses, breaking bondages, and living in the freedom of Christ.

Gevik Hairapetian, Pastor, Persian Speaking Church, Venlo, Holland

Even after growing up in the church, studying at a Christian college, and finishing a year of seminary, I had never been taught the Scriptural principles I learned through the Freedom In Christ materials. Knowing my identity in Christ and understanding the spiritual battle helped me overcome anger, depression, and addiction through the power of Christ. After 20+ years of full-time pastoral ministry, I can honestly say I wouldn't have made it this far, or helped as many people, without the message and ministry of FICM.

Dan Studt, Pastor, Praxis Church, Syracuse, NY, USA

As a pastor, I have read many resources on freedom and discipleship. The Freedom In Christ resource is well written and relevant to every church, no matter what denomination. It really helps church members to know their true identity in Christ and reclaim their freedom in Him.

Rev. Abel A. Akinbode, Zion Baptist Church, Oketunji Area, Osogbo, Osun State, Nigeria

Those of us who have received the teaching and had a Freedom Appointment have been changed by the profound nature of the teaching of God's Word on who we are in Christ, and what this means for us and the church. We highly recommend FIC to churches looking for a teaching of the Gospel that will disciple and change the hearts of church members, so that they are free to look outwards and help build God's Kingdom.

Aidan Tod, St. Josephs Roman Catholic Church, Guildford, UK

We are spiritual beings who need spiritual freedom. But we may not experience it to the full if we fail to resolve our inner spiritual conflicts, such as unforgiveness, sinful practices, believing lies about ourselves and God. This course enabled me to identify and resolve these conflicts.

Dainis Pandars, Preacher, Trinity Baptist Church, Ogre, Latvia

It has given us the tools for spiritual growth and imparts a sense of personal responsibility in being a disciple of Jesus.

Helcio & Angela Lange da Silva, Evangelical Church, Mondim de Basto, Portugal

The material is not new but is good old-fashioned Christianity. What Neil Anderson and Steve Goss have done is to package it in a very accessible and usable way.

Nick Cooper, Pastor, Frome Baptist Church, UK

Freedom In Christ is a discipleship course that helps bring to light your identity in Christ, challenges you to tap into the power of God within you, and leads you to a life full of victories.

Steve Silberman, Director, Alternative Missions, Cofradía de Cuyutlán, Nayarit, Mexico

We are seeing lives changed by the foundational truths of who we are in Christ. I am thrilled to see people being set free and finding release from the things that have kept them in bondage! As a pastor, I highly recommend this ministry and its resources.

Darryl L. Craft, D.Min., Senior Pastor, Temple Baptist Church, Hattiesburg, MS, USA

Praise the Lord for this course! The strong Biblical teaching and truth about our identity in Christ is life-transforming. We have seen blessing with the youth and with the church and plan on using it each year. Simple as it may be, The Steps weekend always seem to bring release and change.

Colin Stephen, Resurrection and Life Evangelical Church, Shkodër, Albania

The *Freedom In Christ Course* helped us evaluate what we really believe and we now understand our Christian life and purpose much better. As a result we can talk about our faith with much more power and freedom.

András Bencze, Lutheran Church Pastor, Székesfehérvár, Hungary

We consider the *Freedom In Christ Course* to be the best material on the market to build Christians up in their walk with Jesus. It encourages personal responsibility and helps people to go deeper with God and discover His blessings. The impact on our church and community has been enormous.

Adrian Pike, Beacon Church, Camberley, UK

As a pastor I thought a great deal about how to disciple our believers in a practical way. The *Freedom In Christ Course* is an answer to my prayers.

Pastor Tekilu, Bishoftu, Ethiopia

Welcome!

Discipleship has often been seen as "teaching Christians to behave in the right way." But in his letters to the churches, the Apostle Paul does not mention anything about how to **behave** or what to **do** until the second half of each letter. In the first half, he helps us understand who we now **are** and what we already **have** in Christ. When we know these things, the rest follows: we live for God not because we feel we **have** to but because we love Him and really **want** to.

Freedom In Christ Ministries has equipped tens of thousands of church leaders to put this "identity-based discipleship" approach into practice. Our passion is to see churches full of Christians who are free, fruitful, and fearless.

I am so grateful to Dr. Neil T. Anderson for trusting me to take his amazing Biblical teaching and use it as the basis for the *Freedom In Christ Course*. I am astounded that it is now in over 30 languages and has been used to help hundreds of thousands of Christians grow as disciples.

Our aim is definitely not merely to give you a nice course to fill ten weeks of your church calendar! I hope we can work with you to develop a strategy for making disciples that will work right across your church for years to come. Our role is to create the best possible resources, put them into your hands, and assist you any way we can.

We do not offer a "one size fits all" approach but have a whole array of different resources and training. We'd love to help you select the ones that are best for your situation.

If we can help you with any matter related to discipleship, do please get in touch (page 285).

In the meantime, enjoy leading the *Freedom In Christ Course*!

Steve Goss
Executive Director,
Freedom In Christ Ministries International

Contents

Checklist Of Resources

This page contains a summary of the different publications and other elements available to run your course. You can get them from Freedom In Christ Ministries or other retailers.

For course leaders:

❑ *Freedom In Christ Leader's Guide* (this book)
We recommend that everyone leading a group has their own copy of this Leader's Guide.

❑ *Freedom In Christ DVD* or subscription to FreedomStream, our on-demand service (see page 27)
Even if you are planning to present the course yourself rather than use the video presentations, watching them aids preparation enormously.

❑ *The Steps To Freedom In Christ DVD* or subscription to FreedomStream

❑ Customisable Publicity Poster (optional)

❑ Customisable Invitations (optional)

❑ Freedom In Christ Songs And Lyric Videos (optional — see page 26)

For participants:

❑ *Freedom In Christ Participant's Guide*
Each participant will need this Guide which contains comprehensive notes for each session, Pause For Thought and Reflection questions, and the lists of Biblical truths.

❑ *The Steps To Freedom In Christ* book
Each participant will need their own copy of this booklet for the ministry component of the course.

❑ Set Of Three Biblical Truth Bookmarks (optional)
Sessions 1, 2, and 6 each have a key list of Biblical truths. Participants love having these bookmarks to keep in their Bible or stick on their refrigerator to remind them of the truths, and it's great to have them to hand out to participants.

❑ Freedom In Christ app (optional)
The comprehensive app that accompanies the course is hugely helpful to participants — see page 25 — and highly recommended. It's free to download and use with a small cost to unlock all the features.

❑ FREEDOM IN CHRIST DISCIPLESHIP SERIES books (optional)
Steve Goss has written four books that accompany the course, one to go with each section. They are straightforward and easy to read and help participants take what is taught deeper. See page 24.

Quick Start Guide

Pages 11–27 contain all the background information you will need to run the course and we recommend you read them thoroughly. On this page we've summarised the main things you will need to do and consider.

1. Register as a course leader

Simply go to: FICMinternational.org/register

It costs nothing and you will receive:
- download of PowerPoint® slides for each session
- download of logos and artwork to publicize your course
- links to the accompanying Freedom In Christ app (see page 25)
- links to the optional Freedom In Christ songs and song videos (see page 26)
- download of time calculator spreadsheet for your sessions

2. Decide how you are going to teach

In small groups, whole church, or large group?
Teach it yourself or use the video?
If video, will you use the DVD or take a subscription to the on-demand service (page 27)?
Will you use individual Freedom Appointments or an away day (page 14)?

3. Familiarize yourself with the session format

Will you use the optional Introductory session (see pages 11–12)?
Will you incorporate Session 7 into an away day (see page 11)?
Which elements of each session will you use (see pages 15–16)?

4. Understand the additional elements available

We have produced a number of optional additional elements that are designed to help participants take the truths taught into their hearts (not just their heads). You will need to familiarize yourself with them:
- FREEDOM IN CHRIST DISCIPLESHIP SERIES books (page 24)
- The Freedom In Christ App (page 25)
- Songs with lyric videos for use in the sessions (page 26)
- Songs that participants can download for personal use (page 26)
- Bookmarks with the three key lists of Biblical truths featured in Sessions 1, 2, and 6

5. Prepare your publicity material

Logos can be freely downloaded once you have registered.
Customisable posters and invitations are available from Freedom In Christ Ministries.

Freedom In Christ Ministries is always happy to offer advice to course leaders. Feel free to get in touch if you have a question (page 285).

Meet The Presenters

You can watch a 16-minute film in which the presenters of the video introduce themselves and tell you something about their journey (available on the DVD, on Freedom Stream, and on the app).

Steve Goss has a background in business and started Freedom In Christ's UK office in 1999, thinking that he could do it on Friday afternoons only. He is "still somewhat surprised" to find himself in full-time Christian ministry. Neil Anderson, Founder of Freedom In Christ Ministries, handed the international leadership of the ministry to Steve in 2012 and it now operates in around 40 countries. He and Zoë have been married for over 30 years and have two grown-up daughters and a pug. They are based in Berkshire, west of London, but travel extensively to minister on all five continents.

In the late '80s and early '90s you would have found **Daryl Fitzgerald** in a Christian hip-hop group called Transformation Crusade — he insists their music was better than their name! He and his wife Stephanie live in Nashville, Tennessee, USA, and have a passion for helping families and marriages. Daryl was a Family Pastor until 2016 when he and Stephanie joined the field staff of Freedom In Christ Ministries. They are the proud parents of five children, the three youngest of whom are in a pop, soul, and rock-n-roll band called The New Respects (which, some might say, is really quite a good name.)

Nancy Maldonado was born in the Andes mountains of Ecuador where she built forts and caught tadpoles with Rob, her childhood friend. Years later, the Swiss Alps would witness their engagement. They lived many adventures as missionaries in Spain, but they say their greatest adventure has been parenting Josue and Sofia in a postmodern secular society. Nancy is part of Freedom In Christ's international team and is specifically responsible for translating FIC materials into Spanish. She loves trying new recipes, discipling women, bright colors, and Earl Grey tea with milk.

Preparing Your Course

How can the course be used?

Most churches use the course to disciple every member (no matter how long they have been a Christian) so that a common foundation of discipleship principles is established across the church. It is flexible enough to be used in a variety of ways:

In Small Groups
In our experience, this is the most effective way to deliver the material and the material is geared toward this setting. A small group ideally needs 90 to 120 minutes per session.

Teaching In Larger Groups
The teaching can equally well be delivered to large groups which can then be divided into smaller groups for the discussion times.

Systematic Preaching With Small Group Follow-Up
The teaching content of each session can be delivered as a straight talk (in three sections lasting typically 40 minutes or so in total), either by using the video or by presenting it yourself (this Leader's Guide contains scripts for you to use as a basis for that). You could, therefore, use it as a main church teaching program, ideally with follow-up in small groups during the week.

After An Outreach Course
Many churches run the *Freedom In Christ Course* directly after an outreach course and find that most people who have been on the outreach course want to continue on to the *Freedom In Christ Course*. Even if people have not become Christians on the outreach course, they can happily go on to the *Freedom In Christ Course*, which will show them clearly in the first session the differences that take place when someone becomes a Christian. Often people make a commitment at that point.

What Is The Structure Of The Course?

The *Freedom In Christ Course* contains ten main teaching sessions which are usually run on a weekly basis.

In addition, there is an essential ministry component called *The Steps To Freedom In Christ*, which runs between Sessions 7 and 8. Most churches run this as an "away day" on a different day of the week between two normal weekly sessions. You can, if you wish, incorporate Session 7 into the away day which means you will only need nine weekly sessions.

There is also an optional Introduction Session designed to run right at the start of the course before Session 1 meaning that, if you choose to use it, your course will have eleven sessions in total. The main objective of the Introduction Session is to help people with very little Christian background understand why it is perfectly reasonable to believe that the Bible is the inspired Word of God. Whether you run it or not depends largely on the make-up of your group. If you have participants with very little Christian background or if it is a new group, you will probably want to include this session.

A description of the various sessions is set out on the following pages.

Optional Introductory Session

Introduction: Why Believe The Bible?

This optional session is designed to introduce the course and create a sense of expectation but there is one overriding thing we want to achieve: to help participants understand that it is perfectly reasonable to believe that the Bible is God's message to the people He created. Without this, as the course progresses, participants with very little Christian background may struggle to understand why we put so much emphasis on the truth in the Bible. This session pre-empts the legitimate questions they are likely to have.

Part A — Key Truths

Jesus said that we will know the truth and the truth will set us free! In the first two sessions we look at some of the key truths we need to know about what it means to be a Christian.

Session 1: Who Am I?

When Adam and Eve were created, they had life in all its fullness. They were perfectly accepted, secure, and significant. When Adam sinned, they lost their relationship with God. The result for us is that we were born physically alive but spiritually dead and with a huge need for acceptance, security, and significance. Jesus came to restore the very same life, acceptance, security, and significance that Adam and Eve had originally, and those who receive His free gift of life become brand new creations in Christ. Knowing that we are now "holy ones" who can come boldly into God's presence without condemnation changes everything.

Session 2: Choosing To Believe The Truth

Everyone lives by faith, even those who are not Christians. It's who or what we put our faith in that determines whether or not it will be effective. As Christians, it's essential that what we believe is in agreement with what God has revealed in His Word which shows us how things really are.

Part B — The World, The Flesh, And The Devil

Every day we struggle against three things that conspire to push us away from truth. Understanding how the world, the flesh, and the devil work will enable us to renew our minds and stand firm.

Session 3: The World's View Of Truth

The world tries to make us look at reality in a way that is opposed to how God says it actually is. It makes its appeal to us through "the lust of the flesh, the lust of the eyes and the pride of life." It also paints a complete but false picture of our reality — our worldview — that varies according to where and when we were brought up. When we become Christians we need to make a radical decision to stop looking at the world in the way we used to and start seeing it from God's perspective by adopting the Biblical worldview which is "how God says it is."

Session 4: Our Daily Choice

Christians have a new heart and a new spirit, but we still struggle with many of the unhelpful ways of thinking and behaving that we grew up with (a primary characteristic of what the Bible calls "the flesh"). However, we don't have to give in to the flesh. We can choose day by day and moment by moment whether to live according to the flesh's urges or according to the promptings of the Holy Spirit.

Session 5: The Battle For Our Minds

It's important to understand that we are in a spiritual battle, and that it is a battle between truth and lies with our minds as the battleground. Every day we face a battle for our minds. However, understanding how Satan works and our amazing position in Christ will equip us to win.

Part C — Breaking The Hold Of The Past

God does not change our past but by His grace He enables us to walk free of it. In this section of the course we look at how we can take hold of what Christ has done for us in order to do just that. This section includes going through *The Steps To Freedom In Christ*.

Session 6: Handling Emotions Well

We can't control our emotions directly but they are, in a general sense, the result of what we choose to believe. If we don't have a proper understanding of God and His Word, and who we are in Christ, or if we have developed faulty life-goals, it will be signaled to us through our emotions. Failure to handle emotions well may make us vulnerable to spiritual attack. The more we commit ourselves to the truth and choose to believe that what God says is true, the less our feelings will run away with us.

Session 7: Forgiving From The Heart

(often combined with *The Steps To Freedom In Christ* on an away day)

Our relationship with others must have the same basis as our relationship with God. Nothing keeps you in bondage to the past more, or gives the enemy more entrance to your life, than an unwillingness to forgive. The crisis of forgiveness is not so much between you and the person who has offended you, but between you and God. Learning to forgive from the heart sets us free from our past and heals our emotional pain. It's really for your own sake that you do it.

Leading People Through *The Steps To Freedom In Christ*

This is the "ministry" component of the course. Participants will be led through a confession and repentance process using *The Steps to Freedom in Christ*, so that they can resolve their personal and spiritual conflicts by submitting to God and resisting the devil, and thereby experience their freedom in Christ (James 4:7). It is a straightforward process that is kind and gentle. During the process participants will uncover strongholds that have developed in their thinking that they can work on in the future.

We recommend that you either take people through The Steps as a group on an away day or (the ideal) give everyone the opportunity to have their own personal Freedom Appointment. It is envisaged that this takes place between Sessions 9 and 10. Participants will need their own copy of *The Steps To Freedom In Christ*.

Session 8: Renewing The Mind

The environment in which we grew up, traumatic experiences in the past, and giving in to temptation have led to the development of "strongholds" in our minds, which prevent us living according to the truth, and we probably became aware of some of these during *The Steps To Freedom In Christ*. We can demolish strongholds by choosing actively to renew our minds to the truth of God's Word, and we will learn a strategy — stronghold-busting — to help us do this. Walking in freedom now needs to become a way of life.

Part D — Growing As Disciples

Having taken hold of our freedom in Christ, we now need to concentrate on growing to maturity. In this final section we will understand the critical importance of relating well to others, and how to ensure that we stay on the path of becoming more and more like Jesus.

Session 9: Relating To Others

The one thing that Jesus prayed for those who came after His first disciples — that's us — is that we would be one, so that the world would know that we are His disciples. His great commandment says we are to love the Lord our God with all our hearts, souls, and minds, and to love our neighbor as ourselves. A right relationship with God should lead to a right relationship with our neighbors. In this session we will consider rights, responsibilities, judgment, discipline, and the needs of others.

Session 10: What Next?

God's life-goal for us is that we become more and more like Jesus in character. Bringing our own goals into line with that will enable us to live a life of true freedom. If we want to be truly successful, fulfilled, and satisfied, we need to uncover and throw out false beliefs about what those things mean and commit ourselves to believing the truth in God's Word. In this session we will examine what we believe concerning eight aspects of our own personal lives in the light of God's Word. The purpose is to help participants understand how faith works in their daily lives, and to encourage them to stay on the path towards becoming more like Jesus.

What Are *The Steps To Freedom In Christ*?

The Steps To Freedom In Christ form the ministry component of the overall Freedom In Christ approach to discipleship. They are simply a tool that provides an opportunity for participants to put the whole of their life before God and deal with anything that might be impeding their walk with Him.

The process is based on James 4:7, "Submit yourselves, then, to God. Resist the devil and he will flee from you." Participants start by asking God to show them any area in their life where an issue needs to be resolved. They then choose to confess and repent of everything He shows them, which removes any ground the enemy may have had in their life. Very simple and gentle — but amazingly effective!

The Steps To Freedom In Christ are fundamental to the course. Please do not be tempted to skip them and make every effort to encourage all of your participants to go through them.

The very best way for participants to go through *The Steps To Freedom In Christ* is in a personal appointment where they are led through by an "encourager" with a prayer partner in attendance. It typically takes three to five hours. Offering every participant their own Steps appointment may well seem impossible if you have a lot of people in your course so personal appointments are not the only route to taking people through. It's worth saying, however, that leaders are surprised how quickly they can build a team of Steps encouragers, especially if they start by training key leaders in the church, so don't rule it out completely.

The alternative is to process The Steps as a group on an away day (or away weekend). It fits between sessions 7 and 8.

There is much more information in The Steps To Freedom In Christ section beginning on page 193.

What Changes Are There In This Version?

This is the third version of the *Freedom In Christ Course*. Previous versions have been used by well over 300,000 Christians and translated into 30+ languages. However, there is always scope for improvement and we are so grateful to leaders from around the world who fed back to us various comments on the content and made suggestions.

In making this revised version, we have endeavored to take the comments and feedback into account whilst preserving the essential elements of the original course. Every part of the course has been revised but the main changes are:

- There are now ten main sessions rather than thirteen (plus the optional Introduction Session and *The Steps To Freedom In Christ*) which makes it easier for most churches to fit it into their schedule. We have been careful to preserve the logical progression of previous versions that works so well and to keep all of the main teaching points, though some are necessarily covered in less detail. To make up for this, two additional short teaching sessions have been included on the optional app that participants can watch in their own time. These are signposted in the main teaching material.

- The notes in the Participant's Guide have been considerably lengthened in order that participants can use them to revise the material more easily and do not have to take so many notes as they go through the teaching.

- The addition of the Freedom In Christ app (see page 25) with lots of additional information, extra teaching films, daily nuggets of truth, and a "stronghold-buster builder" will help participants as they go through the course, especially in the crucial area of renewing the mind. It has a similar format (but different content) to the much-loved app that goes with *Disciple* (our discipleship course for 20s to 30s) that participants have rated extremely highly.

- An album of new songs based on the teaching in the course has been specially produced in Nashville by professional musicians who have had their own lives changed by the Freedom In Christ message (see page 26). Lyric videos are available for download (the first three are included on the DVD and in FreedomStream and the others can be purchased). Each session has had one or two songs specifically written for it which significantly enhance worship in small group settings. Participants find them really helpful in their own devotions. As they listen to the songs and use them in worship, the truths taught go that much deeper. They are also ideal for your church's general worship to help spread the key truths taught across the whole congregation.

- The Pause For Thought questions have been thoroughly revised and a new Reflection section included at the end of each session to make space for personal response to what has been taught.

- The video presentations are still available on DVD but churches can now sign up to a subscription-based on-demand service that gives online access to the video component from all of Freedom In Christ's discipleship courses for a low monthly subscription (see page 27). We are delighted to have a whole new batch of amazing filmed testimonies from all over the world to illustrate the teaching points.

- The video sections are not presented by Steve Goss alone. He is joined by Nancy Maldonado and Daryl Fitzgerald for the main teaching and by Neil Anderson for The Steps To Freedom In Christ session. Steve says, "Nancy brings a lovely female perspective and Daryl brings a great injection of vibrant African American culture. And it was wonderful to be joined by Neil for The Steps — he brings so much wisdom and experience."

What Is The Format Of Each Session?

Each session follows the same format and contains the following elements:

Leader's Notes
An introduction for the leader of the session to help you prepare.

Welcome
For small-group settings — an opening question designed to help group members develop deeper relationships with each other and, usually, to help them to start talking about the theme. During this part of the session, it's more important to encourage group participation and interaction than to do any teaching. The main objective is to build relationships.

Worship

For small-group settings. We have suggested a theme but it is only a suggestion. The main thing is that Jesus is at the center of each session. The songs specially written to accompany the course (see page 26) are very helpful in this time and the words are printed in the Participant's Guide. There are lyric videos to help people learn the songs and to accompany the worship times so that you do not need your own musicians.

Word

This is the main teaching input. It lasts around 40 minutes per session in total split into three sections, each of which is presented by a different person on the video. In addition, Pause For Thought discussions take place between the sections and a Reflection time comes at the end.

If you choose to present the material yourself, you will find the talk written out in full with some useful additional material. We recommend that you stick as closely as possible to the notes (but without reciting them parrot fashion), ideally supplementing them with illustrations from your own experience. There is a PowerPoint® presentation for each session available for you to download (just register with us to access it). The notes show the presentation slides in their correct position and indicate when to move on to the next bullet point or slide. Note that the presentations cannot be edited — our apologies to those of you who quite reasonably prefer to do that but we have found it necessary to make sure that the presentations stay absolutely faithful to the message of each session.

Pause For Thought And Reflection Times

The Word section contains two groups of Pause For Thought questions between sections and one Reflection time at the end. It is in these times that the real learning often takes place and they are of crucial importance. The Pause For Thought questions are designed to be done in groups. The Reflection times are designed to be more of a space for personal response at the end of each session, though some involve group work too. In the time plan at the beginning of each session, we have suggested timings — do guard against shortening them if at all possible. For settings where the Word section has been delivered elsewhere (for example, in a Sunday service) and follow-up only is required, you can plan a session based exclusively on the Pause For Thought and Reflection times. It is not necessary for people to do all of the questions listed. The most important thing is that they spend the time grappling with what has been taught and if that means looking at just one question in more depth, that's fine.

Witness

This question is intended to get small groups thinking about how what has been learned could impact those who are not yet Christians and to encourage them to apply it. In practice it functions like an additional Pause For Thought question and can either be used in addition to the existing questions or as a replacement. The Witness question is not included as a separate element in the time plans.

In The Coming Week

One or two suggested activities for participants to do before the next session. We especially want to encourage people to set aside a time each day to pray and read the Bible if they don't already. Please make sure, however, that participants know that the suggestions are completely optional so that they feel no pressure whatsoever to follow them. It's worth noting that the Freedom In Christ app incorporates these activities into its daily message to participants.

Note: you are unlikely to have time to include every single element. You will need to decide what works best for your setting.

What Can I Do Practically To Prepare Myself To Lead?

Go Through The Teaching In The Course For Yourself

The very best way of preparing yourself to lead the course is to go through it for yourself. You may be able to sit in on a course at another church or you could simply watch the video. Failing that, we recommend that you read the FREEDOM IN CHRIST DISCIPLESHIP SERIES of books by Steve Goss which were specifically written to accompany the course and correspond to the four course sections (see page 24) or *Victory Over The Darkness* and *The Bondage Breaker*, the foundational books written by Neil Anderson, founder of Freedom In Christ Ministries.

We also recommend *Discipleship Counseling* by Neil Anderson which provides the theological basis for *The Steps To Freedom In Christ* process as well as excellent practical advice.

Have A Personal Steps To Freedom In Christ Appointment

A critical part of your own preparation is to experience *The Steps To Freedom In Christ* for yourself. It sends a powerful message to participants that "this is for everyone" when the leader says, "I did it and I benefitted from it." Ideally, this is something that you will go through in your own church, but, if that is not possible, Freedom In Christ can often put leaders in touch with a local church that will be happy to serve them in this way, provided that it is with a view to getting started in their own church.

Work Out And Use A "Stronghold-Buster"

"Stronghold-busting" is a strategy to renew your mind, outlined in Session 8 and is a key tool that participants will take from the course. If you are able to speak from personal experience about how you have used it in your own life, the impact on participants will be that much greater.

Familiarize Yourself With The App

Participants will be encouraged to download the Freedom In Christ app. It would be helpful if you have used it and understand how it works. It is free to download and use with a small cost if you wish to unlock additional features and content. It would be particularly useful to watch the additional teaching films so that you get an overview of all of the teaching that participants can potentially receive and also to use the stronghold-buster builder section.

Register With Freedom In Christ

It's free to register with us and doing so will provide you with access to a number of helpful downloads such as the PowerPoint® presentations, logos etc. for publicity material, and a spreadsheet you can use to plan the timings for each session. Go to FICMinternational.org/user/register.

Any Other Hints And Tips?

- Leaders — set an example and send a message that "this is for everyone" by going through the teaching and *The Steps To Freedom In Christ* yourself first.
- Although the results can be dramatic, avoid portraying this as a "quick fix."
- Emphasise that every freedom-seeker will need to apply ongoing effort to maintain the freedom gained and continue to grow as a disciple.
- Take it slowly — this is not generally something that a church does as a "one-off" but becomes part of "business as usual."
- Look out for the enemy's attack — often through the least expected people.
- Surround your course with prayer — registered users can download a Prayer Action Plan to help with this and there are some suggested prayers on pages 22–23.

- Decide early on how you are going to approach running *The Steps To Freedom In Christ* (there are more details in The Steps To Freedom In Christ Session). If you decide on the away day approach, ensure that you book a suitable venue in good time and give everyone the dates as early as you can. Make sure that participants understand that this is an integral part of the course and not to be missed!

- Keep emphasising that this is discipleship for everyone — not just for "people with problems" or any other section of the church.

- Some may ask just to do *The Steps To Freedom In Christ* or say that they have to do The Steps "now." Resist that and insist that people complete the basic teaching before going through *The Steps To Freedom In Christ* — otherwise they will not know how to stand firm afterwards. If there is no course running, they could watch the video or read the FREEDOM IN CHRIST DISCIPLESHIP SERIES books but it's crucial for their ongoing freedom that they understand the key principles for themselves and don't see this ministry as "something that somebody else does to them or for them."

- "Transformed lives transform lives" — be prepared for the course to make a positive difference throughout your church and beyond as people take hold of their freedom. Think about how it could impact your community as Christians discover afresh for themselves that Jesus really is the answer to the issues out there.

- Remember that Freedom In Christ Ministries exists to equip leaders to disciple others. Don't hesitate to get in touch if you have a question or need any advice (page 285).

How Do We Get Started With Our First Course?

If you see the *Freedom In Christ Course* purely as a one-off course, your church will get benefit from it. The real lasting benefit comes, however, when churches understand and take hold of the Biblical principles behind this approach and implement them consistently so that they become part of how they "do" discipleship. Churches that take the time and trouble to lay good foundations are likely to reap benefits for many years to come. Freedom In Christ Ministries' passion is to equip churches to implement effective church-wide discipleship and has many tools you can use. Getting your first course right is crucial and here are some tips to help you do that.

Get the commitment of leadership

In our experience perhaps the most crucial factor in whether the Freedom In Christ approach to discipleship takes root as a "way of life" is the commitment of the leadership, especially the main leader. We strongly recommend that leaders go through the teaching and *The Steps To Freedom In Christ* ahead of everyone else. If your leaders are not yet fully committed we would advise you wait patiently until they are.

Get key people up to speed

You will want to make sure that other key people are with you: cell or small-group leaders; those responsible for pastoral care; and so on. Your local Freedom In Christ office runs training events and can also provide online and video-based training. FreedomStream (page 27) includes two video-based courses specifically to train your team. Alternatively, you could give them Neil Anderson's main books (*Victory Over The Darkness* and *The Bondage Breaker*) or the FREEDOM IN CHRIST DISCIPLESHIP SERIES books (see page 24) or refer them to Freedom In Christ's website. Then take them through the *Freedom In Christ Course*. In our experience you will reap huge benefits from having leaders do the whole course themselves before leading it. We well understand the time pressures and other difficulties but good preparation will stand you in good stead for years to come and lead to many changed lives.

Get experience of taking people through *The Steps To Freedom In Christ*

In an ideal situation the first people to have their own personal Freedom Appointments (going through *The Steps To Freedom In Christ*) will be leaders. They can then take other people through who in turn can take others through. You will learn as you go along that it does not depend on the skill of the encourager but on the fact that Jesus always turns up. Freedom In Christ Ministries can usually arrange for up to two leaders to have Freedom Appointments in churches who are already up and running in order that they can then go back and take others through.

Run your first course

We recommend starting small, perhaps with one or two small groups, but, if your leaders are well prepared, there is no reason why you could not introduce it to the whole church in one go if that suits you better. If you start small, you will generally find that demand for more courses builds as people see the results in the lives of others. If you run it across the whole church, you will find some who want to go through it again and others will be keen to become part of a team that will run it again. It's unusual in our experience for the course to run just once.

Set up a process for running Freedom Appointments

As you teach the material, introduce the concept of going through *The Steps To Freedom In Christ* and plan how you are going to administer appointments. As the teaching nears an end, start to offer individual appointments — gain some experience with people who are likely to be relatively straightforward before tackling those with deeper needs. We recommend you do this even if you are planning to use an away day for the bulk of participants in your course.

Build your team of encouragers

Those who have been through the teaching and had their own appointment can often become encouragers (those who lead appointments) fairly quickly so that you build a team. You can equip them by inviting them to a training event or running the online training.

Emphasize the need to make this a way of life

Put a lot of emphasis on helping people maintain the progress they have made by encouraging them to keep renewing their mind using "stronghold-busting" (see Session 8). You might run nurture groups. Encourage people to have Freedom Appointments on an annual basis just as they have an annual service for their car.

Using The Video Testimonies

One of the major advantages of using the video presentations is that they contain testimonies from previous course participants. It is often only when people see these that they start to believe that the truths being taught might actually work for them. Even if you are doing the main teaching yourself, it would be well worth showing the video testimonies to illustrate it.

We have deliberately drawn the testimonies from a variety of English-speaking countries and cultures. This means that there are a lot of different accents and it is inevitable that, at some point or other, your participants will struggle to understand what is being said. Remember that there are subtitles in English that you can switch on and off to aid understanding where an accent is particularly difficult to understand.

Leading Your Course
What Advice Do You Have For Leading A Small Group?

A good structure for an evening would be something like this:

Getting Started
Start with coffee and get people to chat and mingle for a while. You could use the Welcome question during this time.

Welcome
The Welcome question functions as an icebreaker and is designed for a bit of fun and to get people interacting at the start of the session. It works well to split people into twos or threes. There is no need to feel that you have to do any teaching at this stage. It can be helpful at this point to invite feedback from the previous session. What struck people particularly from last week? Have they benefited from what they learned during the week in any practical ways? Have they been using the app or reading the FREEDOM IN CHRIST DISCIPLESHIP SERIES books?

Worship
For small-group settings — it is recommended that someone other than the person doing the talk leads this short time of worship. Include worship songs — the songs specially written to accompany the course are the obvious ones to choose and lyric videos are available so people can sing along. The lyrics can also be found in the Participant's Guide. You could also consider reading the Bible verses out loud together.

Focus Truth and Verse
Introduce the Focus Verse and the Focus Truth for the session. There is no need to say more than is written in the Leader's Guide. Then go straight into the Word section.

Word
Play the video or start the talk, pausing for discussion at the Pause For Thought questions as indicated. If you are presenting yourself, keep an eye on time and try to resist the temptation to deviate too much from the notes so that the main points are not lost. The small group time plans for each session will help with timekeeping. Registered users can download a customisable version of these on a spreadsheet so that you can insert your own start time and adjust the timings to your own preferences.

Pause For Thought Discussions
If your group is larger than eight, split people down into sub-groups of no more than seven or eight for the discussion and mix the groups up each week. Occasionally it is helpful to split people up by gender. For variety, consider some discussions in smaller groups of three to four to allow quieter ones to talk. As a leader of a discussion group, one of your main roles is to try to get others to talk. Don't be afraid of silences and feel you have to fill them!

In addition to the questions given, you could start any Pause For Thought with the following open questions:

- What do you think about what you just heard?
- Was there anything you heard that you didn't understand or that needs further clarification?
- How do you think what you have heard applies to you?

You do not have to cover every Pause For Thought question. It can be more valuable to go into depth on one question than cover three questions in a cursory manner. Try not to let the conversation wander too far from the main points and keep an eye on the time (a suggested time for each Pause For Thought section is given at the start of each session). Draw the discussion to a close at the appropriate time by summarizing briefly. The Pause For Thought objectives in this Leader's Guide make a good basis for that summary.

Reflection Times
The point of these times is to give people an opportunity to respond to what the Holy Spirit is saying to them. Ideally they will feel like unhurried times in God's presence during which key truths sink in and people make their own response to Him. Sometimes there are discussion times in groups or activities with another person. Sometimes there are times where individuals spend time quietly with God. This can feel a little strange to some but it is good to encourage them in this. It can help to play soft instrumental worship music during these times (music with words or music that is too lively can be distracting however).

At The End
Discuss the Witness question, point out the In The Coming Week suggestion (but remember that it is completely optional), encourage people to keep using the app, and give out any notices such as the away day details.

Any Tips For Presenting From The Notes In The Leader's Guide?

The notes in the Leader's Guide are self-explanatory. There is also space for you to write your own notes. The boxes with a '+' symbol contain additional information that you may like to include.

Representations of slides from the slide presentation are shown but not at the level of individual bullet points. In the text, whenever you see this symbol ▶ it's an indication that the slide presentation should be moved on to the next bullet point or slide.

The black boxes contain additional notes and points of explanation that you may find helpful.

What Help Is There For Participants With Hearing And Sight Impairment?

The videos have optional subtitles for those with hearing impairment (also useful for those whose first language is not English).

The Torch Trust makes the Participant's Guide and *The Steps To Freedom In Christ* available in large print and braille for those with sight impairment. For details go to www.torchtrust.org.

What Help Is There For Those Whose First Language Is Not English?

The videos have optional subtitles in a number of different languages.

Personal Prayer Of Preparation

God, You're the bedrock under my feet and I depend completely on You. You protect me and clear the ground under me so that my footing is firm. You're the one true and living God. You're a tower of salvation, a shield to all who trust in You, my refuge and my deliverer.

I humbly accept Your call to lead this *Freedom In Christ Course*. On my own I can do nothing whatsoever that will make a difference but I stand in the truth that all authority in heaven and earth has been given to the resurrected Christ, and because I am in Christ, I share that authority in order to make disciples and set prisoners free.

Thank You that You have cleansed me and washed away my sin. As I declare Your Word in Your strength and power, please fill me afresh with Your Holy Spirit.

Strengthen me by Your Spirit, so that I'll be able to take in to a greater degree the extravagant dimensions of Your love and grace and pass that on to others on the course.

I declare that I have a spirit of power and love and a sound mind, and that the Word of Christ dwells in me richly. I've been made holy by Your Word of Truth. The anointing I've received from You abides in me.

Your Word is an indispensable weapon to me, and in the same way, prayer is essential in ongoing warfare. So I declare that because I've made You my dwelling place, no evil shall come upon me. Your promise is that You will give Your angels charge over all that concerns me, and You will keep me in all my ways.

I welcome the kingdom of the Lord Jesus Christ afresh today into my life, my home, my family, my work, and into all I do within the ministry of making disciples in my church.

I pray all of this in the name of Jesus Christ. Amen.

Based on: 1 John 4:4; 2 Samuel 22; Psalm 51; Psalm 19:14; Ephesians 3:16; 2 Timothy 1:7; Colossians 3:16; John 17:17; 1 John 2:27; Ephesians 3:8; Psalm 91:9–11; 2 Corinthians 4:1–7.

Team Declaration

We declare that Jesus is our Lord. He's greater than the one who is in the world and He came to destroy all the devil's works, having triumphed over him by the cross.

We declare that God has given us the *Freedom In Christ Course* at this time to share His Word, and the gates of hell will not prevail against it. The words that come out of God's mouth will not return empty-handed. They'll do the work He sent them to do.

As those who are seated in the heavenly realms, we agree that Satan and every enemy of the Lord Jesus must not in any way interfere with the running of this course. We commit the place where the sessions will take place to Jesus. We cleanse it in Jesus' name from any impure thing.

We declare that the truth of God's mighty Word will be planted and established in [name your church or organization] and that those who come will know the truth and be set free.

We will use our powerful God-given tools for tearing down barriers erected against the truth of God, and for building lives of obedience into maturity.

We announce that what God has promised gets stamped with the "yes" of Jesus. We declare that our God can do anything – far more than we could ever imagine or guess or request. Glory to God in the Church! Glory down all the generations forever and ever!

God is striding ahead of us. He's right there with us. He won't let us down. He won't leave us. We won't be intimidated and we won't worry. The battle belongs to Him!

Based on: Colossians 2:15; John 10:10; John 8:32; Matthew 16:18; Isaiah 55:11; 2 Corinthians 10:4; 2 Corinthians 1:20; Ephesians 3; Deuteronomy 31:8, 1 Samuel 17:47.

The Freedom In Christ Discipleship Series Books

Steve Goss has written four slim, easy-to-digest books specifically as optional additional reading for participants on the course. Each one corresponds to a section of the course. They prove highly effective in helping participants grasp the principles. Churches are encouraged to have the books available at the start of the course for participants to purchase if they want to. They are published by Monarch and are available from Freedom In Christ Ministries and other booksellers.

Free to be Yourself — Enjoy your true nature in Christ
Many Christians focus on trying to act as they think a Christian should act — and find that they simply can't keep it up. They either drop out or burn out. True fruitfulness comes from realizing that we became someone completely new the moment we became Christians. Now we really can be the people God always intended us to be! **Corresponds to Part A (Sessions 1 and 2) of the course.**

Win the Daily Battle — Resist and stand firm in God's strength.
If you are a Christian you are in a raging battle, whether you like it or not. Your only choice is to stand and fight or to become a casualty. Arrayed against you are the world, the devil, and the flesh. They seem formidable. However, once you understand just who you are in Christ and how your enemies work, you can expect to emerge victorious from every skirmish with them. **Corresponds to Part B (Sessions 3 to 5) of the course.**

Break Free, Stay Free — Don't let the past hold you back
Every Christian has a past. It can hold us back big-time. Those of us carrying a lot of "stuff" know that only too well. But even those who have had a relatively trouble-free existence thus far will benefit from understanding how to identify and resolve past sin and negative influences that stop us from moving on. **Corresponds to Part C (Sessions 6 to 8) of the course.**

The You God Planned — Don't let anything or anyone hold you back.
Once we have claimed our freedom in Christ, how do we remain in it and become the people God is calling us to be? How do we know what God is calling us to be anyway? Are the goals we have for our lives in line with His goals? How can we stop other people getting in the way of our growth to fruitfulness? And how do we avoid getting in their way? **Corresponds to Part D (Sessions 9 and 10) of the course.**

The Freedom In Christ App

The Freedom In Christ app is a fantastic help to participants in the course. It helps keep them motivated, encourages them to think a little every day about what is being taught, provides a really useful tool for "stronghold-busting," and has some great additional teaching on key areas.

- Enter the start date of your course and the app will send you a daily nugget of truth tailored to where you are in the course.
- Access the three key lists of Biblical truths.
- Extra teaching films:
  "*Overcoming Temptation*" (Steve Goss)
  "*Taking Personal Responsibility*" (Steve Goss)
- Powerful Stronghold-Buster Builder tool: find your Bible verses, create your stronghold-buster, and set when you wish to be reminded to use it.
- Meet the presenters: see a filmed introduction to Steve, Nancy, and Daryl.
- Extra testimony films to encourage you: there is a particularly helpful longer version of the testimony of escaping from the clutches of porn addiction used in Session 4.
- Sample the Freedom In Christ songs.
- See films of the song writers, Wayne and Esther Tester and Nicole C. Mullen, sharing why Freedom In Christ is so important to them personally and why they wanted to write the songs.
- Get the daily devotional from Neil Anderson.

The app is free to download and use. There is a small charge to unlock some of the content. Search for "Freedom In Christ" in your app store. In case of difficulty, go to **FICMinternational.org/app** where you will find the app store links.

Songs That Help Take The Truths Deeper

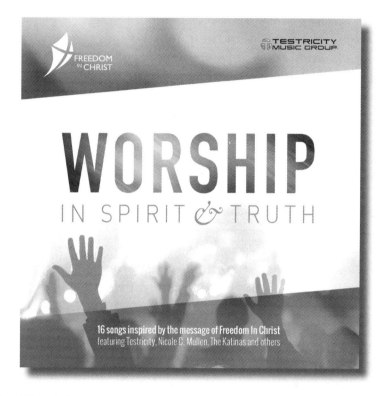

Worship In Spirit And Truth is an album of 16 powerful new songs inspired by the *Freedom In Christ Course*. These brand new songs reflect the truths taught and will help participants take them from head to heart. They will enrich your course sessions and also your church's worship. The album was produced in Nashville by Testricity Music Group and features Testricity, Nicole C. Mullen, The Katinas, and other artists. The Leader's Notes for each session contain details of the songs that go with that session.

Wayne Tester and his wife Esther Tester formed the band Testricity and the record label Testricity Music Group out of their desire to see people set free in Christ. They have written and produced over 500 songs for Universal, Garth Brooks, Disney, Dreamworks, LifeWay, and others. Wayne wrote the theme song for the Sydney Olympics which was seen by 3.6 billion people at one time and has won many awards, (Dove, Platinum records, ASCAP, etc.). But when he went through the *Freedom In Christ Course*, he realized he had issues with pride and performance and had made God's gifts an idol. So he put all of his awards in the trash and put on his eternal true identity in Jesus Christ. Their story is on the Session 3 video.

Nicole C. Mullen is a singer-songwriter who has been inducted into the Christian Music Hall of Fame. She is the only African-American artist to win a Dove Award for both Song of the Year and Songwriter of the Year. On the app she shares the story of how her son was hugely helped by Freedom In Christ's teaching.

- The songs are available for purchase on CD or download.
- The songs are also available as lyric videos to make them easy to use in worship.
  Three of the lyric videos are included on the accompanying *Freedom In Christ Course* DVD and in the FIC Video Online subscription. The others are available for purchase and download.
- The song lyrics are printed at the back of the Participant's Guide to aid in worship during your course and to enable participants to meditate on the truths in them.

For further information and to download go to: FICMinternational.org/songs

On-Demand Videos For All Our Courses

FREEDOM**STREAM**

You can access all of our video material for small groups studies online — including the teaching sessions for this course — for one low monthly subscription. Try it for free!

- Access to all the main Freedom In Christ small group courses so you can browse or use the entire range including:
  Freedom In Christ Course
  Freedom In Christ For Young People
  Disciple (the FIC message for 20s to 30s)
  The Grace Course
  Freed To Lead

- Free video training courses for course leaders and their teams:
  Making Fruitful Disciples — the Biblical principles of discipleship
  Helping Others Find Freedom In Christ — using *The Steps To Freedom In Christ*

- No need to buy several DVD sets if you have multiple groups running.

- Enable users to catch up if they miss a session.

For further information, pricing, and to start your free trial go to:
FICMinternational.org/FreedomStream

Note: features and offers may change from time to time. Please check the website for up-to-date information.

Why Believe The Bible?

Introduction: Why Believe The Bible?

FOCUS VERSE:

Hebrews 4:12: For the word of God is living and active. Sharper than any double-edged sword, it penetrates even to dividing soul and spirit, joints and marrow; it judges the thoughts and attitudes of the heart.

OBJECTIVE:

This optional session is designed to introduce the course to participants and create a sense of expectation but there is one overriding thing we want to achieve: to help participants understand why it is perfectly reasonable to believe that the Bible is God's message to the people He created.

FOCUS TRUTH:

When it comes to books, the Bible is in a league of its own and there are several very good reasons for believing that it is God's message to the people He created.

POINTERS FOR LEADERS:

This is an optional introductory session that turns Freedom In Christ into an 11-session course (plus *The Steps To Freedom In Christ* ministry component). Although every participant will find something of interest in this session, we recommend especially that you use it if you have people in your group who do not have much Christian background, for example those who may have come straight from an introduction to Christianity course.

The main sessions in Freedom In Christ assume that participants believe that the Bible is the inspired Word of God, His message to the people He created. However, not-yet-Christians and some new Christians have not yet come to that conclusion so this introductory session sets out clearly some of the reasons why that is a perfectly reasonable position to take.

The teaching in this session does not pretend to be an in-depth apologetic for the truth of the Bible. It is essential that you have thought through the questions raised in this session for yourself because some will want to talk further about them. It would be helpful to have books and other resources available that they can use to look into them in more depth. Your local Bible Society would be a good source of information on what is available. The American Bible Society can be found at americanBible.org, the UK Bible Society is at Biblesociety.org.uk, and links to equivalents in other countries can be found at unitedBiblesocieties.org.

The session is also an opportunity for people who have been on the course previously to share their own testimony about the change it has made in their lives and we suggest you find an appropriate place for that. Some testimonies appear on the video but "live" testimony can have even more impact. It would be helpful to prepare one or two people in advance to share their story. It doesn't have to be "dramatic" but should show a clear change for the better.

If you are using the video to present the course, note that there is an additional video (lasting just over 16 minutes) that introduces the three presenters, Steve Goss, Nancy Maldonado, and Daryl Fitzgerald (available on the DVD and also on the app). In our suggested timings we have included a 30-minute Welcome time which provides opportunity to show it. Or participants can watch it later on the app.

SMALL GROUP TIMINGS:

(see page 50 for further notes on the timings)

SONGS:

The song from *Worship In Spirit And Truth* (see page 26) that has been written to accompany this session is *Come Closer*. See page 207 of the Participant's Guide for the lyrics and background info.

 WELCOME

What is the best book you have ever read (apart from the Bible)?

 WORSHIP

Suggested theme: putting God right at the center of the course and opening our hearts to Him.

Read one or two of the following passages:
Jeremiah 29:11–13, Psalm 33:4–7, Hebrews 4:12

Suggest that each person turns to Philippians 1:6. Speak the verse out loud together, then ask everyone to personalize it and say in faith, "He who began a good work in me will carry it on to completion."

Encourage the group to spend a few moments thanking God for His faithfulness and opening their hearts to Him.

 WORD

▶Why Should We Trust The Bible?

What we will be talking about throughout this course is based firmly on what is written in the Bible. We can take no credit for it. We're just passing on to you what it says in the Bible.

Since that's the case, we need to ask a fundamental question before we get started on this course: ▶ Why should we trust the Bible? Some people think the Bible is simply a collection of myths and legends. Others think it's a good religious book with some wise thoughts or sayings. Others have no idea because they've never thought about it.

For some of you, the Bible might be a new book. Maybe you've only just become a Christian or perhaps you're still considering it.

Before we start, we're going to take some time to explain briefly some of the reasons why we believe it's totally rational and reasonable to believe that the Bible really is God's message to the people He created.

▶ Whatever facts and figures you look at when it comes to books, the Bible, by a long way, consistently sets itself apart. It is easily the most influential book ever written.

It always tops the best-seller lists — so much so that the best-seller lists just leave it out. Billions of copies have been printed — probably around 6 billion. However, the Bible had a head start because it was the first book ever printed.

Which book would you say has been translated into the most languages? Yes, you guessed it! How many languages? Well, let me give you a clue. The third most translated book is the fairy tale called Pinocchio and that's been translated into 260 languages. The Bible? Over 2,500 languages! The second on that list is *Pilgrim's Progress* — which is a book based on the Bible — with 2,000 languages.

The Bible contains over 750,000 words and it would take you about 70 hours to read the whole book out loud.

Even though it was written by 40 different people (from kings to fishermen) who lived over a period of 1,500 years on three different continents, the great claim of the Bible as a whole is this: it is the message of God Himself to the people He created. To quote the Bible itself, "All Scripture is breathed out by God" (2 Timothy 3:16 ESV). The word "Scripture" refers to the Bible. The idea is that, although there were many human writers, God inspired them to write what they wrote down. They wrote in their own language in their own style but what they wrote was divinely inspired and was written down for us so that we would know what God Himself wanted to say to us. If that is true, it really does make the Bible unique among all other books.

But that's quite a claim. It's an unusual claim. And I'm not expecting you just to believe it because I said it. To be perfectly honest with you I really have no interest in believing it unless it really is true.

PAUSE FOR THOUGHT 1

OBJECTIVE:

TO HELP PEOPLE UNDERSTAND THAT THERE IS SOMETHING SPECIAL ABOUT THE BIBLE.

▶ **QUESTIONS:**

When was the first time that you heard about the Bible, read the Bible, or had it read to you?

Is there a Bible passage or verse that is particularly special to you? If so, read it to the group and explain briefly why it is so meaningful.

Why do you believe — or why do you currently struggle with the concept — that the Bible is "the inspired word of God"?

Let me give you a few reasons why I am one of hundreds of millions of people who have come to the conclusion that believing that the Bible really is God's message to us is a perfectly reasonable, credible position to take based on hard evidence.

1. History Confirms The Bible

▶ The Bible contains a vast amount of historical background and information. If it is what it claims to be, you would expect that information to be accurate.

However, for many years, some experts maintained that the Biblical writers had invented a lot of that detail and that the Bible was not therefore accurate.

One of the oldest stories in the Bible relates to two cities called Sodom and Gomorrah which God destroyed. For years that was considered a myth because there was no evidence of those cities having ever existed. Yet in the mid-1970s a team of Italian archaeologists came across a library of 15,000 clay tablets dating back to around 2,500 BC and discovered that these tablets mention the two cities.

The Old Testament, the first part of the Bible, talks about a people called the Hittites over 50 times. Yet for years people did not believe that they really existed because there was no evidence for their existence outside the Bible. This was an important point because, if they really didn't exist, it calls into question the accuracy of the whole thing. Yet, during the 19th and 20th centuries, archaeologists found evidence that backed up the Bible's claims in spades (or even with spades!). They even found the Hittites' capital city, Hittusa, in Northern Turkey and a treaty between Pharaoh Ramses the Second and the Hittites. Nobody now doubts what the Bible says about them.

In the New Testament, the second part of the Bible, in the Gospel of John (John 5:2–15), John gives quite a detailed description of a particular pool mentioning that it had five covered walkways supported by columns. He says that it was a place where invalids gathered hoping for a miracle because folklore said that occasionally the waters in the pool would be supernaturally stirred up and the first one into the water when that happened would get healed. John tells how Jesus passed by the pool, got into conversation with a man who had been severely disabled for 38 years and then healed him. The man got up and walked for the first time.

To me it's very important that what John says in his description of the pool is correct. It may not be a fundamental part of the story but if it isn't true, then why should we believe his account of the miracle? You can't test the miracle scientifically but you can investigate the place and events around it historically. If it can be shown that John can't be trusted in his historical detail, then I wouldn't want to trust what he says in areas that can't be directly verified.

For centuries, there was absolutely no evidence of this pool in Jerusalem. There were other pools but they didn't have the covered walkway. However, in the late 1800s, a pool with five covered walkways supported by columns was discovered 40 feet or so underground. It was just as John described it. It came complete with an inscription about the supposed healing properties of the waters.

Putting the argument I've just used around the other way, if the authors of the Bible are proved to be accurate in their historical detail, how can we pick and choose and say they cannot be right when they report things that were out of the ordinary such as a healing just because we suppose that "it can't have happened"? That would point to a pretty closed mind wouldn't it?

The reality is that, up to now, the findings of archaeology have done nothing but verify the Bible's historical accuracy. There isn't a single case where they have disproved it. That's quite remarkable.

2. What The Bible Said Would Happen Did Happen

▶ Another thing that sets this book apart is that the Old Testament is full of predictions — prophecies — of things that hadn't happened which then amazingly took place.

Perhaps the most astonishing examples are prophecies about Jesus Christ. There are dozens of them. They predict where He would be born, what He would do, how He would be killed and how He would rise from the dead. And they all came true. But there are plenty of other examples too.

In 586 BC a guy called Ezekiel predicted the destruction of an ancient city called Tyre. He told them that God was saying this: "I will bring many nations against you, like the sea casting up its waves. They will destroy the walls of Tyre and pull down her towers; I will scrape away her rubble and make her a bare rock." (Ezekiel 26:3–4). Shortly afterwards Nebuchadnezzar began a siege that lasted 13 years. The city fell as predicted, the inhabitants fled to a fortified island off the coast and set up a new city.

Ezekiel added (in verse 12) that the invaders would "throw your stones, timber and rubble into the sea."

250 years later, Alexander the Great attacked the island fortress. In order to do so, he had to build a causeway which involved scraping the old city back to a bare rock — a specific prediction — and throwing it all into the sea.

But my favorite Old Testament fulfilled prophecy came from Jeremiah, a guy who was born around 645 BC. He along with other prophets warned the Jewish people that, if they did not

A purely scientific study of how Alexander managed to carry off the feat of breaching the offshore city's defenses was carried out in 2007 and published in the Proceedings Of The National Academy Of Science in the USA (pnas. org). Its conclusion was that he cleverly exploited a natural geographical feature (a sand spit), supplementing it with rubble from the original city to build a causeway.

turn back to God, they would be carried off into exile. This is what he actually said (Jeremiah 25:11): "This whole country will become a desolate wasteland, and these nations will serve the king of Babylon seventy years."

Just as he predicted, the Jews were carried off into exile in Babylon in 605 BC. Things in Babylon weren't too bad as it turned out. Yes, they were slaves. But they weren't generally badly treated. They did not have a bad life. They were able to settle down and get married. That sort of thing has happened many times in history. It is generally the end of that particular people group — they intermarry and are absorbed into the dominant culture.

But Jeremiah had said the exile would be for 70 years only. How likely was it that they would return to their own land as prophesied by Jeremiah? Incredibly unlikely.

Guess what happened at about year 66. Babylon, this mighty superpower that seemed absolutely untouchable, was conquered by a new superpower, the Persians, under the leadership of Cyrus.

The very next year Cyrus issued a decree permitting the Jews to return to their land. He even permitted the Jews to rebuild their temple — and paid for the work from the royal treasury. Wow!

PAUSE FOR THOUGHT 2

OBJECTIVE:

TO HELP PEOPLE NEW TO THE BIBLE SEE SOME OF THE STRIKING PROPHECIES IN IT AND ALSO TO LEARN HOW TO START USING IT.

LEADER'S NOTES:
SPLIT PEOPLE INTO GROUPS OF THREE OR FOUR. MAKE SURE EACH GROUP HAS GOT MEMBERS WHO ARE LIKELY TO KNOW THE GOSPEL STORIES WELL.

IF YOU HAVE PEOPLE WHO MAY BE NEW TO THE BIBLE, TAKE SOME TIME TO EXPLAIN A LITTLE ABOUT HOW IT WORKS: OLD TESTAMENT AND NEW TESTAMENT; HOW CHAPTERS AND VERSES WORK; HOW TO LOOK UP A REFERENCE.

RECOMMEND AN APPROPRIATE TRANSLATION FOR THEM TO BUY IF THEY DON'T ALREADY HAVE A BIBLE AND TELL THEM WHERE THEY CAN GET IT. SUGGEST THEY MIGHT LIKE TO READ A SMALL AMOUNT EACH DAY, PERHAPS STARTING WITH ONE OF THE GOSPELS.

▶ QUESTIONS:

Look up some of the following Old Testament prophecies: Micah 5:2; Isaiah 7:14; Jeremiah 31:15; Psalm 41:9; Zechariah 11:12–13; Psalm 22:16-18 and Zechariah 12:10; Exodus 12:46 and Psalm 34:20; Psalm 22:18. From your knowledge of the story of Jesus, how were these prophecies fulfilled?

"History confirms the Bible and things predicted in it later happened." How do these two things help you believe the Bible really is God's message to us?

What are some of the reasons that people dismiss the claims of the Bible?

3. The Bible's Claim That Jesus Rose From The Dead Is Credible

I don't care how fond I may be of the Bible stories about Jesus, I want to know if they're just a fairy tale, if they're the combination of some fact and a lot of fiction, or if they're actually true.

▶ The defining claim of the New Testament is that Jesus Christ rose from the dead. This is a startling claim, and many may simply dismiss it as impossible without even looking at the facts. But those with a genuinely open mind will surely want to look at the evidence.

Well, let's look at it! The medical evidence seems to indicate that Jesus was, in fact, dead before He was put in the tomb — professional Roman soldiers with plenty of execution experience gave this verdict. It seems equally clear from the evidence that three days later His tomb was indeed empty. Even the authorities admitted it and said that the disciples must have stolen Jesus' body.

Jesus appeared to His disciples a few days after being subjected to the most brutal execution method known at that time. And He seemed absolutely fine, not like someone who'd nearly escaped death. In fact He appeared to over 500 people at the same time.

Peter, one of Jesus' disciples, wrote: "We did not follow cleverly devised stories when we told you about the coming of our Lord Jesus Christ in power, but we were eye-witnesses of his majesty." (2 Peter 1:16).

Even more convincing for me is that many of those eye-witnesses went on to die for their belief that Jesus rose from the dead. Peter himself was crucified upside down at the spot where St. Peter's in the Vatican now stands.

You don't go to your death for something that you're not absolutely certain about, do you?

4. The Church Has Never Stopped Growing

Finally, to determine if the Bible is trustworthy, you can look at the people who follow the Bible. If it is God's Word, then its teachings would have an effect on their daily lives — which in turn would lead to more and more people wanting to join them. Is that happening? Is the Church growing?

Around the turn of the millennium, a group called the Lausanne Statistical Task Force launched a study of the available historical evidence to estimate how many real Christians there have been in the world throughout the history of the church. They weren't interested in saying,

> **i** This important research by the Lausanne Statistical Taskforce is not easy to find. It is quoted in *Be A Hero: The Battle For Mercy And Social Justice* by W. Campbell and S. Court (Destiny Image 2004), p. 156.

"That's a Christian country" and counting everyone in it. Instead, they estimated the number of people committed to follow Jesus.

► Their conclusions might surprise you. The worldwide church took until 1900 to reach 2.5% of the world population. Then, in just 70 years it doubled to reach 5%. In the next 30 years — between 1970 and 2000 — it more than doubled again to reach 11.2% of the world population.

Back in the early 1800s, when the world population reached 1 billion, there would have been around 20 million Christians. Right now with the population heading rapidly for 7.5 billion, we get that many in just a few months. About a million people a week are becoming Christians. In fact, there are probably more Christians alive right now than have ever lived and died throughout the whole of history.

The Church is the most dynamic organization the world has ever seen. It's never stopped growing and is growing faster today than ever before.

Now, if you live in a Western country, you may be shaking your head because the church has been in decline here in recent decades. But, that's a historical anomaly which is outweighed by the growth elsewhere. In just about every developing country, the Church is growing.

Let's take Communist China, for example, where despite Government opposition, 28,000 people a day are becoming Christians. There are 80 to 100 million in total there now. There are more Christians in China than members of the Communist party.

Look at Africa — the number of Christ-followers there has risen from three in a hundred a century ago to 45 in a hundred today.

Over the last few decades, South Koreans have been flocking to Jesus by the million. The UN has officially reclassified it from a Buddhist nation to a Christian one.

Jesus predicted all this in the Bible. He said, "I will build my church, and the gates of Hades will not overcome it." (Matthew 16:18)

i The *Operation World* book and resources are good sources of information on the spread of Christianity in different countries. See operationworld.org.

5. The Truths In The Bible Change Lives Today

As I said before, I'm really not interested in believing this stuff if it's not true.

But if the Bible is true, you'd expect to see an impact in people's daily lives too. Let's hear what happened to some people after they came to Freedom In Christ and accepted the challenge to believe the Bible and put their trust in Jesus.

[Do you have some people who could give testimonies here? Alternatively use the video testimonies or quote from the letters on page 49.]

Those of us who believe that the Bible consists of a message from God Himself are not taking some blind "leap of faith." There is a perfectly logical and reasonable basis for what we believe. We've only had time to skim the surface, but there are plenty of resources available if you want to find out more.

About The Rest Of The Course

Why is this so important? Because, if the Bible is true, then we'll find the principles it gives us for living truly life-changing. And so they are.

Do please join us for the rest of the course where we'll be looking at some straightforward principles from the Bible. The focus won't be a bunch of rules — do this, don't do that, no. Our focus will be what we **believe**, not so much how we **behave**. Because when we get that right, our behavior will come into line. Jesus said, it is when we know the truth that we will be truly free (John 8:32).

We will learn how becoming a Christian is the defining moment in our lives, how we became brand new people from the inside out; and how that means we can come to God any time we like without fear; how nothing we do can make God love us any more or any less.

We'll find out how we can resolve the effects of even the deepest issues from the past; how we can deal with repeating patterns of getting stuck in stuff we'd rather not be in.

We'll get to understand what God's purpose is for our life. It may not be what you think.

These principles have certainly changed my life. And so many others have told us that their lives have been changed too. We're really excited about sharing them with you. ▶

REFLECTION

OBJECTIVE:

TO GIVE AN OPPORTUNITY FOR PARTICIPANTS TO AFFIRM TO GOD THEIR COMMITMENT TO HIS WORD.

LEADER'S NOTES:
THERE IS A "REFLECTION" TIME AT THE END OF EACH SESSION. THE EMPHASIS IS ON AN INDIVIDUAL MAKING A PERSONAL RESPONSE TO GOD RATHER THAN ON GROUP DISCUSSION. PLEASE FEEL FREE TO LEAD PEOPLE IN THIS TIME IN A WAY THAT THEY WILL FEEL COMFORTABLE WITH BUT DO MAKE SURE THEY HAVE SPACE TO MAKE A PERSONAL RESPONSE.

YOU MIGHT LIKE TO PLAY SOME INSTRUMENTAL MUSIC SOFTLY IN THE BACKGROUND AS PEOPLE GO THROUGH THIS TIME.

▶ REFLECTION

Spend some time thanking God for the Bible.

Then ask Him to continue to develop in you a thirst and longing to read and understand His Word in your day-to-day life.

WITNESS

If someone told you that they thought the Bible was "just a collection of myths and legends" what would you say to them?

IN THE COMING WEEK

If you have never got to grips with reading the Bible regularly before, why not try reading a little bit each day? You could start with one of the Gospels: Matthew, Mark, Luke, or John. As you read, remind yourself of the truths we have looked at and that the Creator of the universe wants to speak to **you** through His Word, the Bible, **today**. Wow!

Part A

KEY TRUTHS

Jesus said that we will know the truth and the truth will set us free!

In the first two sessions we look at some of the key truths we need to know about what it means to be a Christian.

Who Am I?

Session 1:
Who Am I?

FOCUS VERSE:

2 Corinthians 5:17 (ESV): Therefore, if anyone is in Christ, he is a new creation. The old has passed away; behold, the new has come.

OBJECTIVE:

To realize that deep down inside we are now completely new creations in Christ, "holy ones" who are accepted, secure, and significant.

FOCUS TRUTH:

Your decision to follow Christ was the defining moment of your life and led to a complete change in who you now are.

POINTERS FOR LEADERS:

In this first session you will be helping people answer the question, "Who am I?" The way Christians respond to the question reveals what they believe about the gospel and their spiritual heritage. This is a delightful session to lead because you will see people who for years have believed that deep down they are somehow a disappointment to God start to realize the truth of what Jesus has done for them — He has changed their very nature from someone who was displeasing to God to someone in whom He delights.

Some people may struggle because they do not **feel** like a holy one. Keep emphasising that the critical thing is not what you feel but what the Word of God actually says. If you want to explore this topic in more detail, we recommend that you read *Victory Over The Darkness* by Dr. Neil T. Anderson (Bethany House).

This session contains the first of three key lists of Biblical truth that we will share with participants during the course. They can be life-transforming if people make the choice to believe them. The lists are readily accessible via the app and in the Participant's Guide. You can also order from Freedom In Christ a set of color bookmarks that many really find helpful to keep in their Bible or pin on their fridge.

If you are planning an away day after Session 7, remember to inform people of the date so that they can keep it clear. We recommend that, at an appropriate point during the session, you share testimonies from yourself or others who have been through the *Freedom In Christ Course* previously. If you are using the video presentations, some will be shown on that but it would be even more effective to supplement those with 'live' testimonies if you can. If you are not using the video and you do not yet have any testimonies of your own, you might like to read the extracts from letters sent to Freedom In Christ Ministries on page 49.

If you are using the video to present the course, there is an additional video lasting just over 16 minutes that introduces the three presenters, Steve Goss, Nancy Maldonado, and Daryl Fitzgerald (available on the DVD, and also on the app). If you didn't show it during the Introduction Session, suggest that participants have a look at it on the app.

Participants will find it beneficial to read the four FREEDOM IN CHRIST DISCIPLESHIP SERIES books alongside going through the course (see page 24). We recommend that you have some available for people to buy or refer them to Freedom In Christ's website. There are details in the Participant's Guide on page 6. At the start of each session (in the Word section) we have listed the relevant pages from the book series.

THE APP

We strongly encourage you to recommend the Freedom In Christ app to participants. It has been specifically designed to accompany participants through the course so that they really connect with the life-changing truths they will encounter.

They can enter the dates of the sessions and for seven days after each session the app will send them short daily nuggets to reinforce the teaching in that week's session.

It also contains additional teaching films on important areas such as handling temptation and working out who is responsible for what in the Christian life.

One of the key features is the Stronghold-Buster Builder. Stronghold-busting is a tool to help participants renew their mind which is taught in Session 8. The app will prompt participants to use their stronghold-busters on a daily basis.

It also gives participants access to the Freedom In Christ Daily Devotional, a year's worth of daily encouragements that will remind them of the principles they will learn on the course.

It's available as a free download giving access to the first three sessions and the lists of Biblical truth. There is a small charge to unlock the other sessions. Try it for yourself first! See page 25 for more details.

TESTIMONIES

The following are extracts from communications sent to Freedom In Christ Ministries. They can be read out as testimonies of people's experiences on the course if you do not have any of "live" testimonies of your own yet and are not using the video.

1. "I can truly say that, after finding Jesus as my Savior, entering into the fullness of my spiritual freedom in Christ has been the most significant moment of my life — I recommend it."

2. "Finding my freedom in Christ has changed my life."

3. "I have been a Christian for many years, been to all the right meetings, done the right actions, worn all the T-Shirts! For a long time now I have been feeling quite despondent, thinking that there must be more to church life than this, and that if I were prayed for by the right person or had a 'dramatic experience or manifestation' then I would be more spiritual and would be a better Christian.

But listening to all the teaching last week I began to realize that actually I already knew all the truths that were spoken and this was so encouraging.

Then on Saturday going through *The Steps To Freedom In Christ* I didn't actually 'feel' anything, but later realized that I didn't have any deep-seated issues that needed dealing with (only a few minor ones) as they had already been dealt with by God before. I just hadn't believed it. Any other issues I now know how to deal with. I wept through our worship time on Sunday morning."

4. "I wanted to contact you with thanks and praise! For the first time, I went to bed last night just praising God, telling him that I loved him. And I woke up this morning with my heart full and pounding with his love.

The truths that I encountered in the course were liberating. Although much of it I 'knew,' it was not true in my heart. I was separated from the truth of God's love and Jesus' liberation by a large wall of pain, wounds, and lies — so many lies about God. But the wall came tumbling down this week."

SMALL GROUP TIMINGS:

The following plan is designed to help those leading the course in small groups. It assumes a meeting of around two hours in length and suggests how long each part of the session should last and also indicates the cumulative elapsed time (in minutes). You will find a time plan in each session.

Welcome	12 minutes	12
Worship	12 minutes	24
Word part 1	14 minutes	38
Pause For Thought 1	18 minutes	56
Word part 2	14 minutes	70
Pause For Thought	88 minutes	88
Word part 3	15 minutes	103
Reflection	17 minutes	120

Note:

The time allocated for the Word sections is based on the length of the corresponding section of the accompanying video sessions.

The Witness section is not included in the time plan as it tends to be used in place of a Pause For Thought section. You will need to add on five to ten minutes if you want to include it separately.

Registered users of the course can download a spreadsheet with these timings. Simply enter your own start time, adjust the length of the various components as desired, and you will have a timed plan of your session.

SONGS:
The song from *Worship In Spirit And Truth* (see page 26) that has been written to accompany this session is *That's Who I Am* (Part One of Four). See page 208 of the Participant's Guide for the lyrics and background info.

If this is a new group you might like to extend this time and ask the pairs to introduce each other to the whole group.

WELCOME

Spend a couple of minutes in pairs finding out as much as you can about each other. Then, in no more than 30 seconds, answer this question about your partner. "Who is he/she?"

WORSHIP

Suggested theme: God's plans and promises.

Read one or two of the following passages: Psalm 33:10–11, Job 42:2, Proverbs 19:21

Suggest that group members speak out in worship and praise the attributes of our God — for example, wisdom, sovereignty, holiness, faithfulness — or God's various names.

WORD

I highly recommend you download the Freedom In Christ app which will really help you as we go through the course.

Before we begin the session, let me recommend two ways you can reinforce the Biblical principles we will consider.

There is an accompanying app that you are likely to find very helpful. You might like to go to your app store and search for "Freedom In Christ" right now. It's free to download. You can enter the date of today's session and for seven days it will give you some short nuggets of truth to consider. It also contains some extra teaching films and a lot of other features that I'll mention in due course. The first three sessions are free and there's a small charge to unlock the others. See page 7 in your Participant's Guide for more information.

In case of difficulty finding the app, participants can go to FICMinternational.org/app to get the correct link.

Also, Steve Goss has written four short books, collectively known as the Freedom In Christ Discipleship Series, that correspond to the four parts of the course (see page 6 in your Participant's Guide). The first in the series, *Free To Be Yourself*, corresponds to Part A of the course (the first two sessions). Read up to page 59 in the book for the material that relates to this session.

Welcome to Freedom In Christ!

In your Participant's Guide there are notes you can use as we go through each session. This session starts on page 21.

▶   Our focus over these ten sessions together is making sure that we really *experience* the truth in God's Word, not just as "head knowledge" but in our hearts.

Who Are You Really?

Perhaps the most fundamental truth we need to know is who we are.

So, who are you?

It sounds like a simple question.

▶   If you were to meet me at a party and say "Who are you?" I might say "Well, I'm [name]." But you might rightly point out, "No, that's just your name. Who are you?"

"I am a [job title]." "No, that's what you do."

"I'm [nationality]." "No, that's where you were born or where you live."

Is this person that you are looking at really me? [List some physical characteristics: height, hair color, etc.].

▶   You could put me on an operating table to try to find out who I really am.

▶   If you chopped off one of my arms, would I still be me?

▶   If you chopped off one of my legs as well, would I still be me?

What if you transplanted my heart, kidneys, and liver, would I still be me?

Where am I then? If you keep chopping will you eventually find me? I must be in here somewhere!

The question is: what makes up the real "me," the real "you"?

The Original Design

You Were Created In The Image Of God

► The Bible says that we were made "in God's image" (Genesis 1:26), and God is spirit.

So at the most fundamental level of our being we too have a spiritual nature. It is not our body, our outer person, that is created in the image of God; it's our inner person.

"God is spirit" — John 4:24. "Jesus answered, 'Very truly I tell you, no one can enter the kingdom of God unless they are born of water and the Spirit. Flesh gives birth to flesh, but the Spirit gives birth to spirit.'" — John 3:5-6

There's a TV series in which celebrities trace their family tree. It seems that every family has its share of success, shame, and secrets. In the TV series, people have become very emotional as they found out about their ancestors as if this additional knowledge somehow helps them understand themselves a little better.

But if we really want to understand why we are as we are and why we have the in-built drives that we do, we need to go a lot further back than that and start with the couple that we are all descended from.

► Scientists confirm that our mitochondrial DNA proves that we are all descended from the same woman and our Y-chromosomes prove that we are all also ultimately descended from the same man. Look around the room. . . . We're all related to each other. . . . What a terrible thought!

The Bible tells us that our ultimate ancestors were called Adam and Eve. Christians disagree about exactly how God created them but we all agree that God inspired their story to be written down to communicate some very significant truth.

Adam's spirit — his inner person, the core of his being — was connected to his body. In other words he was physically alive. Just as we are.

But Adam's spirit was also connected to God. Which meant that he was also spiritually alive.

That is how we were designed to be too: on the one hand our spirit is connected to our physical body, and on the other hand our spirit is connected to God.

Note: Some theologians believe that the human spirit and the soul are the same thing. Others believe that the human spirit is distinct from the soul. From this point on we will tend to use the term "inner person" that incorporates both concepts.

This spiritual life, this connection to God gave Adam three very significant things:

▶ 1. Acceptance

Adam had an intimate relationship with God. He could talk with Him at any time and have His full attention.

▶ 2. Significance

Adam was given a purpose for being — to rule over the birds of the sky, the beasts of the field and the fish of the sea (Genesis 1:26).

▶ 3. Security

He was totally safe and secure in God's presence. Everything he needed was provided for — food, shelter, companionship — everything!

Here's the key thing to get hold of. You were created for that kind of life: complete acceptance by God and other people; significance — a real purpose; and absolute security — no need to worry about a single thing.

The Consequence Of The Fall

Adam and Eve were told, "You must not eat from the tree of the knowledge of good and evil, for when you eat of it you will surely die" (Genesis 2:17). They did eat. Did they die? Physically? No. Physical death did eventually come but not until 900 years later. They died spiritually.

The connection that their spirit had to God was broken and they were separated from God. Consequently, all their descendants including you and me were born physically alive but spiritually dead.

▶ The acceptance they enjoyed, that amazing intimate moment-by-moment relationship with God, changed into a crushing sense of rejection, and we all know that feeling.

That sense of significance was replaced by a sense of guilt and shame and we're all born with it.

This little piece of wisdom comes from the internet:

> If you can start the day without caffeine or pep pills,
>
> If you can be cheerful, ignoring aches and pains,
>
> If you can eat the same food every day and be grateful for it,
>
> If you can conquer tension without medical help,
>
> If you can relax without alcohol,
>
> If you can sleep without the aid of drugs,
>
> Then you must be the family dog.

Dogs don't seem to have this need to feel significant, to make their life worth something. In fact as long as they can eat, sleep, and sniff other dogs occasionally, they seem quite happy. I've tried it and it's not enough for me!

▶ And that sense of security turned to fear. The first emotion expressed by Adam was, "I was afraid" (Genesis 3:10). "Don't be afraid" is the most repeated commandment in the Bible.

So all of us are born into an environment that's not at all like the one we were designed for.

▶ But instinctively we want to find our way back to the acceptance, significance, and security we were meant to have.

It is often said that the command "Do not be afraid" appears 365 times in the Bible, one for every day of the year.

That would be a nice concept — if it were true! In fact there are about 170 occurrences.

PAUSE FOR THOUGHT 1

OBJECTIVE:

TO GET PEOPLE TALKING AND TO START TO REINFORCE THE IMPORTANT CONCEPT THAT ADAM AND EVE WERE ORIGINALLY COMPLETELY CONFIDENT IN THEIR SIGNIFICANCE, SECURITY, AND ACCEPTANCE BUT LOST THOSE THINGS.

▶ QUESTIONS:

What prompted you to come to the *Freedom In Christ Course* and what are your hopes for it?

What were the consequences of Adam and Eve's sin? What are the ways it caused their relationship with God to change?

What sort of things in our daily lives promise to make us feel accepted, significant, and secure?

What Jesus Came To Do

The only solution to the predicament that we've looked at is to restore our relationship with God, to become spiritually alive again. That's why God sent Jesus.

Jesus was like Adam at the very beginning — He was both physically and spiritually alive. But unlike Adam, Jesus never sinned. He showed us how a spiritually alive person can live in this fallen world if they live dependently upon their heavenly Father.

However, Jesus came to give us more than an example, He came to . . . well, why did He come? What would you say?

Most people say, "He came to forgive my sins" and, yes, that's true. But that was just a means to an end. What if we asked Jesus? Actually someone did and Jesus Himself said,

▶ "I have come that they may have life, and have it to the full" (John 10:10).

Other verses in John referring to the life that Jesus came to bring: John 6:48; 11:25; 14:6.

Throughout the course the difference between Christians and not-yet Christians is shown to be a stark one. Depending on the group, it may well be worth emphasizing at this stage that you only get the "life" back if you become a Christian. You may like to say something like: "If you are not sure that you are a Christian, then it's a matter of choosing to receive God's free gift and making Him your Lord. Simply thank God that He sent Jesus to die for you when you were in a completely hopeless state and accept Him as your Lord and Savior. There'll be an opportunity to do this at the end of the session."

In some traditions it might be helpful to add: "Although we commonly use the word 'saint' to refer to a Christian role-model whose life on earth is complete, the Bible uses it to refer to Christian believers in local churches."

What did Adam lose? **Life**. What did Jesus come to give us? **Life**.

When we become Christians our spirit is reconnected to God's Spirit. At that moment we get back the life we were always meant to have with its acceptance, significance, and security.

▶ Eternal life is not just something you get when you die. It's a whole different quality of life **right now** (John 5:24).

So, who are you?

The moment you became a Christian was the defining moment of your life. Everything changed for you. And the language the Bible uses is very dramatic:

> Therefore, if anyone is in Christ, he is a new creation. The old has passed away; behold, the new has come. (2 Corinthians 5:17 ESV)

Can you be partly old creation and partly new? No!

> For you were once darkness, but now you are light in the Lord. (Ephesians 5:8)

Can you be both light and darkness? Not according to that verse.

A Saint — Not A Sinner

Many of us have come to think of ourselves as "a sinner saved by grace."

You certainly **were** a sinner, and you were saved by grace alone. But, here's an interesting verse:

> While we were still sinners, Christ died for us. (Romans 5:8)

Past tense. This verse seems to imply that we're no longer sinners.

In the New Testament, the word "sinner" appears over 300 times. But it's clearly a shorthand way of referring to people who are not yet Christians. You never see it applied to a Christian, at least not in terms of who they are **now**, only in terms of who they used to be.

There's another word that is shorthand for believers and you'll find it over 200 times. Traditionally in English this word has been translated "saint" but it really means "holy one."

Languages such as Spanish, Portuguese, Italian, and French don't have this problem — the same word still means both "holy one" and "saint."

▶ Yes, you are holy. Set apart for God. Special. At the moment you became a Christian — even if you can't pinpoint the exact moment — you became completely new in your inner person. Who you are deep down inside changed from being someone who couldn't help but displease God to someone who is accepted, significant, and secure in Christ.

Galatians 3:27 says that we have "clothed ourselves with" Christ. Perhaps you have understood that to mean that you're still the same dirty, rotten no-good person deep down inside, but it's all covered up by Christ, so that when God looks at you, He doesn't really see you, He sees Jesus.

But that's not at all what the Bible says. ▶ It's more like the story Jesus told about a son who messed up badly and came crawling back home dirty, smelly, and broken, expecting to be punished.

▶ His father unexpectedly welcomed him with open arms and within a few minutes of his arrival gave him a fine, expensive robe to wear (Luke 15:22).

▶ Did the robe make him acceptable because it covered up all the dirt? No. The dirt was on the outside. It wasn't the robe that made him a son, was it? He was given the robe because he was already a son and it was the appropriate dress for a son.

Regardless of the mess you may have made or how bad you feel about yourself, the truth is that, if you have accepted Jesus as your Lord, you are now a son or daughter of God Himself. You're righteous, clean, and holy on the inside. You can clothe yourself with Christ because at the deepest level of your being He's already made you holy. When God the Father looks at you now, He doesn't see Christ covering your mess. He sees you just as you are: His child, a new creation, holy, wonderful. And He delights in you.

[Do you have a personal story you can tell to illustrate how in your own life you came to the understanding that you are a holy one rather than a sinner?]

Understanding this is crucial, not so much for our salvation but if we want to become the people God created us to be.

The story of the prodigal son forms the basis of the *Grace Course* (Goss, Miller, Graham — Monarch 2012) which is designed as a follow-up to this course and the illustrations are taken from there.

▶ Suppose you were an orphan who became a thief and you heard one day that the king had decreed that all thieves were forgiven. Good news . . . but if that's all the decree said, would it change how you saw yourself? No — you'd still be an orphan and a thief. Would it change your behavior? Probably not. If you think of yourself as a forgiven sinner (but still a sinner) what are you likely to do? Sin! Because, by definition, that's what sinners do!

But what if the decree mentioned your name and said that the king not only forgave you, but also wanted to adopt you, wanted to make you a prince? ▶ Would that change how you saw yourself? Of course. Would it change your behavior? Of course: "Why would I ever want to go back to the life I had now that I am a prince?"

You are not only forgiven, you are adopted. You have become a son or daughter of the King of Kings!

▶ Who you are now is a **fact** and Satan can't change it. But if he can get you to believe a lie about who you are, he can cripple your walk with God.

No child of God is inferior or useless, but if Satan can get you to believe that you are, that's how you'll act.

No child of God is dirty or abandoned anymore. But if Satan can get you to believe that you are, that's how you'll act.

You might say, "You don't know what's been done to me."

It doesn't change who you are in Christ.

"You don't know what failures I've had as a Christian."

It doesn't change who you are in Christ. Jesus loved you when you were still a sinner. He's not going to stop now that you're a saint.

"But what about my future sins?"

When Jesus died once for all, how many of your sins were future? All of them!

You're not saved by how you **behave** but by what you **believe**. And life as a Christian is more of the same. It's not about trying to behave differently. It's about knowing the truth, which then works out into your behavior. This course is not about learning to behave differently but to believe differently.

PAUSE FOR THOUGHT 2

OBJECTIVE:

TO REINFORCE THE KEY TRUTH THAT WE ARE NOW HOLY ONES WHO HAVE BACK THE LIFE WE WERE CREATED TO HAVE.

▶ QUESTIONS:

John 10:10 says that Jesus came to bring us life in all its fullness. What do you think that might look like in practice?

How might knowing that we are "saints" or "holy ones" instead of "sinners" change how we see ourselves?

What are some of the things that could prevent us from fully knowing that we are now new creations in Christ who are completely forgiven?

What Happens When I Go Wrong?

One of the main problems we have with seeing ourselves as saints rather than sinners is: we are painfully aware that we still sin.

Let me tell you a secret. I snore / burp. ▶ But when I introduce myself to you, I don't have to say, "Hi, my name is [Name] and I'm a snorer / burper!" I may snore / burp but that's not who I **am**. It's what I **do** and there is a big difference between the two.

It's what we are deep down in our inner person that defines our identity, not what we do. If you are a Christian, at the very core of your being you now share in God's divine nature. We are now new creations; the old has gone; the new has come.

However, that doesn't mean that we are living in a state of sinless perfection. The Bible is clear: "If we claim to be without sin, we deceive ourselves and the truth is not in us" (1 John 1:8). We will go wrong from time to time.

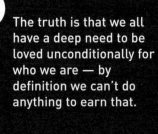

The truth is that we all have a deep need to be loved unconditionally for who we are — by definition we can't do anything to earn that.

Perhaps an accurate way to describe us would be "saints who sometimes sin."

And sin is a serious matter. It gives the devil a foothold in our lives and stops us being fruitful. It disrupts the harmony of our fellowship with God. But it doesn't fundamentally change our relationship with Him.

When you were born again, you became God's child. Spiritually speaking you received His DNA — God's own Spirit lives in you (Romans 8:9) and you now share His very nature (2 Peter 1:4). Nothing can separate you from God's love (Romans 8:39). No one can snatch you out of His hand (John 10:28). If you are truly born again, your relationship with God is settled no matter what you or anyone else might do.

Let me give you an illustration. You know the fairy tale of the princess who decided to kiss a frog? When she kisses the frog, it changes into a handsome prince. Now imagine they go out to dinner to celebrate at a fancy restaurant and suddenly a fly starts to buzz around their table. The prince leaps out of his chair and catches the fly with his tongue. Does his frog-like behavior make him a frog again? No, he's still a prince. He's just **acting** like a frog. That's how it is when we sin as Christians. It doesn't mean we have gone back to being a sinner. We are still saints. We're just **acting** like sinners.

When we do wrong, we need simply to go to our loving Father, agree with Him that we were wrong, change our thinking about the sin, turn away from it, and know our sin is already forgiven because of Christ's death.

The truth is: nothing you do can make God love you any more — or any less. If you were the only person in the whole world who needed Christ to die, He would have died just for you. That's how special you are!

On pages 33–34 of your Participant's Guide you will find the "Who I Am In Christ" list. We've taken a variety of verses from the Bible that tell us who we really are if we have decided to follow Jesus and we've put them in the "I" form. Let's read them aloud together:

▶ I Am Accepted

I renounce the lie that I am rejected, unloved, or shameful. In Christ I am accepted. God says:

I am God's child.

I am Christ's friend.

I have been justified.

▶ I am united with the Lord and I am one spirit with Him.

I have been bought with a price: I belong to God.

I am a member of Christ's body.

I am a saint, a holy one.

▶ I have been adopted as God's child.

I have direct access to God through the Holy Spirit.

I have been redeemed and forgiven of all my sins.

I am complete in Christ.

▶ I Am Secure

I renounce the lie that I am guilty, unprotected, alone, or abandoned. In Christ I am secure. God says:

I am free from condemnation.

I am assured that all things work together for good.

I am free from any condemning charges against me.

▶ I cannot be separated from the love of God.

I have been established, anointed, and sealed by God.

I am confident that the good work God has begun in me will be perfected.

I am a citizen of heaven.

▶ I am hidden with Christ in God.

I have not been given a spirit of fear, but of power, love, and self-control.

I can find grace and mercy to help in time of need.

I am born of God and the evil one cannot touch me.

I am accepted

I renounce the lie that I am rejected, unloved, or shameful. In Christ I am accepted. God says:

I am God's child.

I am Christ's friend.

I have been justified.

9 SLIDES IN TOTAL

ℹ Some may not be familiar with the word "renounce." It would be worth checking that it is understood. If you prefer, you could use an alternative such as "reject," "refuse," or "say no to."

▶ I Am Significant

I renounce the lie that I am worthless, inadequate, helpless, or hopeless. In Christ I am significant.

God says:

> I am the salt of the earth and the light of the world.
>
> I am a branch of the true vine, Jesus, a channel of His life.
>
> I have been chosen and appointed by God to bear fruit.

▶   I am a personal, Spirit-empowered witness of Christ's.

I am a temple of God.

I am a minister of reconciliation for God.

I am a fellow worker with God.

I am seated with Christ in the heavenly realms.

▶   I am God's workmanship, created for good works.

I may approach God with freedom and confidence.

I can do all things through Christ who strengthens me!

I am not the great "I Am," but by the grace of God I am what I am.

You may have been sitting here thinking "Does all this apply to me?" If you are a Christian the answer is a definite yes — but if you are not a Christian it doesn't. If you are not quite sure you are a Christian or you know you are not, it's very easy for you to make a decision to make Jesus the Lord of your life. You can do it simply by asking for the forgiveness of your sins and accepting the free gift of life He came to give. You can do that by speaking to Him in your own heart. If you want to, you can pray it with me. Let's pray: "Thank You, Jesus, for dying in my place to take away all of my sin. Right now I accept Your free gift of life. I choose to make You Lord of my life so that I can become someone completely new. Thank You that I belong to You and now I am Your child."

If you prayed that prayer for the first time, go and tell someone. It will make their day. It means that the list of Biblical facts we read now definitely apply to you.

There was a pastor who loved skiing. One season he was given a brand new electronic pass you don't even have to take out of your pocket to get through the gate to the ski lift. But sometimes when he tried to go through the gate the screen said "not valid." However, he found that if he jumped around in front of the gate long enough, it would eventually let him through. He finally discovered the problem. In another pocket in his ski jacket, he was carrying the old card from the previous year and the machine was sometimes reading the old card rather than the new one. The moment he got rid of the old card, the problem disappeared.

As a believer in Christ you now have a new card, a new identity. Get rid of your old way of thinking because your old identity has gone and your new identity has come. Begin to recognize who you really are in Christ! ▶

REFLECTION

OBJECTIVE:

TO HELP PEOPLE GRASP THE TRUTHS IN THE "WHO I AM IN CHRIST" LIST AT A DEEPER LEVEL.

LEADER'S NOTES:
HEARING SOMEONE ELSE READ THESE TRUTHS SPECIFICALLY TO YOU IS A POWERFUL WAY OF GRASPING THEM.

ENCOURAGE PEOPLE TO FACE EACH OTHER AND LOOK AT EACH OTHER AS THEY SPEAK. ASK THEM TO SPEAK SLOWLY, DELIBERATELY, AND MEANINGFULLY. SOME WILL FIND THIS A LITTLE UNCOMFORTABLE BUT IT CAN BE INCREDIBLY POWERFUL.

▶ **REFLECTION**

Get together with one other person and have the first person read the "Who I Am In Christ" statements to the other changing "I am" to "You are." Then swap around.

Spend a few minutes discussing the statements and the verses they are based on. Share which ones impacted you and why. Spend some time praying for each other, that you will have a deeper understanding that your significance, security, and acceptance are found in Him.

WITNESS

If you were asked by a neighbor to explain the difference between a Christian and someone who is not yet a Christian, what would you say? Do you think that a Christian is in any way better than a non-Christian? What would you say to someone who asks you, "Why should I become a Christian?"

IN THE COMING WEEK

Read the "Who I Am In Christ" list out loud every day. Then pick one of the truths that is particularly meaningful to you and spend some time reading it in its context and asking God to help you understand it more fully.

Who I Am In Christ

I Am Accepted

I renounce the lie that I am rejected, unloved, or shameful. In Christ I am accepted.

God says:

I am God's child (John 1:12)

I am Christ's friend (John 15:5)

I have been justified (Romans 5:1)

I am united with the Lord and I am one spirit with Him (1 Corinthians 6:17)

I have been bought with a price: I belong to God (1 Corinthians 6:19–20)

I am a member of Christ's body (1 Corinthians 12:27)

I am a saint, a holy one (Ephesians 1:1)

I have been adopted as God's child (Ephesians 1:5)

I have direct access to God through the Holy Spirit (Ephesians 2:18)

I have been redeemed and forgiven of all my sins (Colossians 1:14)

I am complete in Christ (Colossians 2:10)

I Am Secure

I renounce the lie that I am guilty, unprotected, alone, or abandoned. In Christ I am secure.

God says:

I am free from condemnation (Romans 8:1–2)

I am assured that all things work together for good (Romans 8:28)

I am free from any condemning charges against me (Romans 8:31–34)

I cannot be separated from the love of God (Romans 8:35–39)

I have been established, anointed, and sealed by God (2 Corinthians 1:21–22)

I am confident that the good work God has begun in me will be perfected (Philippians 1:6)

I am a citizen of heaven (Philippians 3:20)

I am hidden with Christ in God (Colossians 3:3)

I have not been given a spirit of fear, but of power, love, and self-control (2 Timothy 1:7)

I can find grace and mercy to help in time of need (Hebrews 4:16)

I am born of God and the evil one cannot touch me (1 John 5:18)

I Am Significant

I renounce the lie that I am worthless, inadequate, helpless, or hopeless. In Christ I am significant.

God says:

I am the salt of the earth and the light of the world (Matthew 5:13–14)

I am a branch of the true vine, Jesus, a channel of His life (John 15:1, 5)

I have been chosen and appointed by God to bear fruit (John 15:16)

I am a personal, Spirit-empowered witness of Christ's (Acts 1:8)

I am a temple of God (1 Corinthians 3:16)

I am a minister of reconciliation for God (2 Corinthians 5:17–21)

I am a fellow worker with God (2 Corinthians 6:1)

I am seated with Christ in the heavenly realms (Ephesians 2:6)

I am God's workmanship, created for good works (Ephesians 2:10)

I may approach God with freedom and confidence (Ephesians 3:12)

I can do all things through Christ who strengthens me! (Philippians 4:13)

I am not the great "I Am," but by the grace of God I am what I am (Exodus 3:14; John 8:24, 28, 58; 1 Corinthians 15:10)

Choosing To Believe The Truth

Session 2: Choosing To Believe The Truth

FOCUS VERSE:

Hebrews 11:6: Without faith it is impossible to please God, because anyone who comes to him must believe that he exists and that he rewards those who earnestly seek him.

OBJECTIVE:

To understand that everyone lives by faith in something or someone and that faith in God is no more than finding out what is already actually true and choosing to believe and act on it.

FOCUS TRUTH:

God is truth. Find out what He has said is true and choose to believe it, whether it feels true or not, and your Christian life will be transformed.

POINTERS FOR LEADERS:

In this session we hope to encourage participants to make a definite commitment to believe what God says is true no matter what their feelings tell them.

It will come as a surprise to some to realize that everybody lives by faith and that faith is simply making a choice to believe what God says rather than believing in ourselves, others, and what our feelings are telling us.

If you are teaching this yourself, note that a key part of the teaching is the sharing of personal stories that illustrate how our faith grows and how God is always faithful. Although you could simply tell the stories from Steve Goss and Nancy Maldonado that feature in the script, it would be preferable to consider what stories you could include from your own experience to replace them.

This session contains the second of three key lists of Biblical truth we will share with participants during the course. They can be life-transforming if people make the choice to believe them. The lists are readily accessible via the app and in the Participant's Guide. You can also order from Freedom In Christ a set of color bookmarks that many really find helpful to keep in their Bible or pin on their fridge.

If you are planning an away day after Session 7, remember to inform people of the date so that they can keep it clear.

THE APP

We strongly encourage you to recommend the Freedom In Christ app to participants because it really helps them take the principles taught to a deeper level. You might consider asking people who have tried it since the last session to share their experiences.

SMALL GROUP TIMINGS:

Welcome	15 minutes	15
Worship	12 minutes	27
Word part 1	13 minutes	40
Pause For Thought 1	20 minutes	60
Word part 2	10 minutes	70
Pause For Thought 2	20 minutes	90
Word part 3	15 minutes	105
Reflection	15 minutes	120

Registered users of the course can download a spreadsheet with these timings. Simply enter your own start time, adjust the length of the various components as desired and you will have a timed plan of your session.

SONGS:

There are two songs from *Worship In Spirit And Truth* (see page 26) that have been written to accompany this session: *Eyes of Faith* and *That's Who I Am* (Part Two of Four). See pages 209–210 of the Participant's Guide for the lyrics and background info.

 WELCOME

Have you had a prayer answered recently? Share the story briefly.

Do you believe that an atheist has more or less faith than a Christian? What about a Hindu or a Muslim? What about someone who "just doesn't know"?

 WORSHIP

Suggested theme: realizing just how much God loves us and delights in us.

Read one or two of the following passages:
Ephesians 3:16–19, Zephaniah 3:17, 2 Corinthians 3:18, Hebrews 12:1–2

Suggest that each person turns to Psalm 103:8–17 and reads it quietly. Then encourage people to speak out the truths of God's amazing, unfailing, and unchanging love for us and thank Him for them.

WORD

If you are reading the FREEDOM IN CHRIST DISCIPLESHIP SERIES books, read pages 60–93 of *Free To Be Yourself* for the material that corresponds to this session.

Choosing To Believe The Truth

SESSION 2

So, who are you? ▶   As we saw in the last session, if you know Jesus, you are a holy one. Whether it feels like it or not!

Does God love you? Yes! If you performed better, would God love you more? No. Does God love me more than you? No, He doesn't. God's love has nothing to do with what we **do**. It doesn't make any difference whether you perform great one day, and mess up the next. God will still love you because that's His nature. He is love. He couldn't not love you.

However, God's love for you on its own doesn't mean that you will be the person He wants you to be and that you will do the things that He has prepared for you. That's all about the choices you make. And the choices you make come down to what you believe; what you really believe, not necessarily what you think or what you say you believe. If you want to know what someone really believes, don't listen to what they **say** but look at what they actually **do**.

Faith Is Simply Believing What Is Already True

The Bible tells us: "Without faith it is impossible to please God" (Hebrews 11:6).

But what is faith? One little boy put it like this: "Faith is trying hard to believe what you know isn't really true!" Sounds reasonable but actually it's the very opposite of that. Faith is just finding out what is **already** true and making a choice to believe it.

▶ Look at the story in 1 Samuel 17 where the Israelites were in a battle with the Philistine army. The Philistines were saying, "We don't want a blood-bath. Just have your best soldier fight our best soldier one-on-one, and the winner takes all." Well, the Philistines thought they were setting a trap because they had a secret weapon, a giant called Goliath. They thought no one could fight against him and win. The Israelite army was completely afraid.

But then comes a young boy, David, pulls out his sling, and says, "How dare you challenge the armies of the living God?" and kills Goliath.

David and the Israelite army were threatened by the same situation. The Israelite army saw the giant in relationship to themselves and were in a panic.

▶ But David saw the giant in relationship to God and was at peace. Who saw the situation as it really was? David. He saw what was actually true!

Faith is simply recognizing what is already actually true.

As Christians we want our life to matter so if we hear of someone who is doing amazing things for God, what do we usually do? We go buy the book, watch the film. We see what they are doing and then try to do what they do. There is some value in doing this but it is not the key issue. Hebrews 13:7 says: "Remember your leaders who spoke the word of God to you. Consider the outcome of their way of life and imitate their faith." In other words, look at the people you admire, but don't copy what they **do**, copy what they **believe**. Why? Because what we do comes from what we believe. If we don't get our beliefs right, our actions won't be right.

The message of this session is simple: find out from God what is already true; choose to believe it whether it feels true or not; and it will transform your Christian life.

By the way, it's worth noting in passing that not believing in something doesn't make it false. For example, Jesus taught very clearly about hell but some Christians say they don't believe in it. However, not believing in hell doesn't make it go away. It doesn't lower the temperature there by one single degree!

Everyone Lives And Operates By Faith

The issue of faith is not that we believe. Everyone believes in something or someone. Practically every decision and every action you make demonstrates your faith in something.

▶ For instance, the last time you were driving your car and came to a green traffic light, what did you do? You probably drove right through it. Even though you couldn't see that the traffic light in the other direction was red, that the other drivers saw it and had stopped. You drove right through by faith.

Some people choose to believe that there's no such thing as a God, that we've evolved from animals. That's faith. In fact, when you look at this universe or at how amazing our human bodies are I think it takes a lot more faith to believe that there is no God than to believe in God.

The Critical Issue Is Who Or What We Believe In

▶ You might believe that you can fly a plane across the Atlantic Ocean by pedaling it. You might have more faith to believe that it will work than anyone who has ever lived. But actually it won't work.

The critical issue with faith is not so much **that** we believe but **what** we believe.

A true story: There was a hypnotist who announced that he was going to give a public demonstration of his psychic powers by driving a car blindfolded. He put the blindfold across his eyes, and with conviction and confidence he climbed into his car and started driving. After 20 yards he drove confidently into the back of a parked police van. He may have had an enormous amount of faith but what he believed in — his psychic powers — let him down. His beliefs didn't reflect reality (and he probably got a ticket too!)

It's who or what we believe in that determines whether our faith will actually work.

Let's look at another true story in the Bible. In 1 Kings 18 you read the story of Elijah and the prophets of Baal. Elijah and the prophets decided to hold a competition to see whose God was real.

▶ They both set up altars and threw a dead bull on it to be sacrificed. They were both to ask their god to send fire from heaven to burn it up. There were about 450 prophets of Baal and they won the toss and went first. They danced and danced and called out to Baal but nothing happened. Then they cut themselves with spears and called out louder. Nothing. It went on all day but they didn't get an answer.

Then it was Elijah's turn.

▶ He called on God and immediately fire came from heaven and burned up not only the bull but the wood and the stones!

Who had more faith? Actually we don't know. The prophets of Baal clearly had great faith in Baal but it made no difference — because Baal wasn't real.

▶ Jesus said that we only need faith the size of a mustard seed to move a mountain (Matthew 17:20). Elijah may only have had a little bit of faith but his offering was immediately burned up. Because he was calling on the true and living God. It doesn't depend on how large our faith is but on who we put our faith in. It's not our power that moves the mountain — it's God's.

Traffic lights can go wrong. Other faith objects like our parents, the church, friends, husbands, and wives can let us down.

▶ Hebrews 13:8 says: "Jesus Christ is the same yesterday and today and forever." That's why He is the one thing we can put our faith in who will never fail us. He has never failed to be and do all that He said He would be and do. And He never changes.

PAUSE FOR THOUGHT 1

OBJECTIVE:

THE MAIN OBJECTIVE IS TO UNDERSTAND THAT THE IMPORTANT THING IN DETERMINING WHETHER OR NOT FAITH WORKS IS WHERE OUR FAITH IS PLACED NOT HOW MUCH FAITH WE HAVE. AIM TO SHOW THAT FAITH REQUIRES US TO TAKE A STEP OF TRUST AND THAT MEANS ACTING ON IT, NOT JUST AGREEING WITH IT MENTALLY. FAITH WILL WORK IF WE FIND GOD'S WAY IN A SITUATION AND ACT ON IT WHETHER WE FEEL LIKE IT OR NOT.

► QUESTIONS:

"If you want to know what someone really believes, don't listen to what they say, but look at what they actually do." Spend some time discussing this thought.

God asks us to believe what the Bible says is true, even when it might not feel true. Share about a time when you chose to override your feelings and acted by faith instead.

"It takes more faith to believe that there is no God than to believe in God." What do you think about this statement?

People might sometimes say to us, "I wish I could have your faith," as if it were some mystical thing that might one day come over them. Christians might say, "Oh, if only I could have faith like so-and-so." Are we given a certain amount of faith so that some are destined to have lots of faith and others not very much? No! Faith is just making a choice to believe what God says. So let's try to understand how we can increase our faith.

► Let's say you have a two-year-old and you put her on a table, stand back a little bit and say, "Come on, jump into my arms." She may waver a little bit but then jump and you would catch her. What do you do next? Go a little further back and say, "Come on, jump into my arms." Let's say she does and you catch her and you go even further back. She will continue to jump provided you continue to catch her. As long as you don't let her down, her faith in you will keep growing and growing.

That's how faith grows. As you find out what God has said, choose to believe it and find that it works, you will get to know God better and will be able to trust Him with bigger and bigger things.

It's great to memorize Bible verses and take part in a Bible study. But your faith grows when you take that verse or that truth you learned and put it into practice, when you jump and find that God catches you. It's all very well learning the verse that says that God loves a cheerful giver, for example, but your faith will grow when, perhaps for the first time, you take a deep breath and give beyond what you feel you can afford in response to a prompt from God — and you find, of course, that God does not let you down.

As you get to know that God, the object of your faith, really can be trusted with absolutely anything, you will trust Him for bigger and bigger things. But start where you are right now.

Have you ever wondered how Abraham could contemplate sacrificing his son Isaac? He had come to learn through experience that God was loving and could be trusted.

You start with what God has said is true and you choose to believe it. Don't start with what you feel — you'll be all over the place! You don't feel your way into good behavior — you behave your way into good feelings. Your feelings will follow in due course.

[Can you replace this story from Steve Goss with one of your own?]

I'm not at the Abraham level of faith yet but as I look back I can see that God has deliberately engineered circumstances to build my faith. If I look back to the first time I heard about Freedom In Christ Ministries, for example, I can see that the Lord led me on a journey that increased my faith. We had a couple in our church who had a lot of problems and my pastor asked me to disciple them. I found it a frustrating process because we didn't seem to make much progress. I knew Jesus was the answer for their problems but I didn't know how. I didn't know what I could do apart from praying for them and that didn't seem to change anything.

One day I was in a Christian bookshop and I came across *The Bondage Breaker*, a book by Neil Anderson. The teaching in this course is based on that book and another book by Neil Anderson, *Victory Over The Darkness*, but at that time I hadn't heard of them. I just sensed that God was telling me to buy the book. Odd really — but I took a small step of faith and bought it. That was the start of a radical change in the direction of my life as it turned out — I had no idea at the time. I read it and it made a lot of sense. I was intrigued with a process in the back called "The Steps To Freedom In Christ" which claimed to help people resolve personal and spiritual conflicts.

One evening my pastor and I tried it out very tentatively with this couple — nothing else had worked. We didn't do it the way I would do it now but it didn't seem to matter. To cut a long story short, the wife got cancer and was dying. Before they went through The Steps we weren't even sure that she was a Christian. Yet as she faced death it was clear that there had been a major change in her after The Steps: she knew where she was going and when she finally died it was practically with a big grin on her face. Her husband, who had a history of mental breakdowns, was my concern at that time. I couldn't see how he would survive the premature death of his wife — but he did. He didn't have another breakdown.

We then started teaching the material from the books in our church using a forerunner to this course and going through The Steps with each other. What surprised us is that it was the so-called "good" Christians who suddenly started changing and getting new testimony of what God was doing. So much so in fact that people asked us to run the course again . . . and again. Unheard of! Soon we had people coming from lots of different churches and it was getting bigger and bigger.

About that time I felt the Lord saying that we should bring this teaching to the UK. I discovered that FIC had a website and sent an e-mail in asking if there was a UK office. The answer I had back said that they didn't feel it was right to open any more overseas offices. They did say, however, that if we wanted to test it we should invite Neil Anderson over to run a conference. That just seemed completely impossible to a small church like ours — we didn't have the facilities or the cash. So we just left it on the shelf.

Well the next thing we knew we got another e-mail saying that Neil Anderson was coming to the UK, his first visit for seven years. We asked where he was going to be and heard with interest that he was coming to Reading — which is where we live! Then we got a call from the church that had invited him, our local large conference-running church, saying that they understood we knew something about Neil Anderson's ministry and would we be willing to run the conference with them! So the Lord brought Neil Anderson to us — and we were able to meet face-to-face and tell him what we thought God was saying.

As I look back at those events with the benefit of hindsight it really helps my faith. I now know that I never need to manipulate events but can trust God to deliver what He promises. I just need to wait. God has been gracious enough to me to show me clearly that He is real. I think He is ready to do that in all of our lives. We simply start where we are and do what He has told us to do no matter how small it seems.

PAUSE FOR THOUGHT 2

OBJECTIVE:

WE WANT TO HELP PARTICIPANTS UNDERSTAND THAT IT IS HOW WELL WE KNOW GOD THAT DETERMINES OUR LEVEL OF TRUST IN HIM AND THAT GOD ALLOWS OUR FAITH TO BE TESTED BECAUSE HE PRIZES IT SO HIGHLY.

▶ QUESTIONS:

What are some of the ways our faith grows?

In what circumstances or seasons in your life have you noticed your faith grow the most?

What are some of the ways you have discovered that help you get to know God better?

Faith Is Demonstrated By Actions

In the Bible, the words "faith," "trust," and "believe" are all the same word in the original Greek. That's important to know because in English when you say that you believe something, it doesn't carry the same connotation as to trust in something, does it? But faith is not simply agreeing with something intellectually. It's a reliance that you demonstrate by actions.

James says, "Faith by itself, if it is not accompanied by action, is dead. But someone will say, 'You have faith; I have deeds.' Show me your faith without deeds, and I will show you my faith by what I do" (James 2:17–18).

No matter what we say, it's what we do that shows what we really believe. ▶   It's like standing at the train station wanting to go to Barcelona. You find out all about the times of the trains, you learn all the technical details, you even study

the train map, and you say you believe them to be true — but you never actually get on a train.

If you want to know what you really believe, look at what you do.

As we have seen, our faith grows when we make that choice to put it into practice. But it's when we find ourselves in difficult times that it can potentially grow the most. Maybe a health scare, financial concerns, or an uncertain future perhaps.

It's in these times that we have to choose whether to put our faith in God or in something else.

[Can you replace this story from Nancy Maldonado with one of your own?]

When our son Josué was 3 years old, Rob & I received crushing news. He was diagnosed with Fragile X Syndrome, a genetic and hereditary condition that affects his development, speech, emotions, and mental capacity. If you're a parent, you know that having and raising kids is always an adventure in faith — we are obviously so out of control. But this special child pushed us further. I remember Rob and I looking at each other and wondering, "When will he walk? When will he talk? Will he talk at all? When will he be potty-trained? Will he be potty-trained at all?" At every stage in his life we had questions no one could answer with certainty. We were missionaries at the time and wondered, "Should we leave the mission field and go back home to look for the best special needs programs?" More recently, when he became a teen, "Will he ever have any friends of his own?" And the hardest question of all, "Who will take care of him when we're gone?"

I tend to forget because he's brought so much joy to our life, but it's been tough. At every stage we've had to choose between relying on our own efforts to search and access the best resources or resting in God's care and provision. Yes, God has been faithful time and again, so when I get anxious about the present or the future, I remember that His promise of care and provision is for both His able and disabled children.

So, you can see that the question of how much faith you have is in your hands. It all depends on choosing to believe the truth and putting it into practice.

A young woman grew up with very abusive parents and had been exposed to witchcraft through her grandmother. Sadly, as a young Christian she was led to believe that she needed someone with a special spiritual discernment and anointing to help her overcome the spiritual oppression she had experienced since she was a child. How was she to find such a person? How long was she to wait? Who knew? She waited passively, stunted in her growth, unfruitful. Many times she received prayer and sometimes it helped but it had no lasting effect. She did eventually come through. But it wasn't through some special person. It was when she took active responsibility for her own spiritual growth.

The outcome of your Christian life is in **your** hands. On the Freedom In Christ app, you'll find a film containing some additional teaching from Steve on this.

The truth is that there's no one here who can't become a mature, fruitful disciple. There's no one here who can't resist temptation, get out of hopelessness, leave behind negative behavior and past influences and move on. You don't need some special anointing from God or others. You just need to know what is already true, choose to believe it, and act on it.

Now, we have another list of truths from the Bible that will help us with this. It's called The Twenty "Cans" Of Success and you'll find it in your Participant's Guide on pages 44–45 or on the app. Let's read it aloud together.

▶   Why should I say I can't when the Bible says I can do all things through Christ who gives me strength?

Why should I lack when I know that God shall supply all my needs according to His riches in glory in Christ Jesus?

▶   Why should I fear when the Bible says God has not given me a spirit of fear, but of power, love, and a sound mind?

Why should I lack faith to fulfill my calling knowing that God has allotted to me a measure of faith?

Why should I be weak when the Bible says that the Lord is the strength of my life and that I will display strength and take action because I know God?

▶   Why should I allow Satan supremacy over my life when He that is in me is greater than he that is in the world?

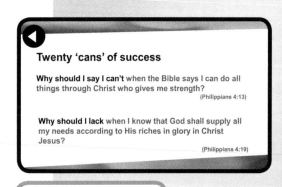

Twenty 'cans' of success

Why should I say I can't when the Bible says I can do all things through Christ who gives me strength?
(Philippians 4:13)

Why should I lack when I know that God shall supply all my needs according to His riches in glory in Christ Jesus?
(Philippians 4:19)

7 SLIDES IN TOTAL

Why should I accept defeat when the Bible says that God always leads me in triumph?

Why should I lack wisdom when Christ became wisdom to me from God and God gives wisdom to me generously when I ask Him for it?

▶ Why should I be depressed when I can recall to mind God's loving kindness, compassion, and faithfulness and have hope?

Why should I worry and fret when I can cast all my anxiety on Christ who cares for me?

Why should I ever be in bondage knowing that, where the Spirit of the Lord is, there is freedom?

▶ Why should I feel condemned when the Bible says I am not condemned because I am in Christ?

Why should I feel alone when Jesus said He is with me always and He will never leave me nor forsake me?

Why should I feel accursed or that I am the victim of bad luck when the Bible says that Christ redeemed me from the curse of the law that I might receive His Spirit?

▶ Why should I be discontented when I, like Paul, can learn to be content in all my circumstances?

Why should I feel worthless when Christ became sin on my behalf that I might become the righteousness of God in Him?

Why should I have a persecution complex knowing that nobody can be against me when God is for me?

▶ Why should I be confused when God is the author of peace and He gives me knowledge through His indwelling Spirit?

Why should I feel like a failure when I am a conqueror in all things through Christ?

Why should I let the pressures of life bother me when I can take courage knowing that Jesus has overcome the world and its tribulations?

We'll have one more list to share with you later in the course. Keep in mind that there's nothing magical about reading these lists out. The truth in them will only have an effect on your life to the extent that you decide to believe it. But reading the lists out loud — as soon as you wake up in the morning for several weeks — is a great way to commit yourself to affirm and believe the truth. I've known many people who say that their lives have been completely transformed just by doing that.

Elijah said: "How long will you waver between two opinions? If the Lord is God follow Him; but if Baal is God, follow him" (1 Kings 18:21). Will you take this opportunity to make a new commitment to base your life completely on what God says is true, regardless of your feelings and regardless of the opinions of others? ▶

REFLECTION

OBJECTIVE:

TO HELP PEOPLE GRASP THE TRUTHS IN THE TWENTY "CANS" OF SUCCESS LIST AT A DEEPER LEVEL.

LEADER'S NOTES:

THE FIRST QUESTION SHOULD BE COVERED IN A GROUP. FOR THE SECOND ONE, GIVE EACH INDIVIDUAL SOME TIME AND SPACE ON THEIR OWN.

▶ REFLECTION

In your group read the Twenty "Cans" Of Success. Pause after each one to allow people to share why that truth is particularly meaningful to them.

Which truth is most significant to you? Write it down and personalize it, for example, "Why should I, Nancy, say I can't when the Bible says I can do all things through Christ who strengthens me? (Philippians 4:13)" Take time to digest and enjoy this truth, asking God to help you receive it in your spirit.

 **WITNESS**

Think of someone you know who is not yet a Christian. What does the Bible say about why they don't yet believe (see 2 Corinthians 4:4, Romans 10:14–15)? Write a prayer you could pray that specifically asks God to do something about the things that are stopping them from believing. Then take God at His word and pray it!

 IN THE COMING WEEK

Every day read the Twenty "Cans" Of Success list out loud. Then pick one of the truths that is particularly appropriate to you and make a decision to believe it regardless of feelings and circumstances. If you can find a way of stepping out in faith in some practical way based on that truth, so much the better!

Twenty "Cans" Of Success

1. Why should I say I can't when the Bible says I can do all things through Christ who gives me strength (Philippians 4:13)?

2. Why should I lack when I know that God shall supply all my needs according to His riches in glory in Christ Jesus (Philippians 4:19)?

3. Why should I fear when the Bible says God has not given me a spirit of fear, but of power, love, and a sound mind (2 Timothy 1:7)?

4. Why should I lack faith to fulfill my calling knowing that God has allotted to me a measure of faith (Romans 12:3)?

5. Why should I be weak when the Bible says that the Lord is the strength of my life and that I will display strength and take action because I know God (Psalm 27:1; Daniel 11:32)?

6. Why should I allow Satan supremacy over my life when He that is in me is greater than he that is in the world (1 John 4:4)?

7. Why should I accept defeat when the Bible says that God always leads me in triumph (2 Corinthians 2:14)?

8. Why should I lack wisdom when Christ became wisdom to me from God and God gives wisdom to me generously when I ask Him for it (1 Corinthians 1:30; James 1:5)?

9. Why should I be depressed when I can recall to mind God's loving kindness, compassion, and faithfulness and have hope (Lamentations 3:21–23)?

10. Why should I worry and fret when I can cast all my anxiety on Christ who cares for me (1 Peter 5:7)?

11. Why should I ever be in bondage knowing that, where the Spirit of the Lord is, there is freedom (2 Corinthians 3:17; Galatians 5:1)?

12. Why should I feel condemned when the Bible says I am not condemned because I am in Christ (Romans 8:1)?

13. Why should I feel alone when Jesus said He is with me always and He will never leave me nor forsake me (Matthew 28:20; Hebrews 13:5)?

14. Why should I feel accursed or that I am the victim of bad luck when the Bible says that Christ redeemed me from the curse of the law that I might receive His Spirit (Galatians 3:13–14)?

15. Why should I be discontented when I, like Paul, can learn to be content in all my circumstances (Philippians 4:11)?

16. Why should I feel worthless when Christ became sin on my behalf that I might become the righteousness of God in Him (2 Corinthians 5:21)?

17. Why should I have a persecution complex knowing that nobody can be against me when God is for me (Romans 8:31)?

18. Why should I be confused when God is the author of peace and He gives me knowledge through His indwelling Spirit (1 Corinthians 14:33; 1 Corinthians 2:12)?

19. Why should I feel like a failure when I am a conqueror in all things through Christ (Romans 8:37)?

20. Why should I let the pressures of life bother me when I can take courage knowing that Jesus has overcome the world and its tribulations (John 16:33)?

Part B

THE WORLD, THE FLESH, AND THE DEVIL

Every day we struggle against three things that conspire to push us away from truth. Understanding how the world, the flesh, and the devil work will enable us to renew our minds and stand firm.

The World's View Of Truth

Session 3:
The World's View Of Truth

FOCUS VERSE:

Romans 12:2: Do not conform to the pattern of this world, but be transformed by the renewing of your mind. Then you will be able to test and approve what God's will is — his good, pleasing, and perfect will.

OBJECTIVE:

To understand that Christians need to make a definite decision to turn away from believing what the world teaches and choose instead to believe what God says is true.

FOCUS TRUTH:

The world we grew up in influenced us to look at life in a particular way and to see that way as "true." However, if it doesn't stack up with what God says is true, we need to reject it and bring our beliefs into line with what is really true.

POINTERS FOR LEADERS:

It's very easy for people to accept uncritically the version of truth that the world throws their way. In this session you will be helping people get to grips with the fact that the world's various versions of "truth" are opposed to what God says is true. You will also help them come to understand that they have almost certainly grown up with beliefs that they need to take a definite step to abandon in favor of the Biblical worldview, "how God says it is."

The concept that they have a worldview will be new to some who have unthinkingly accepted what they have been taught and what they have absorbed from their culture.

If you are planning an away day after Session 7, this would be a good point to remind people of the date so that they keep it clear.

SMALL GROUP TIMINGS:

Welcome	12 minutes	12
Worship	12 minutes	24
Word part 1	12 minutes	36
Pause For Thought 1	20 minutes	56
Word part 2	15 minutes	71
Pause For Thought 2	20 minutes	91
Word part 3	14 minutes	105
Reflection	15 minutes	120

Registered users of the course can download a spreadsheet with these timings. Simply enter your own start time, adjust the length of the various components as desired, and you will have a timed plan of your session.

SONGS:

There are two songs from *Worship In Spirit And Truth* (see page 26) for this session: *We Choose Life* and *That's Who I Am* (Part Three of Four). See page 211–212 of the Participant's Guide for the lyrics and background info.

WELCOME

If you could go anywhere in the world, where would you choose?

Do you think that the way you look at the world and what you believe would be very different if you had been brought up in a different culture?

WORSHIP

Suggested theme: the uniqueness of Jesus.

Read John 14:6: "Jesus answered, 'I am the way and the truth and the life. No one comes to the Father except through me.'"

Then read one or two of Ephesians 1:17–23, 1 Corinthians 1:30, Philippians 2:5–11.

Pause between each passage and invite people to tell Jesus how amazing He is.

WORD

For background information on this section of the course, read the book *Win The Daily Battle*. Read pages 11–42 in the book for the material that relates to this session.

The World's View Of Truth

SESSION 3

What Is "The World"?

We've looked at some fundamental truths: who we are in Christ and the fact that faith is simply a choice to believe what God tells us is already true. In the next three sessions we're going to turn our attention to the things that try to deflect us from the truth. We have three distinct enemies: the world, the flesh, and the devil.

First, in this session, we'll look at the world and how it tries to make us look at reality in a way that is opposed to how God says it actually is.

The world is the system or culture we grew up in and live in. That will vary greatly according to where you are from and when you were born. I'm going to talk about it almost as if it were a person with its own thoughts and deeds. It isn't. However, there is someone behind it, Satan, whom Jesus called (John 12:31) "the ruler of this world." To a significant extent, he is the one who pulls the strings behind the world and works through it.

Let's look at the three main tactics the world uses to try to divert us from the truth.

Tactic 1: Promising To Meet Our Deepest Needs

Its first tactic is promising to meet those deep needs we all have. We were created to have the kind of life Adam had: 100% acceptance, the highest significance, perfect security. But that wasn't the life we were born into. From our first breath we didn't have the spiritual connection to God that we were meant to have. Yet we were created with those in-built needs for acceptance, significance, and security that our connection with God would have fulfilled.

When we were growing up and instinctively started looking to fulfill those deep needs for acceptance, significance, and security, up popped the world and said, ▶ "No problem! I'll show you how to get those."

It feeds us false formulas:

Performance + accomplishments = significance

Status + recognition = security

Appearance + admiration = acceptance

Those are lies. But in the absence of a spiritual connection to God, we naturally fell for them. Or as Paul put it, we naturally "followed the ways of this world" (Ephesians 2:2).

[Can you replace this story from Nancy Maldonado with one of your own?]

In Ecuador I won a scholarship to a fine, expensive school where I got a really good education, but where I fit in like a fly in milk (a Spanish saying). I was a low-middle-class pastor's kid in a rich kids´ school. There I absorbed this worldly value related to social class and status: connections and appearance are of utmost importance. My world expanded at university and I joined a young adults church group where I made good friends. But I was embarrassed by my new friends who, if I'm honest, seemed shabby nobodies. When I started hanging out with them I would pray that I wouldn't run into my former classmates.

You see, the world has a kind of one-two punch. On the one hand it makes us feel insignificant, insecure, and that nobody likes us (It told me: "You're a poor nobody, you don't fit in.") Then it offers ways that promise to fix it: dress in fashionable brands, hang out with the elite. But they don't work.

1 John 2:15–17 is a key passage in understanding how the world tries to suck us in:

> Do not love the world or anything in the world. If anyone loves the world, love for the Father is not in them. For everything in the world — the lust of the flesh, the lust of the eyes, and the pride of life — comes not from the Father but from the world. The world and its desires pass away, but whoever does the will of God lives forever.

According to the passage, there are three channels through which the world works: the lust of the flesh, the lust of the eyes, and the pride of life. They are the same channels that Satan used when he tempted Eve and again when he appeared to Jesus in the wilderness and tempted Him.

The Lust Of The Flesh

▶   We'll look at the flesh as an enemy in its own right in the next session. But let's just notice for now that the lust of the flesh is linked to the world. The more we buy into the world's lies and act on them, the more unhelpful patterns of thinking become established in our minds, which then become default ways of behaving.

The Lust Of The Eyes

▶   The world also works through the lust of the eyes. It shows me things that it claims will meet my needs — those legitimate needs for acceptance, significance, and security that God created me to have.

It's interesting and sad that a number of pieces of research have shown that more Christian men regularly use porn than don't. And quite a few women use it too.

🛈 A good source of information on porn use amongst Christians is *The Porn Phenomenon*, research commissioned by Josh McDowell Ministry from Barna Group in 2016. Available from barna.com.

If you are teaching the Word section yourself rather than using the video, you might consider showing the testimony on porn that features there. It is also included in a longer form on the app so that participants can watch it at a time of their choosing.

Such testimonies give people real hope that this issue can be resolved in Christ (and it can!)

The world is always trying to get our attention with bright, new, attractive things. Airbrushed models make us feel we have to look a certain way and create anxiety about aging. Ultimately they don't lead us into the bright future they promise but into darkness and confusion.

The Pride Of Life

▶   Then there's the pride of life. This is simply the temptation the world throws at us to boast about our life, based on the lie that it's possessions or achievements or connections that make us significant.

Even as a Christian I'd swallowed the world's lies about social class and status. There I was, embarrassed by my friends who loved Jesus and loved me, before people who I had no meaningful connection with — ridiculous!

The truth is, when we feel the need to boast about what we have, our achievements or who we know, we show our insecurity. We're using those things as a crutch to bolster our self-image. But you don't need to do that any more (and neither do I). We are now holy and pleasing to God. We are accepted and completely secure in Him.

PAUSE FOR THOUGHT 1

OBJECTIVE:

TO HELP PEOPLE UNDERSTAND THEIR VULNERABILITY TO THE WORLD'S PROMISES TO MEET OUR GOD-GIVEN NEEDS FOR SIGNIFICANCE, SECURITY, AND ACCEPTANCE.

▶ QUESTIONS:

In what ways has the world tried to make you feel insignificant, insecure, and unloved?

In what ways has the world promised you significance, security, and acceptance? Do you recognize these "false formulas"?

Performance + accomplishments = significance
Status + recognition = security
Appearance + admiration = acceptance

How can you counteract "the lust of the flesh, the lust of the eyes, and the pride of life" (1 John 2:15–17)?

Tactic 2: Painting A Complete But False Picture Of Reality

▶ Have you ever put on a virtual reality headset? Rather than simply watching a movie or a sporting event you can have the impression that you are right in it — if you move your head to the right or the left, the scene will change accordingly and you can interact with this 360 degrees virtual world as you do with the real world.

One of the pioneers of virtual reality says that the goal is to make technology that's as real as real life with none of the limitations. But of course it won't be real. It will just **feel** real.

▶ And that's essentially the second tactic of the world: to give you a distorted view of reality but feed it to you as the real thing. In effect it gives you a virtual reality headset but you don't know you're wearing it. This virtual reality headset is called your "worldview."

I have two daughters. Anyone care to guess what language they speak? English! But if they had been brought up in a French home they'd speak French. Just as we pick up things like language from our environment, we also pick up beliefs, values, and ways of behaving. We are influenced by our family, our schooling, our friends, the media.

So without even realizing it we all develop a way of looking at reality that we believe is true. But if your worldview is faulty, it will lead to faulty judgments about what happens in your life.

There are thousands of different worldviews but let's look at the most common to understand how they work.

1. A Non-Western Worldview

If you were brought up in Africa or Eastern cultures you may well have absorbed the belief that the universe is controlled by a kind of universal power that runs through everything and by spirits of many types.

If something bad happened to you — let's say you suddenly became ill — you would pass that bad experience through your virtual reality goggles to make sense of it and you would probably begin to suspect that someone might be manipulating this universal power or the spirits against you by cursing you or doing some kind of magic.

▶ Just as you might turn to an electrician to sort out problems with the power in your house, you would probably turn to a sort of cosmic electrician — a shaman or witch doctor — to sort out the problems with this universal power.

If this is how you see reality, chances are that you will be living in constant fear that someone else might have a better control of the powers or that you might somehow unwittingly upset a spirit that would then turn against you.

2. The Western Worldview

Most people brought up in the West don't turn to a witch doctor if things start to go wrong. Instead we tend to look for logical reasons and try to fix the problem.

▶ That's because we have been fed a different view of reality by the world. It's a worldview that tells us that what is real can only be known through scientific methods. If we're ill we'll turn to a doctor who will use scientific methods to try to make us better.

In this worldview, it's still just about OK to believe in God and other supernatural things but we come to believe that they have no real bearing on our daily life. It's generally thought, for example, that we can leave spiritual questions out of our children's education without losing anything that really matters.

I heard of someone who said, "I believe in God. But I'm a practicing atheist" and that would be true of many people.

3. The Postmodern Worldview

▶   But culture is always changing and another worldview — usually called the "Postmodern" worldview — has been emerging in the West in recent decades, which is something of a reaction against past generations' reliance on scientists and experts. After all, what experts say has all too often turned out to be wrong.

The younger you are, the more likely you are to be suspicious of experts in general but particularly suspicious of those who make strong claims to certainty. In fact you may well have come to see anyone who has strong convictions as being on a dangerous line that ends with extreme, fanatical terrorists.

Whereas previous generations saw truth as something revealed by God or discovered by science, increasingly we test whether an idea is valid or not purely on the basis of our own personal experience. If it feels good to me, it's OK. Each person is free to make up their own version of truth based on their own experience.

So politicians can say what people want to hear even if it flies in the face of facts and get a strong following. Groups on social media promote even the most outlandish views and members reinforce each other's beliefs.

That is why Christians are under pressure to agree that all religions are equally true. Saying that we respect the right of other people to different beliefs and that we are happy to dialogue with them is no longer enough. There is a pressure to agree that their beliefs are just as "true" as our own.

Younger Christians are happy to say that Jesus is **their** truth but hesitate to go further and talk about Him as **the** truth.

This has led to what you might call "extreme tolerance" where practically any behavior is acceptable. People in previous generations used pornography, indulged in binge drinking, used drugs, or had multiple sexual partners, but would usually have acknowledged that those things were wrong. Increasingly, people don't see these things as inherently wrong as long as they make them feel good. In fact the only thing that is seen as wrong is saying that what someone else is doing is wrong!

The bottom line is that people are increasingly absorbing into their worldview a belief that there is no real, solid, undergirding truth.

The Biblical Worldview: Truth Does Exist

So, what is true? That there is a spiritual power flowing through the universe that we can manipulate? Something that only science can uncover? Whatever feels good to you?

Which worldview is right?

None of them!

If we were to take that virtual reality headset off, get rid of the values and beliefs that our own particular culture instilled in us, what would the world actually look like?

▶ The Bible claims to be God's revelation of reality to the people He created. If that is right, then taking off that headset would mean that what we would see would correspond exactly to what the Bible tells us. That what the Bible says is "how it really is."

Jesus said, "I am the way and the truth and the life. No one comes to the Father except through me" (John 14:6).

What! Are we saying that only one view of reality can be right? Isn't that a bit, well, intolerant?

▶ Consider the most important question facing everybody in the world: What happens when you die?

Hinduism teaches that when a soul dies it is reincarnated in another form.

Christianity teaches that souls spend eternity in either heaven or hell.

Spiritists think we float around as ghosts.

Atheists believe that we have no soul and that when we die our existence simply ends.

Can all those things be true at the same time? To put it another way, does what you believe will happen to you when you die make any difference to what will actually happen? Or will the same thing happen to everyone when they die regardless of what they believed before the event?

Surely, if Hindus are right, we will all be reincarnated. If Christians are right, we will all stand before the judgment seat of God. If atheists are right, all of our existences will come to an end. If spiritists are right we'll all float around as ghosts. But they simply can't all be true at the same time.

So it's clear that there is such a thing as real truth that exists whatever individuals may choose to believe.

We are not proposing a version of truth that we have made up ourselves. The Bible has been tested and found reliable by millions of people over thousands of years. In fact many of those ordinary people have found that, by choosing to believe it, they have been able to accomplish, or be a catalyst for, extraordinary things: starting and running hospitals that are open to everyone, providing education, helping to abolish slavery, helping people get free from drugs.

We may find it difficult to advance an unfashionable argument. But are we really being helpful if we encourage people in their view that there is no truth when Jesus has said very clearly that He is **the** truth?

PAUSE FOR THOUGHT 2

OBJECTIVE:

TO REINFORCE THE CONCEPT THAT WE HAVE ALL BEEN HEAVILY INFLUENCED BY A NON-BIBLICAL WAY OF LOOKING AT REALITY.

▶ **QUESTIONS:**

How different would your worldview be if you had grown up in another part of the world or at a different time?

In what ways do you identify with one of the three worldviews discussed here?

When we talk to people about Jesus' claim to be the only way to God, how can we not come across as arrogant?

Tactic 3: Not Replacing Core Beliefs

▶ All of us were raised wearing a virtual reality headset of one kind or another — it's our original worldview. But it's crucial to understand that these headsets give us a distorted view of reality.

The third tactic of the world is to get us to **add** our Christian beliefs to our existing worldview rather than **replace** it, so that our core beliefs remain the same.

▶ Gold leaf is real gold that is beaten until it is 200 times thinner than a human hair, then it is applied to books, ornaments, buildings, and sometimes even food. Something that is covered in gold leaf looks as if it is made from solid gold but it's actually just a thin covering.

Imagine your Christian beliefs as a beautiful gold ornament. If we were to take a saw and cut it in half, what would you see inside?

▶   Would it be solid gold all the way through?

▶   Or would there just be a thin layer of gold with some cheap and nasty metal inside?

It's much easier to see how deeply our core beliefs affect us when we look at the lives of other people who have different worldviews from our own. For example, in an African country, the leadership of a missionary organization was ready to hand the church they planted over to African leadership. Two men were candidates for the position. Now what I'm about to say might sound silly to you, if you were not brought up with an African worldview, but one of them went to a witch doctor to get a charm to enhance his chances of being chosen as the church leader. Why did he do that? He was simply reverting back to his core beliefs, because they were deeper than his newer Christian beliefs.

How are those brought up in the West affected by the Western worldview which in effect denies the reality of the spiritual world? Some parts of the Church have tried to get rid of what they consider to be unnecessary supernatural "baggage." They deny the miraculous and the existence of angels and demons.

Most of us recognize the reality of the spiritual world, at least intellectually. However, the Western worldview can still influence us. It encourages us to live our lives and exercise our ministries as if the spiritual world didn't exist. Now we don't need to go around seeing a demon behind every bush, but if you leave demons out of the equation you are setting yourself up for some problems because you don't have a complete view of how this world operates.

When something goes horribly wrong in our lives, many Christians blame God. Why? Influenced by the Western worldview, they leave Satan out of the equation who, the Bible says, is a thief who "comes only to steal and kill and destroy" (John 10:10).

What about when someone has a mental or psychological problem? The medical profession, influenced by the Western worldview, tends to ignore the reality of the spiritual world.

[Can you include an example of your own to replace the following story from Daryl Fitzgerald?]

For instance I was explaining the gospel to a young man who came into my office. I could tell by his body language and the look in his eyes there was a battle going on for his mind. I asked him to tell me what was going on in his head. He said there were voices in his head telling him, "The gospel is not true. The gospel is not true."

Is that a chemical imbalance, maybe some kind of problem with his brain? Or should we at least consider the possibility that the voices in his head might be coming from a demon? A healthy view of reality would acknowledge both possibilities.

The Church is often divided into two camps: one group who ignore the reality of the spiritual world and just look at psychological and emotional treatment; and the other group who see a demon behind everything. We are whole people — spirit, soul, and body — and we need to have a healthy balanced view that takes into account both the natural world and the spiritual world.

We say we believe the Bible, but isn't it true that many of our decisions are made on the basis of what we think rather than on what God is saying? We say we believe in the power of prayer but do we spend time praying, or do our actions really demonstrate that we believe that we can sort out our lives on our own and use prayer only as a last resort?

Holding on to our core beliefs leads to a shaky foundation for our faith.

For example, consider this question: Why are you a Christian?

Christians who are still operating according to their old worldview might say something like:

"I believe because it seems to work"; or

"I feel it is true in my experience"; or

"I sincerely believe it is true for me."

But what happens when it no longer seems to work or when it doesn't feel true any more, or when another attractive belief system comes along?

Os Guinness says: "The Christian faith is not true because it works; it works because it is true. . . . It is not simply "true for us"; it is true for any who seek in order to find, because truth is true even if nobody believes it and falsehood is false even if

Time For Truth, Os Guinness (Baker Books 2000), pp. 79–80

everybody believes it. That is why truth does not yield to opinion, fashion, numbers, office, or sincerity — it is simply true and that is the end of it."

▶ Each of us needs to come to a point where we realize that what the world has caused us to believe is so contrary to what is really true that we make a conscious decision to throw it away. We need to make a conscious choice to believe what the Bible says, to make the Word of God our core belief system — not just something we add on like a coating of gold leaf to a faulty belief system.

If we don't, it will lead us to compromise and we'll be "double-minded" and "unstable in all our ways" (James 1:8).

I'm going to say a prayer that you can pray with me if you want to make a firm decision to base the rest of your life on what God says is true.

Lord Jesus, no matter what the world throws at me, I am making a decision today to believe only what You say is true in Your Word, the Bible. I choose not to be double-minded any longer but to trust You and make the Bible the core of what I believe. I renounce and turn away from my previous worldview and make a new commitment today to base my life on the truth in Your Word. I trust that You will be faithful to me. In Jesus' name. Amen.

REFLECTION

OBJECTIVE:

TO GIVE PEOPLE AN OPPORTUNITY TO REJECT ASPECTS OF THEIR ORIGINAL WORLDVIEW AND EMBRACE THE TRUTH IN GOD'S WORD.

LEADER'S NOTES:

YOU COULD EITHER DO THIS IN A GROUP OR HAVE PEOPLE DO IT INDIVIDUALLY.

THE CONCEPT OF "RENOUNCING" AND "ANNOUNCING" IS FUNDAMENTAL TO THE *FREEDOM IN CHRIST COURSE* AND PARTICIPANTS WILL BECOME WELL USED TO IT. YOU MIGHT LIKE TO EXPLAIN AGAIN THAT TO RENOUNCE SOMETHING IS TO REJECT IT OR TURN AWAY FROM IT.

▶   REFLECTION

Spend some time in prayer throwing out your old worldview and choosing to see the world as God says it actually is.

You might find it helpful to say "I renounce the lie that [my old false belief], and I announce the truth that [truth from God's Word]." For example:

"I renounce the lie that the unseen spiritual world is not real, and I announce the truth that it is just as real as the physical world we can see."

"I renounce the lie that financial success brings real security, and I announce the truth that I am already perfectly secure because no one can snatch me out of God's hand."

"I renounce the lie that I should be worried that someone may have cursed me, and I announce the truth that I am seated with Christ in the heavenly realms far above all other spiritual powers."

WITNESS

How will understanding that we all grow up with a particular way of looking at the world help you as you talk to people who are not yet Christians?

 # IN THE COMING WEEK

At the end of each day take five minutes to review how your old worldview has reared its head during the day to try to persuade you to compromise the truth of the Bible. When you identify it happening, take time to renounce the false belief from your previous worldview and make a commitment to base your life on the truth of the Bible.

Our Daily Choice

Session 4:
Our Daily Choice

FOCUS VERSE:
Romans 8:9a ESV: You, however, are not in the flesh but in the Spirit, if in fact the Spirit of God dwells in you.

OBJECTIVE:
To understand that, although we still have urges that tend to pull us away from relying completely on God and following the promptings of His Spirit, we no longer have to give in to them but are free to make a genuine choice.

FOCUS TRUTH:
Although you are a new person in Christ with a completely new nature, and are free to live according to what the Holy Spirit tells you, obeying Him is not automatic.

POINTERS FOR LEADERS:
This session helps us to understand our second enemy, "the flesh," our default way of thinking and behaving. Christians have a choice whether to walk according to the flesh, or to the Spirit.

The Biblical term "flesh" is used in this course because it avoids confusion. Some Bible translations, notably the very popular New International Version (NIV), went through a phase of interpreting the Greek word "sarx" as "sinful nature" (although they put an explanatory footnote: "or flesh"). This can be confusing in the light of the first session, in which it was taught that Christians are new creations in Christ whose fundamental nature is now that of a "holy one."

When Christians read their NIV Bible, they could easily have concluded (wrongly) that their core nature is still sinful. There are two significant places where the New Testament uses the Greek word that actually means "nature" ("phusis") and these helpfully bring out the key truth. Ephesians 2:3 describes our nature ("phusis") before we came to Christ: "we **were** by nature objects of wrath." In contrast to this, 2 Peter 1:4 reads that we now "participate in the divine nature" — we share God's nature ("phusis").

Christians are no longer "in Adam," they are alive "in Christ" (see Romans 8:5–10). The "old self" (old man) was crucified with Christ (Galatians 2:20). "Old self," "nature," and "flesh" are not interchangeable terms. The old self refers to the natural person, who we were in Adam or in the flesh. Christians are no longer "in the flesh" because they are "in Christ." Every new creation in Christ has a new heart and a new spirit, thus a new core identity and nature that is directed toward God. However, the flesh remains after salvation and it has been conditioned to live independently of God. The Christian, however, can choose to live either according to the flesh or according to the Spirit.

Thankfully, from the 2011 version onward, the NIV adopted the literal translation "flesh" but you may have participants who are using a pre-2011 version and you may need to explain this point to prevent confusion.

Concept Of "Footholds":
This session introduces the important concepts of how the flesh can lead us into sin and how unresolved sin issues can give the enemy a "foothold" or "opportunity" in our lives. In the next session we will look specifically at the topic of the enemy and how he works and explain more about this.

THE APP

Steve Goss has put an additional short teaching session on the app called "Who Is Responsible For What?" that goes well with this session. We recommend that participants watch it after this session.

SMALL GROUP TIMINGS:

Welcome	10 minutes	10
Worship	13 minutes	23
Word part 1	14 minutes	37
Pause For Thought 1	20 minutes	57
Word part 2	15 minutes	72
Pause For Thought 2	20 minutes	92
Word part 3	13 minutes	105
Reflection	15 minutes	120

Registered users of the course can download a spreadsheet with these timings. Simply enter your own start time, adjust the length of the various components as desired, and you will have a timed plan of your session.

SONGS:

The two songs from *Worship In Spirit And Truth* (see page 26) that have been written to accompany this session are *Living In Colour* and *That's Who I Am* (Part Four of Four). See pages 213–214 of the Participant's Guide for the lyrics and background info.

WELCOME

What would you most like to do if you knew you could not fail?

 # WORSHIP

Suggested theme: worship Him for who He is.

Read aloud the following passages:

"Through Jesus, therefore, let us continually offer to God a sacrifice of praise — the fruit of lips that profess his name." (Hebrews 13:15)

"Then a voice came from the throne, saying: 'Praise our God, all you his servants, you who fear him, both small and great!'" (Revelation 19:5)

"Exalt the Lord our God, and worship at his holy mountain; for the Lord our God is holy!" (Psalm 99:9)

"Yours, Lord, is the greatness and the power and the glory and the majesty and the splendor, for everything in heaven and earth is yours. Yours, Lord, is the kingdom; you are exalted as head over all. Wealth and honor come from you; you are the ruler of all things. In your hands are strength and power to exalt and give strength to all. Now, our God, we give you thanks, and praise your glorious name."
(1 Chronicles 29:11–13)

Suggest that each person worships God in quiet adoration.

 # WORD

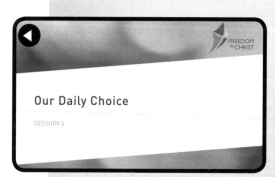

Our Daily Choice

SESSION 4

The second book in the FREEDOM IN CHRIST DISCIPLESHIP SERIES, *Win The Daily Battle*, corresponds to Part B of the course. Read pages 84–111 in the book for the material that relates to the flesh.

We might think that becoming a Christian means that we will automatically do everything right — as if accepting Christ solves all our problems. But it doesn't work that way. As believers we sense the Holy Spirit deep down inside and we want to please God. But we often fail to live the Christian life in the way we want to, and sometimes we don't feel different at all. Our bad habits don't instantly disappear. In fact, the struggle with sin may seem to intensify. Why?

Some have grown up believing that their heart is "deceitful above all things and beyond cure" because that's what it says in Jeremiah 17:9. Why, however, would you take that truth from the Old Testament and apply it to a New Testament believer, especially when one of the great prophecies of the Old Testament is "I will give you a new heart and put a new spirit in you" (Ezekiel 36:26)? Before we were Christians, our hearts were indeed "beyond cure," but now in Christ we have new hearts!

In this session we're going to look at what the Bible calls "the flesh," the second of our enemies.

Paul says:

> For those who live according to the flesh set their minds on the things of the flesh, but those who live according to the Spirit set their minds on the things of the Spirit. For to set the mind on the flesh is death, but to set the mind on the Spirit is life and peace. For the mind that is set on the flesh is hostile to God. (Romans 8:5–7a ESV)

Let's start by looking a little more at what happened — and what did not happen — when we became Christians.

What Changed

We've already seen that the moment we became Christians, some dramatic changes took place.

▶ We have a new heart and a new Spirit within us

One of the great prophecies of the Old Testament is this: "I will give you a new heart and put a new spirit within you" (Ezekiel 36:26). Before we were Christians our hearts were "deceitful . . . and beyond cure" (Jeremiah 17:9) as Jeremiah put it — but now in Christ we have brand new clean hearts!

We have new life "in Christ"

We are new creations and are now alive in Christ.

We have a new master

Our new spiritual authority is God; before our conversion it was Satan (John 8:44, Ephesians 2:1–2).

▶ What Did Not Change

Let's look at some of the things that didn't change when we became Christians.

Our body did not change

Physically we still look the same as before. One day we'll get a new body but, for now, we still have the same old flesh and bones.

Our "flesh" wasn't taken away

When we talk about the term "flesh" we are not referring to our physical bodies but talking about the urges and desires it has. You could think of the Biblical concept of the flesh as "the urge to do what comes naturally to a fallen human being."

As we grew up, independent of God, we learned to react, cope, and think in certain ways. These old ways of thinking and behaving are the primary characteristics of the flesh. When we became Christians no one pressed a "clear" button in our minds.

[Can you replace this illustration from Daryl Fitzgerald with one of your own? There is a further illustration from Steve Goss in the note in the margin.]

Let me give you an illustration of how the flesh works. I used to have a hard time communicating with my father. His face always seemed cold and hard toward me, so when I saw him it made me feel like I had done something wrong. So every time I saw him I learned to feel fear or rejection.

Over the years I learned about how he grew up and what he went through as a child. I learned how he conditioned himself to survive in the Vietnam War. I realized that his tough face didn't mean that he was angry with me. It was just a result of his past. However, I learned to think it meant he was rejecting me. It has taken some time for me to train myself to think differently.

Even now, when I see his face, my initial reaction is to think and feel rejection. Then I have to remind myself of the truth. That's exactly how the flesh works. It's a set of automatic thoughts and behaviors that we have learned over time.

"Flesh" is an unfamiliar word, but it is exactly what the original Bible text says. The Greek word used in the New Testament was the word used to describe meat you would buy from the supermarket or the flesh that makes up your body.

Many modern Bible translations went through a phase where they didn't translate the word "flesh" literally but interpreted it as "sinful nature." I completely understand why they did that because the word "flesh" sounds old. However, using the

Illustration from Steve Goss: I learned early on in life that when I felt low, eating could give me a lift. Eventually it became a coping mechanism. There is nothing wrong with eating or food — but using it as a way to meet a need such as comfort is acting independently of God. He is the God of all comfort and more than ready to pour it into my life. The problem is that these things become flesh patterns, "default" ways of behaving.

Illustration from Steve Goss: I once had someone come to work for me who was fun to have around and outgoing. Yet I noticed that all that changed whenever I called him into my office for a meeting. Although I try to be as pleasant a boss as possible and am, I think, easy to work for, he would always come into my office looking very nervous and tight-lipped. After some months he told me that, in his previous job, whenever the boss called him into his office it was to shout at him and criticize him. Even though his circumstances had changed completely and he didn't work for the nasty boss any more, whenever his new boss called him into his office, the same old thought patterns went to work. It took some time but, as he gradually realized that he never got treated badly any more, he stopped reacting that way. The flesh is like a default way of thinking.

term "nature" is unhelpful and confusing because, as we have seen, Christians no longer have a sinful nature but we share God's nature.

A phrase such as "sinful tendency" might have worked better. Because it clearly communicates the concept that we have something inside of us (that the Bible calls the flesh) that pulls us towards sin without implying that in the core of our identity we have reverted to being sinners.

We are going to stick with the literal translation "flesh" and that's what many Bible translators now do.

Sin did not die

The big question for many is this: how can we defeat sin? The bad news is we can't. The good news is that Christ has already done it for us! Sin itself is not dead. In fact, it is still extremely appealing, and it tempts us every day to try to meet our legitimate needs for security, acceptance, and significance, through things other than God.

Then what has to change so that we don't go round in circles falling into the same old sin patterns?

It won't happen by trying harder. The key to freedom is knowing the truth. We need to know the truth about sin.

Even though sin used to be our master, Paul tells us that it has no power over us any more.

Even though sin is very much alive, Paul tells us that we are to realize that we are alive to God and dead to sin (Romans 6:11).

When we died with Christ, His death ended our relationship with sin.

But sometimes I wake up in the morning feeling dead to Christ and feeling alive to sin. As Paul said in Romans 7:21 "So I find this law at work: although I want to do good, evil is right there with me." What is this law? Paul calls it the "law of sin" (Romans 7:23).

How can you overcome a law that is still effective?

Well, who here can fly? Why can't you fly? Because every time you try, the law of gravity keeps you stuck to the earth.

See the Leader's Notes at the beginning of this session for important information on understanding "the flesh" and clearing up any confusion about Bible translations that interpret it as "sinful nature."

Even though the Bible makes it clear that as a Christian I am "dead to sin but alive to God in Christ Jesus" (Romans 6:11), sometimes I wake up in the morning feeling very alive to sin but dead to God! However, nothing has changed. I simply need to believe what is really true rather than what my feelings are telling me.

▶ But we can all fly by getting into a plane! Has the law of gravity been temporarily suspended? No. It's still working. But we've overcome the law of gravity by a greater law: the law of lift and thrust.

So how do you overcome the law of sin that is still in effect? By a greater law. Romans 8:2 says "Through Christ Jesus the law of the Spirit of life set me free from the law of sin and death."

The law of the Spirit of life that's now at work in me as a child of God is far greater than the law of sin and death. Before I became a child of God, a saint, a holy one, I had no choice but to stay on the ground in my sin, but now in Christ I have the power to choose to fly above the law of sin and death!

PAUSE FOR THOUGHT 1

OBJECTIVE:

TO REINFORCE PEOPLE'S UNDERSTANDING OF WHAT CHANGED AND WHAT DID NOT CHANGE WHEN WE BECAME CHRISTIANS.

▶ QUESTIONS:

What are some of the main things that you notice have changed in you since you became a Christian? And what do you wish would have changed but hasn't?

In what particular type of situation do you recognize that you become more vulnerable to the attempts of the flesh to draw you toward sin? What practical steps can you put in place to help you at those times?

God's Word tells us that we are alive to Christ and dead to sin. Why does this not feel true some days? How can we rise above "the law of sin"?

Our Choices

▶ It is becoming clear that we face some very real choices:

- even though we no longer have to think and react according to our flesh, we can choose to do so

- even though sin has no power over us, we can choose to give in to it

1 Corinthians 2:14–3:3 (ESV) describes three different types of person. See if you can identify which one you are:

▶ The natural person does not accept the things of the Spirit of God, for they are folly to him, and he is not able to understand them because they are spiritually discerned.

This describes someone who is not yet a Christian:

- physically alive but spiritually dead

- separated from God and living independently from Him

- no sense of any kind of direction from the Holy Spirit so they live prompted solely by the impulses of the flesh

Paul continues:

▶ The spiritual person judges all things, but is himself to be judged by no one.

This is supposed to be the normal state for Christians:

- their spirit is now united with God's Spirit

- they choose to walk by the Spirit and therefore demonstrate the fruit of the Spirit (see Galatians 5:22–23)

- they still have the flesh but crucify it daily as they recognize the truth that they are now dead to sin (see Romans 6:11–14) and they submit to God and resist the devil

- their emotions are increasingly marked by joy and peace instead of turmoil

This is the model of maturity to which we are all moving — but don't dismiss it as something that might be possible for others but is not for you.

Finally Paul comes to the third type of person:

> But I, brothers, could not address you as spiritual people, but as people of the flesh, as infants in Christ. I fed you with milk, not solid food, for you were not ready for it. And even now you are not yet ready, for you are still of the flesh. For while there is jealousy and strife among you, are you not of the flesh and behaving only in a human way?

▶ "People of the flesh" describes Christians who have been made spiritually alive just like the spiritual person but, instead of choosing to follow the impulses of the Spirit, follow the impulses of the flesh. They are free to walk according to the Spirit but choose not to, either deliberately or because they are being deceived and don't understand how to.

Their daily life tends to mimic the natural (non-Christian) person more than the spiritual person:

- mind occupied by wrong thoughts

- emotions plagued by negative feelings

- body showing signs of stress

They are living in opposition to their identity in Christ and are likely to be plagued by feelings of inferiority, insecurity, inadequacy, guilt, worry, and doubt.

They will also tend to get "stuck" in sin-confess cycles. In Romans 7:15–24 Paul describes how bad it feels to be stuck and refers to it as "miserable" or "wretched." Because our spirit is joined to God's Spirit, in our inner being we delight in God's law — we really want to go His way. Yet we find that we fail time and again. Maybe we return time and again to comfort eating or gossip or sexual sin. In the end we feel completely hopeless and conclude (wrongly) that we can never escape.

The salvation of fleshly Christians is not the issue. But they accomplish nothing much of eternal value in such a state — a tragedy when in due course they stand before God and look back at what might have been.

Barriers To Growth

If you feel you are more of a fleshly person than a spiritual person right now, don't beat yourself up. Just look at what is getting in the way and deal with it. Here are some of the barriers to growth.

▶ Deception

As fleshly patterns of thinking get more and more ingrained, they become entrenched and we refer to them as "strongholds." They stop us seeing things as they really are and keep us in deception. Common areas of deception for the Christian would include thoughts like these:

- "This might work for others, but my case is different and it won't work for me."

- "I could never have faith like so-and-so."

- "God could never use me."

It takes a determined effort to deal with a stronghold and we'll show you how to do that in Session 8.

▶ Unresolved personal and spiritual conflicts

In Ephesians 4:26–27 Paul says:

> "In your anger do not sin": Do not let the sun go down while you are still angry, and do not give the devil a foothold.

In other words, if we do not deal with something like anger quickly and we let it turn into the sins of bitterness and unforgiveness, we give the devil a foothold, an opportunity to hold us back.

[See note left on this illustration from Steve Goss]

A plane I was traveling on was running late. When it finally arrived I was one of the first on board and headed for my seat. I became aware that it was more and more difficult to move forward and eventually ground to a halt with a load of impatient people behind me. My jacket had some toggles on elastic and one of them had got caught on the first row — I was now at row 11! I couldn't move forward until someone released it for me.

> The illustration of being held back by an elasticated toggle is memorable and works well. If you are presenting the course yourself you may find it helpful at this point to show the section of the video where Steve Goss tells the story. Alternatively we suggest you find a way of explaining the concept of being held back by an elasticated cord.

For example, if you have never truly forgiven someone who hurt you, you are leaving a big door open to the enemy to confuse your thinking and stop you from connecting with truth. If you do not close that door by obeying God and forgiving that person, no matter how well someone preaches the truth to you, you are unlikely ever really to get hold of it in a way that you can grasp and put into practice.

▶ But it's actually straightforward to release the toggle, to get rid of the foothold. You will have the opportunity later in the course to go through a process called *The Steps to Freedom In Christ*, which is a straightforward tool you can use to examine all the areas of your life and ask the Holy Spirit to show you where you have not repented and closed the door to the enemy's influence. You can then, in a controlled and calm way, take the authority you now have in Christ to repent of those things and cut off the capacity of the enemy to confuse your thinking. In our experience there is no Christian that does not benefit from this process and, for many, it's the key to getting hold of the truths that we are teaching. It's something I do every year.

It's not uncommon for people who have been through *The Steps To Freedom In Christ* to be listening to some teaching and say something like, "Why didn't someone tell me this 20 years ago?" Their poor pastor might respond, "I've been telling you for 20 years!" They were just not able to connect with it in any meaningful way until they dealt with their personal and spiritual conflicts.

For many in this course, it's going through The Steps that will suddenly enable them to grasp key truths for the first time in their heart not just their head:

"God really does love me."

"There really is no condemnation for me now."

"God really does want the best for me."

"I don't have to be frightened any more."

"I am not a victim any more."

You could take this opportunity to explain a little about *The Steps To Freedom In Christ* process:
It's a gentle process between you and God in which you ask the Holy Spirit to show you things from the past that have given the enemy ground in your life. You then choose to repent (change your mind), thus removing any right that the enemy had to confuse your thinking. The process is based on James 4:7: "Submit yourselves, then, to God. Resist the devil, and he will flee from you."

Not assuming responsibility for our lives

A final reason that we may not make progress is that we haven't learned to take responsibility for the things that God says are our responsibility.

Steve Goss has put an additional short teaching session on the app on this but here's the bottom line:

▶ Peter says, "His divine power has given us [past tense] everything [not **nearly** everything] we need for a godly life" (2 Peter 1:3). Paul agrees and says we already have "**every** spiritual blessing" (Ephesians 1:3).

So it's not a question of asking God to do something more. And it's not a question of looking for an anointed person to "zap" us or pray the "right" prayer.

It comes down to knowing just who you are: a holy child of the living God who already has everything they need to be the person God is calling them to be. And then understanding how to put it all into practice, which is what this course is all about.

PAUSE FOR THOUGHT 2

OBJECTIVE:

TO DISCUSS THE THREE DIFFERENT TYPES OF PERSON AND SEE THAT MANY CHRISTIANS SWING BETWEEN THE "FLESHLY" AND "SPIRITUAL" PERSON, BUT THAT THERE IS GENUINE HOPE OF CHANGE.

▶ QUESTIONS:

How do you identify with the descriptions of the three different types of people that are mentioned in 1 Corinthians 2:14–3:3?

How have the barriers to growth mentioned caused you to show more of the characteristics of a "fleshly person" than a "spiritual person"?

What practical steps and daily choices can we put in place to ensure we act as a "spiritual person"?

Choosing To Walk By The Spirit Every Day

▶ Once we've committed ourselves to believe the truth no matter what we feel, and once we've dealt with our unresolved spiritual conflicts, we are genuinely free to make a choice every day. We are back in the position Adam and Eve were in before the Fall, able to choose freely. That free will is hugely important to God.

Paul wrote, "Live by the Spirit, and you will not gratify the desires of the flesh" (Galatians 5:16).

The key choice we can make every day is whether to obey the promptings of the flesh or the promptings of the Holy Spirit. The two are in direct opposition to each other.

[Do you have a story of your own to replace this one from Nancy Maldonado that could bring out the eagle/chicken metaphor? If not, consider showing Nancy's story from the video. And see the note in the margin.]

Even if you don't have a story to illustrate the eagle and chicken, it's worth making the point that past experiences can make us see ourselves as spiritual chickens so we think and act like a chicken. But actually our true identity is as an eagle and when we realize that, we will start to think and act like the eagle that we are.

The church my husband and I planted in Spain divided, not once but twice in two years. Like all divisions it was nasty and painful. Our leaders and friends became our enemies. It truly felt like we'd lost a child, our baby. In the midst of this turmoil, I gathered to pray with two women. We prayed and shared our hearts and at one point they stopped me and said: "Nancy, you've got to stop talking like that!" I asked "Like what?" "You always say, 'I'm such a disaster!'" And I responded "But it's true. I'm forgetful, absent minded, I'm always late, I easily feel overwhelmed. I'm a disaster!"

▶ As we continued praying the Lord revealed both my false and my true identity — I'd been living like a chicken when He'd made me an eagle! I certainly didn't feel like an eagle — I don't even like to fly, literally. I identified so much more with a chicken — small, shy, fearful, bound to earth, anxious, and concerned that "the sky is falling."

▶ But no, God said I was an eagle — fearless, free, flying above the storm, living in the heights. Do I feel like an eagle now? Sometimes. Other times, the amount of conflict or pain makes me cry out "Lord, can't you see this is killing me?" And He patiently answers, "Yes, Nancy, for a chicken to fall from this height would be lethal, but you're an eagle and I'm

teaching you to fly." Rarely a day goes by when my flesh doesn't tell me that I'm a chicken. And I can make the choice to listen to it and allow that lie to domesticate me. Or I can choose to listen to the promptings of the Spirit and dare to fly free.

What Is Walking By The Spirit?

Walking By The Spirit Is Not:

▶ **Just a good feeling**

Sometimes the Holy Spirit touches us in such a way that we feel full of joy or peace. That's a lovely gift when it happens, but being filled with the Spirit day-by-day is much more than that. Because if we base our life on having a good feeling, we'll always be looking for "the key" to feeling better and we'll be constantly chasing after a new experience. I've known so many people in our churches addicted to having other people pray for them. They seek a warm tingly feeling inside, or a cathartic emotional release. But there's no fruit in their lives until they realize they are responsible for their own growth in the Lord.

▶ **A license to do whatever we want**

Some think that freedom means we can cast off all the guidelines God has given to help us lead responsible lives. You can try that, and your sin of choice might feel like freedom for a short while, but eventually you realize it's actually bondage. The key question is: can you stop? If you can't, you have become a slave to sin.

▶ Legalism (slavishly obeying a set of rules)

The Old Testament law revealed the moral nature of God but nobody could live up to it. The point of the law was to lead us to Christ by teaching us how much we need Him (Galatians 3:24).

But Paul says, "If you are led by the Spirit, you are not under the law" (Galatians 5:18).

When we see living for God as obeying a set of rules or behaving in a certain way, our walk with Him becomes a joyless trudge. It's hard to keep it up, and very tempting to give up. God isn't blessed by people who obey because they feel they have to. He wants us to obey because we want to, because we delight in doing His will.

So, what **is** walking by the Spirit?

Walking By The Spirit Is:

▶ True freedom

We read in Corinthians: "Where the Spirit of the Lord is, there is freedom." (2 Corinthians 3:17)

The devil can't make you walk in the flesh, although he will try to draw you that way. We have the freedom to be the people God created us to be and to make the choice to live by faith in the power of the Holy Spirit.

▶ Being led

During our time in Spain we lived for a while in a rural area where sheep were abundant. In Spanish, the words for "shepherd" and "pastor" are the same. So when people asked Rob what he did, and he answered, "I'm a pastor," people would ask, "of sheep or goats?"

So, one day I accompanied a friend to pasture her sheep. I stood by the gate while she opened the stable door to let them out. I waited . . . nothing. Then I heard her saying, "Nancy, could you hide behind the wall where the sheep can't see or hear you?" You see, the sheep didn't know me, so seeing and hearing me frightened them. But not so with her.

Jesus said, "My sheep listen to my voice; I know them, and they follow me." (John 10:27)

▶ **Walking at God's pace in the right direction**

"Come to me, all you who are weary and burdened, and I will give you rest. Take my yoke upon you and learn from me, for I am gentle and humble in heart, and you will find rest for your souls. For my yoke is easy and my burden is light." (Matthew 11:28–30)

Being yoked to Jesus doesn't work if only one of us is pulling. Nothing will get done if we expect God to do it all. And neither can we accomplish anything lasting for eternity by ourselves. Only Jesus knows the right pace and the right direction to walk. When we walk with Him we learn that His ways are not hard and we find rest for our souls.

How Can We Tell If We Are Walking By The Spirit?

▶ Just as you can tell a tree by its fruit, you can tell whether you are walking by the Spirit by the fruit of your life. If you're being led by the Spirit, your life will be increasingly marked by love, joy, peace, patience, kindness, goodness, faithfulness, gentleness, and self-control.

If you are living according to your flesh, that too will become evident in your life.

Perhaps you have become aware during this session that you are living according to the flesh. What is the appropriate response? Simply to confess it, deal with any footholds of the enemy, invite the Holy Spirit to fill you, and start obeying the promptings of the Spirit rather than the flesh.

Walking by the Spirit is a moment-by-moment, day-by-day experience. You can choose every moment of every day either to walk by the Spirit or to walk by the flesh, to walk like a chicken or to fly like an eagle. ▶

FREEDOM IN CHRIST

REFLECTION

OBJECTIVE:

TO GIVE PEOPLE AN OPPORTUNITY TO MAKE A PERSONAL COMMITMENT TO WALK BY THE SPIRIT RATHER THAN BY THE FLESH.

LEADER'S NOTES:
THE FIRST PART CAN BE DONE IN GROUPS AND CAN BE COMPLETED IN JUST A COUPLE OF MINUTES — DON'T LET IT GO ON LONG. THE SECOND PART IS FOR INDIVIDUAL RESPONSE.

▶ **REFLECTION**

Paul said this to his younger disciple, Timothy:

> For this reason I remind you to fan into flame the gift of God, which is in you through the laying on of my hands. For the Spirit God gave us does not make us timid, but gives us power, love and self-discipline. (2 Timothy 1:6–7)

Who was responsible for "fanning into flame" the gift of the Holy Spirit in Timothy's life, God, Paul, or Timothy?

Whose responsibility is it to do that in your life? What are some of the ways you could do that?

Take some time on your own in prayer to commit to walk by the Spirit rather than the flesh and to fan into flame the gift of the Holy Spirit in your life.

WITNESS

How would you explain to a not-yet-Christian the benefits of being filled with the Spirit in a way that would make sense to them?

IN THE COMING WEEK

Every day specifically commit yourself to walk by the Spirit rather than by the flesh. Ask the Holy Spirit to fill you and guide you.

The Battle For Our Minds

Session 5:
The Battle For Our Minds

FOCUS VERSE:

Ephesians 6:11: Put on the full armor of God, so that you can take your stand against the devil's schemes.

OBJECTIVE:

To understand that, although our enemy, the devil, is constantly attempting to get us to believe lies, we don't have to believe every thought that comes into our head but can hold each one up against truth and choose to accept or reject it.

FOCUS TRUTH:

We are all in a spiritual battle. It's a battle between truth and lies, and it takes place in our minds. If we are aware of how Satan works, we will not fall for his schemes.

POINTERS FOR LEADERS:

The whole area of Satan and demons has not been well understood by the Western church but it's essential that, without "looking for a demon behind every bush," we equip people to understand that the battle with Satan is real and that it is played out in our minds. Satan is a liar and our defense against him is truth.

Many will be surprised by some of the things they will learn in this session and often many questions are raised. You are advised to be well prepared (perhaps reread *Win The Daily Battle* by Steve Goss or Part 1 of *The Bondage Breaker* by Dr. Neil T. Anderson).

Be aware that Satan very much wants Christians to fear him — guard against any tendency of your group to go in that direction.

You are unmasking Satan's schemes and it is particularly important to pray in the meeting room before you start. Exercise the spiritual authority you have in Christ and commit yourself, the room, and all the equipment to God. Ask for His protection for yourself, and for Him to guard the hearts and minds of those who come. See the personal prayer and team declaration on pages 22–23.

Remind people of the away day dates if you are running an away day after Session 7.

THE APP

Steve Goss has put an extra teaching film on the app called "Overcoming Temptation" that would be helpful for participants to watch after this session.

SMALL GROUP TIMINGS:

Welcome	10 minutes	10
Worship	12 minutes	22
Word part 1	16 minutes	38
Pause For Thought 1	20 minutes	58
Word part 2	12 minutes	70
Pause For Thought 2	20 minutes	90
Word part 3	15 minutes	105
Reflection	15 minutes	120

Registered users of the course can download a spreadsheet with these timings. Simply enter your own start time, adjust the length of the various components as desired, and you will have a timed plan of your session.

SONGS:

The song from *Worship In Spirit And Truth* (see page 26) that has been written to accompany this session is *Standing Stronger*. See page 215 of the Participant's Guide for the lyrics and background info.

 # WELCOME

Has anyone ever played a really good trick on you, or have you played one on someone else? What was it?

 # WORSHIP

Suggested theme: His authority — our authority.

Read Colossians 2:15: "And having disarmed the powers and authorities, he made a public spectacle of them, triumphing over them by the cross."

You may also like to read one or more of Luke 10:19, Colossians 2:20, Matthew 28:18–20.

Suggest that each person rereads the focus verse for this session (Ephesians 6:11) and spends a few moments committing themselves to put on "the whole armour of God" (Ephesians 6:13–18) afresh.

 # WORD

The second book in the FREEDOM IN CHRIST DISCIPLESHIP SERIES, *Win The Daily Battle*, corresponds to Part B of the course. Read pages 43–110 in the book for the material that relates to this session.

The Battle For Our Minds

SESSION 5

The Battle Is Real

We've looked so far in this section of the course at the way this fallen world tries to influence our thinking, and how our flesh has been programmed to predispose us to live independently of God.

But we're not just up against the world and the flesh. The Bible teaches that we're also up against the devil, whom Jesus calls the "father of lies" (John 8:44). The good news is that this is the most resolvable of the three. Jesus came to destroy the devil's work (1 John 3:8).

The tendency, however, of those of us brought up with the Western worldview is to run our lives as if the spiritual world did not exist. But from the beginning of Genesis to the end of Revelation, there's one continuous theme in the Bible: the battle between the kingdom of light and the kingdom of darkness; between the Spirit of Truth and the father of lies; between the Christ and the Antichrist.

"But wasn't that all dealt with at the cross? I'm a Christian — surely I'm immune."

▶ No — the truth is, you're the bull's eye. Is the armor of God for the nonbeliever? No, it's for the believer. We are in the battle whether we like it or not. Paul tells us explicitly that we are not fighting flesh and blood but "the spiritual forces of wickedness in the heavenly realms" (see Ephesians 6:10–18).

▶ If you bury your head in the sand, you leave a great big target exposed!

If we don't understand that we are in a battle or how that battle works, we're very likely to become a casualty — to be "neutralized" in our walk with the Lord.

Satan The Deceiver

So, who is Satan and how does he work?

When God created Adam and Eve to rule over the world the devil had to crawl at their feet in the form of a snake.

But when they sinned, Adam and Eve effectively handed over their right to rule the world to Satan. That's why Jesus referred to him as "the prince [or ruler] of this world" (John 12:31). He's also called "the ruler of the kingdom of the air" (Ephesians 2:2), and we're told that the whole world lies in his power (1 John 5:19).

Satan Is Not Like God

▶   God and Satan are not equal and opposite powers or anything remotely like that, though Satan would like you to think that they are. In fact, it has been said that to compare Satan to God is like comparing an ant to an atomic bomb. The Bible makes a huge distinction between the "Creator" and the "created" (see John 1:3). Like us, Satan is a mere created being.

Satan Can Only Be In One Place At One Time

Because of that, we can infer that he can only be in one place at one time. He rules this world through "rulers, authorities, powers and spiritual forces of evil in the heavenly realms" (Ephesians 6:12), different types or levels of fallen angels. The Bible doesn't bother telling us a huge amount about how they are organized because we don't really need to know.

Only God is everywhere at once. That means that most of us have probably never come up against Satan himself in person. So when I use the term "Satan" I am usually referring not just to Satan himself (who can only be in one place at one time) but using it to refer to evil spirits in general.

Satan's Power And Authority Do Not Even Begin To Compare To God's

At the Cross Jesus completely disarmed Satan (Colossians 2:15) and Satan can only operate within the boundaries that God sets (see Jude 1:6). He can't just walk into your life and inflict damage and destruction.

▶ If a dog is loose, a cat will stay right out of its way. If, however, the dog is on a leash, a cat seems to know just how far it can come and will often delight in parading past slowly just out of reach. Of course, the dog goes wild, snarling, barking, and straining at its leash but the cat knows it is perfectly safe and has great fun standing just beyond the limit of the leash, the picture of calm and tranquillity.

God has put Satan on a leash and he can only act within the boundaries that God has set.

Satan Does Not Know Everything

Every occult practice relates to the mind or the future, but Satan knows neither perfectly.

There's no evidence that Satan can read your mind. For example, all interaction in the Bible between angels and people or demons and people is done out loud.

In Daniel 2 God gave King Nebuchadnezzar some dreams. He demanded that his magicians told him what they meant but first they also had to tell him the content of his dreams. These sorcerers could not do it because their normal sources of power and information were demons and they clearly were unable to read the king's mind. If they had been able to, they would because that would have prevented Daniel from advancing in the king's service.

Only God knows the future. Satan does not know the future except what God has revealed. Many claim that they can see into the future using occult (Satanic) powers. Think about that for a moment. If someone were genuinely able to see into the future, what would they do? I dare say they would make a fortune buying stock-market shares that were about to rise dramatically or betting on rank outsiders in horse races that would then go on to win. What they would not be doing is spending time in tents at carnivals reading palms for a few coins a time.

Have you ever seen the headline "Psychic wins lottery"? Neither have I. I rest my case!

How Satan Works

By Putting Thoughts Into Our Mind

▶   Now this does not mean that Satan cannot put thoughts into your mind, something that the Bible clearly teaches he can do.

[YAWN] Mind you, so can I. . . . In fact I hope that during this course I've been putting lots of thoughts into your mind.

Because he's had so much practice observing people over many years, he can often make a pretty accurate guess about what's going on in your mind — and it's not hard for him to know what you are thinking if he gave you the thought in the first place.

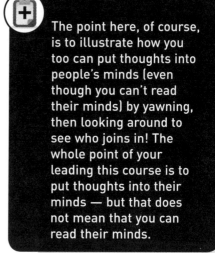

The point here, of course, is to illustrate how you too can put thoughts into people's minds (even though you can't read their minds) by yawning, then looking around to see who joins in! The whole point of your leading this course is to put thoughts into their minds — but that does not mean that you can read their minds.

Some people get spooked because they know someone who went to a medium or some other occult practitioner and was told a detail of their life that no other person — or often only a deceased person — knew. Undoubtedly much of that is explainable through psychology or mind games. However, it would be equally possible that the information was revealed to the medium by a demon which had observed 20 years ago that Great Uncle Bill had a heart-shaped mole on his left buttock.

The Spirit clearly says that in later times some will abandon the faith and follow deceiving spirits and things taught by demons. (1 Timothy 4:1)

Are Christians being deceived into abandoning faith and listening to demons? Let's look at three Biblical examples to try to understand how we can be affected without even knowing it.

> Satan rose up against Israel and incited David to take a census of Israel. (1 Chronicles 21:1)

What's wrong with that? Wouldn't you want to know how many troops you had? But even the captain of his guard tried to persuade him not to do it because it showed that David was putting his confidence in his own resources rather than God.

But why did he listen to Satan? To put it another way, would he have done it if he had thought it was Satan's idea? Of course not! David believed that it was his own idea — even though the Bible makes clear that it wasn't.

> The evening meal was being served, and the devil had already prompted Judas Iscariot, son of Simon, to betray Jesus. (John 13:2)

Weren't these Judas' own thoughts? No. The Bible clearly says that the thought came from the devil. And when Judas realized the implications of what he had done, he went out and hanged himself.

> Then Peter said, "Ananias, how is it that Satan has so filled your heart that you have lied to the Holy Spirit and have kept for yourself some of the money you received for the land?" (Acts 5:3)

Ananias almost certainly thought that this was his own idea, but the Bible makes clear that it originated with Satan. Ananias was deceived and it had terrible consequences — God struck him dead. He sent a powerful message to the early Church about the importance of not compromising the truth.

It's not too much of a leap to think that, if Satan can put thoughts into our mind, he can make them sound like our own. He would not announce the thought with an evil cackle: "Satan here — you're useless." No, he would make it sound very like your own thought: "I'm useless, I'm ugly." Not every thought that comes into your mind is your own. And you don't have to think every thought that comes into your mind.

PAUSE FOR THOUGHT 1

OBJECTIVE:
TO UNDERSTAND WHO SATAN IS AND HOW HE WORKS. TO REALIZE THAT HE IS ONLY A CREATED BEING BUT ALSO A DESTROYER, LIAR, AND THIEF (JOHN 8:44, 10:10).

▶ **QUESTIONS:**

Does the devil seem more or less powerful than you had imagined? In what ways?

"Not every thought that comes into your head is your own" (for example, "I'm useless" or "I'm dirty"). What do you think about this?

Looking back, can you identify occasions when a thought you have had may well have been from the enemy? Are those thoughts always completely false?

Through Temptation, Accusation, And Deception

The strategies Satan uses fall into three categories: temptation, accusation, and deception.

Let's imagine your Christian life as a race, with the racetrack stretching out in front of you. Satan can't block the path or stop you from becoming everything that God wants you to be. All he can do is shout out to you from the sidelines.

▶ He'll try to tempt you away ("Hey! Look what's over here! Come and get it. It'll make you feel better and no one needs to find out. You know you want to.").

▶ Or he'll shout accusations at you ("You blew it again? You useless excuse for a Christian! You might as well sit down and give up.").

▶ He'll also tell you barefaced lies ("Excuse me — you're going the wrong way. The finishing line is back that way.").

Satan is trying to get us into sin, to establish negative patterns of thought ("I'm hopeless" or "I'll never be able to"), and to deceive us into worldly ways of thinking ("I can sort this out on my own" or "All I need is positive thinking").

The most defeated Christians believe the lies and sit down — "Yeah, you're right, it's hopeless."

Others stand while they argue with the thoughts, but they make no progress.

Victorious Christians simply **ignore** them. They take every thought captive to the obedience of Christ and keep running toward the finishing line.

Are we experiencing a battle for the mind? Let's ask three questions to find out. Please raise your hand to indicate your response. If you're watching the video do join in!

- How many of us have experienced some form of temptation this last week? (And are the others being tempted to lie?)

According to the Bible, who's the tempter? Is it the opposite sex, or the porn site, or the chocolate bar? No, those are just objects that Satan uses. But given that Satan himself can only be in one place at a time, we're probably dealing with deceiving spirits.

- How many of us here have struggled with the voice of the accuser in the last week? Or, to put it another way: How many of us have struggled with thoughts like "I'm stupid," "I'm hopeless," "No one understands me," "God doesn't love me," "I'm different from others"?

Every one of us has. Satan accuses us before God day and night (Revelation 12:10).

- In the last week, how many of us have been deceived in some way?

Far fewer hands went up for the third question [if indeed that is the case!] because if I tempt you, you know it and if I accuse you, you know it. But if I deceive you, by definition you don't know it. Deception is Satan's primary strategy.

Ask people to raise their hands in response to these questions. Generally speaking, most hands go up for the first two questions and not many for the third, which emphasizes the point that deception is the most effective weapon Satan has: if we are being deceived, by definition we don't know it.

▶ Remember the illustration of the eagle that thought it was a chicken from the last session? We can be deceived into seeing ourselves as spiritual chickens. We don't repent of that because we think it's reality and we think like a chicken: "I'm a disaster," "This is too much for me," "I'm so overwhelmed." We act like a chicken, taking small, fearful steps forward and then retreating.

▶ But when we realize that the chicken identity is in fact deception, when we're tempted to feel or think like a chicken we can catch ourselves and recognize it as a lie. We can remind ourselves of the truth that we are eagles, even when we don't feel like one.

By Getting Footholds In Our Lives Through Sin

▶ In the last session we looked at Ephesians 4:26–27 which says that if we don't deal with anger quickly, we give the devil a foothold in our life.

You can see the same principle in 2 Corinthians 2:10–11:

> Anyone you forgive, I also forgive. And what I have forgiven — if there was anything to forgive — I have forgiven in the sight of Christ for your sake, in order that Satan might not outwit us. For we are not unaware of his schemes.

We'll look at forgiveness in a later session. But for now I'll just point out that Satan's greatest access to our lives is often through the sin of unforgiveness.

▶ If Satan can lead us into sin, he gains a point of influence in our lives that he can use to hold us back, as if we are on a piece of elastic.

We tend to look for the activity of demons in "dramatic" episodes. But the battle is primarily in the mind.

The Relationship Between Demons And Christians

It's very important to stress at this point that we're not talking about Christians being completely taken over or taken back by demons.

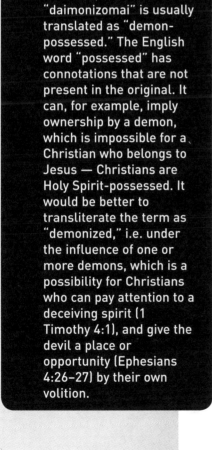

▶ At the center of your being, your spirit is connected to God's Spirit and Satan can't have you back. You have been purchased by the blood of the Lamb (1 Peter 1:18–19). In other words, we're not talking here about ownership or "possession."

If we fall for Satan's temptation, accusation, or deception, he may gain a degree of influence in our minds (1 Peter 5:8). His goal is to neutralize us or even use us to further his agenda (for example, Acts 5:3).

We read in 2 Corinthians 4:4 that Satan "has blinded the minds of unbelievers" and these footholds seem to work in believers in much the same way. They cause a degree of spiritual blindness and make it more difficult for us to "connect" with truth. That's why good teaching on its own isn't enough for us to grow. We may simply be unable to connect with it until we deal with these footholds of the enemy.

The good news is that getting rid of these footholds is not difficult or dramatic, and you'll get an opportunity to do that in a gentle and controlled way when we go through *The Steps To Freedom In Christ*. Many find that they are then able to grasp the truth of God's Word in a completely new way.

In English translations of the Bible, the Greek term "daimonizomai" is usually translated as "demon-possessed." The English word "possessed" has connotations that are not present in the original. It can, for example, imply ownership by a demon, which is impossible for a Christian who belongs to Jesus — Christians are Holy Spirit-possessed. It would be better to transliterate the term as "demonized," i.e. under the influence of one or more demons, which is a possibility for Christians who can pay attention to a deceiving spirit (1 Timothy 4:1), and give the devil a place or opportunity (Ephesians 4:26–27) by their own volition.

PAUSE FOR THOUGHT 2

OBJECTIVE:

TO HELP PEOPLE GET TO GRIPS WITH WHAT IT MEANS PRACTICALLY TO WIN THE BATTLE FOR OUR MINDS.

▶ **QUESTIONS:**

"If you are deceived, by definition you don't know it." What are some of the ways that you might become aware of deception in your life?

What practical steps can you take to "take every thought captive" to obey Christ (2 Corinthians 10:5)?

If we have given the enemy a foothold through sin, how can we take that foothold away according to James 4:7?

Our Defense

Understand Our Position In Christ

▶ Ephesians 1:19–22 says that Jesus is seated at God's right hand, the ultimate seat of power and authority, "far above all rule and authority, power and dominion." God has placed all things under His feet and we are told that He is now "head over **everything**" (our emphasis).

That's a great position of power!

So what is our position?

▶ Ephesians 2:6 says, "And God raised us up with Christ and seated us with Him in the heavenly realms in Christ Jesus."

We are seated with Jesus, **far** above Satan and all demonic powers. Not just slightly above!

Use The Resources We Have In Christ

▶ Now even though Satan is defeated, he still "prowls around, like a roaring lion looking for someone to devour" (1 Peter 5:8).

However, James 4:7 says, "Submit to God. Resist the devil and he will flee from you." As long as you are submitting to God when you resist the devil he has no choice but to flee. This applies to every Christian no matter how weak and frail you feel, or how long or how short a time you have been a Christian. Every believer has the same authority and power in Christ over the spiritual world.

▶ Understanding this concept is the key to escaping from sin-confess cycles. We need to do more than simply **confess** to God that we did wrong. We also need to **resist** the devil so that he flees from us.

Do Not Be Frightened

There's nothing big about a demon except its mouth! They are like dogs with a big bark but no teeth. We don't need to be intimidated by something that goes bump in the night. The truth is that demons are petrified of Christians who understand the magnitude of power and authority they have in Christ. Satan and demons have no power over Christians except what we give them.

Illustration from Steve Goss: One of my daughters' friends was frightened of dogs. When she came round they had to be kept in a separate room. One time the dogs got out. As soon as she saw them, she leapt up onto the table. She was quite a big girl and the dogs were quite small. Now, what power did those dogs have to get her up onto the table? Only what she gave them. How did she get up there? The dogs used her mind, her emotions, her will, and her muscles. What would have happened if she had stood her ground. They would have licked her a little, lost interest, and gone away.
In the same way, demons have no power over Christians except what we give them.

So some of you might be thinking, "Do you mean there might be demons in here?" Yes, the spiritual world is filled with demons, but so what? God has not given us the spirit of fear. You have no reason to be afraid of that. What else is here that you can't see but has the potential to hurt you? [PAUSE]. Germs!

What is the proper response to the fact that there are germs all around?

▶   Do you need to go put on a protective suit and spray disinfectant all over the place? No! The best response is to live a balanced life of diet, exercise, and rest and let your immune system protect you.

What is the best response to the fact that there are demons all around? Simply to fix our eyes on Jesus and by faith live a righteous life in the power of the Holy Spirit. The last thing you need to do is go looking for a demon behind every bush.

However, the danger comes for those Christians who don't realize that demons are there, don't understand how they work, and don't know how to protect themselves. When doctors didn't know there were germs all around us, they didn't sterilize their instruments or scrub their hands and people died. Christians who don't put on the full armor of God are left exposed to the attack of the enemy because they don't understand the reality of the spiritual world.

By the way, your authority does not increase with volume! You don't need to shout the devil away. If you think you have to shout and scream, you're not exercising your authority, you're actually undermining it. The devil's goal is to get you to respond in fear. If you respond in fear you're operating in the flesh and he will defeat you.

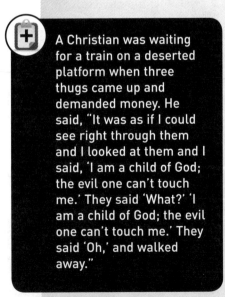

A Christian was waiting for a train on a deserted platform when three thugs came up and demanded money. He said, "It was as if I could see right through them and I looked at them and I said, 'I am a child of God; the evil one can't touch me.' They said 'What?' 'I am a child of God; the evil one can't touch me.' They said 'Oh,' and walked away."

If you're ever tempted to be frightened of the enemy here is a good verse to memorize: "The One who was born of God keeps them safe, and the evil one cannot harm them." (1 John 5:18b).

Guard Our Minds

▶   Then we need to guard our minds, to be careful what we allow into them.

There are a lot of Eastern influences coming into the business world, schools, and even churches, that are spiritually dangerous. A lady wrote to Freedom In Christ saying that she attended an inner-healing seminar in her church and participated in a process called guided imagery. Instead of getting better she got worse and eventually she was taken through *The Steps To Freedom In Christ*.

She says:

> It was an awesome encounter with the love of our heavenly father like I have never experienced before. At the beginning of the session, with the help of the loving, gentle pastor, the Lord revealed a spirit guide that had gained entrance during the inner healing guided imagery. I had learned to look forward to his presence in my prayer life in the form of a purple light that guided me in many situations. I had often shared with my pastor my color purple. He believed it was from the Lord and didn't recognize it as demonic either. We were both deceived.

> As a result of this demonic guide, my marriage ended, my son is alienated from me and I am alienated from my church. Now as a result of an encounter with truth I am free in Christ.

It's concerning when such practices enter our church. The psalmist said, "Search me, God, and know my heart; test me and know my anxious thoughts. See if there is any offensive way in me" (Psalm 139:23–24). It's good to invite God to search our heart. However, we are never told to direct our thoughts inward or passively but always outward and actively. Even in 1 Corinthians 14, the definitive chapter on tongues and prophecy, Paul says if you pray with your spirit, you should also pray with your mind.

We open ourselves up to deception when we put our mind into neutral. That's what other religions do. For example, Maharishi Yogi, a Hindu, says, "The mind is like a snake. You have to get it out of the way so that you can perceive truth directly."

We never want to deny any supernatural work of God in our lives, but He does not bypass our minds — He works through them.

Turn On The Light

Some people are concerned to know whether the thoughts in their mind are from the enemy or not. That's the wrong question. The real issue is not where the thought came from but whether it's true! We are told to, "take **every** thought captive." (2 Corinthians 10:5). I don't care if it is coming from my memory, the TV, the internet, or a deceiving spirit. If it is not true, I'm not believing it!

One lady was constantly rebuking thoughts in her mind — I mean constantly: "I rebuke that thought in Jesus' name." It's good that she was aware of the reality of the spiritual world but do we need to keep checking our thoughts and rebuking the enemy every five minutes to see if he has put a thought into our mind? No.

▶ If you're in a dark room and you want to see, what do you do? Do you try and shoo the darkness away? No — you turn on the light! Don't focus on the enemy, focus on the truth.

▶ Do you know how bank clerks are trained to recognize forged currency? By studying forged notes? No! By studying the real thing. They get to know what real currency looks like so they are able to spot fake ones when they come through. In the same way, our defense against deception is to know the truth.

Satan's lies can't withstand the truth any more than night can withstand the rising sun. It's a truth encounter, not a power encounter.

▶ So let's not focus on the enemy. Instead, as Paul instructs:

> Whatever is true, whatever is noble, whatever is right, whatever is pure, whatever is lovely, whatever is admirable — if anything is excellent or praiseworthy — think about such things. (Philippians 4:8)

▶

FREEDOM IN CHRIST

REFLECTION

OBJECTIVE:

TO FOCUS ON THE PROTECTION WE HAVE FROM SATAN'S SCHEMES. WE RECOMMEND THAT THE FIRST PART IS DONE AS A WHOLE GROUP AND THE SECOND PART INDIVIDUALLY.

▶ REFLECTION

"The One who was born of God keeps them safe, and the evil one cannot harm them" (1 John 5:18b). Spend a few minutes as a group discussing this powerful truth and how it applies to your daily life.

Read Ephesians 6:10–18 pausing after each element of the armor of God to pray. As you pray, visualize yourself putting on — or having on — each piece of the armor and commit yourself to what it represents, for example:

- "I put on the belt of truth. I commit myself to believe the truth, speak only the truth, and live according to the truth."
- "I thank You that Jesus has made me righteous and that the breastplate of righteousness covers my heart."

 ## WITNESS

How do you think Satan works in the lives of your non-Christian friends? What might you be able to do about this?

 ## IN THE COMING WEEK

Meditate on the following verses: Matthew 28:18; Ephesians 1:3–14; Ephesians 2:6–10; Colossians 2:13–15.

Part C

BREAKING THE HOLD OF THE PAST

God does not change our past but by His grace He enables us to walk free of it. In this section of the course we look at how we can take hold of what Christ has done for us in order to do just that. This section includes going through *The Steps To Freedom In Christ*.

Session 6

Handling Emotions Well

Session 6: Handling Emotions Well

FOCUS VERSE:

1 Peter 5:7–8: Cast all your anxiety on him because he cares for you. Be alert and of sober mind. Your enemy the devil prowls around like a roaring lion looking for someone to devour.

OBJECTIVE:

To understand our emotional nature and how it is related to what we believe.

FOCUS TRUTH:

Our emotions are essentially a product of our thoughts and a barometer of our spiritual health.

POINTERS FOR LEADERS:

Throughout the course we have challenged people to believe what God says is true regardless of how they feel. That does not mean, however, that we should deny our feelings. God created us with the capacity to feel emotionally, and that is an essential part of our humanity. In this session we seek to show how our emotions relate to the rest of our lives, in preparation for the emotional healing that will come when people go through *The Steps To Freedom In Christ*.

This session contains the third of three key lists of Biblical truth that we will share with participants during the course. They can be life-transforming if people make the choice to believe them. The lists are readily accessible via the app and in the Participant's Guide. You can also order from Freedom In Christ a set of color bookmarks that many really find helpful to keep in their Bible or pin on their fridge.

Dr Neil T. Anderson has written several books on the areas covered by this session that you could read yourself for further information or recommend to participants, for example, *Freedom From Fear* (Harvest House) and *Overcoming Depression* (Bethany House).

Remember to run through the logistical information for your away day if you are running one.

SMALL GROUP TIMINGS:

Welcome	12 minutes	12
Worship	13 minutes	25
Word part 1	15 minutes	40
Pause For Thought 1	15 minutes	55
Word part 2	15 minutes	70
Pause For Thought 2	25 minutes	95
Word part 3	15 minutes	110
Reflection	10 minutes	120

Registered users of the course can download a spreadsheet with these timings. Simply enter your own start time, adjust the length of the various components as desired, and you will have a timed plan of your session.

SONGS:

The two songs from *Worship In Spirit And Truth* (see page 26) for this session are *Ever Present God* (Psalm 139) and *My Father*. *My Father* goes especially well with the *My Father God* list of Biblical truths that comes at the end of the session. See pages 216–218 of the Participant's Guide for the lyrics and background info.

 # WELCOME

Would you describe yourself as an emotional person? Tell the group about an event in the past that resulted in emotional pain or joy.

 # WORSHIP

Suggested theme: He made us so well, and He knows us so well!

Read Psalm 139 aloud together, have a period of quiet for reflection and then invite people to praise God.

 # WORD

The third book in the FREEDOM IN CHRIST DISCIPLESHIP SERIES, *Break Free, Stay Free*, corresponds to Part C of the course. Read pages 12–55 in the book for some key principles and the material that relates to this session.

God Is Described In Emotional Language

This session marks the start of the third section of the course, where we're going to find out how we can break the hold that the past has on us. The book that accompanies this section of the course, for those who want to go a little deeper, is *Break Free, Stay Free* — you'll find more details in your Participant's Guide.

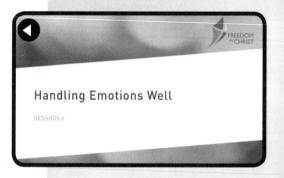

In this session we're going to consider the whole question of our emotions. Did you know that the Bible describes God using emotional language?

He loves us so much that He's described as "jealous" (Exodus 34:14). We are told it is possible to "grieve" the Holy Spirit (Ephesians 4:30).

▶ Jesus wept at the grave of Lazarus (John 11:35) and when He looked at Jerusalem (Luke 19:41).

We Can't Directly Control How We Feel

▶ As we saw in the first session, we're made in God's image so we too have an emotional nature.

We can't simply turn our emotions on and off with a remote control like we do our TV. They aren't like our ability to walk or wave our hand, where we just make a conscious decision to do it. They are more like the way our heart beats or our immune system functions — it just happens.

If you want to check that out, try this simple test. Think of someone you just don't like (try not to look at them right now!) and decide that from now on you're going to like them. Is it working? No. You just can't do it!

The good news is that God doesn't ask us to like people — He commands us to love them. Love is not an emotion — it's a choice we can make. If we make that conscious choice to love them, we may find that we'll eventually come to like them too.

And right there you have a key principle concerning our emotions: although you can't control them directly, you can change them over time, as you make a conscious choice to change what you can control. And you can control what you choose to believe.

Negative Emotions — Our Red Warning Light

Your emotions are to your soul what your ability to feel pain is to your body.

Suppose someone had the power to take away the sensation of pain and offered it to you as a gift. Would you receive it?

It would be tempting, wouldn't it, especially if you were in chronic pain? But it would be dangerous.

[See optional additional illustration in the note overleaf.]

If you go to the dentist for a filling and have an anaesthetic, you will usually be told not to eat anything for a while afterward. You may think that this is so you don't damage the filling.

Dolphins work a little differently. Their heart beat is automatic but they do have to control their breathing consciously. That's logical because they spend most of their lives underwater and would not want to take a breath unless there was air to breathe in. It does, however, mean that they can never sleep because if they did, they would suffocate. They have an ingenious way around this — they only let half of their brain sleep at one time while the other half ensures that breathing and other functions, such as looking out for danger, continue. That is why you may see a dolphin with just one eye open. It's not winking at you. It's just that the half of its brain that controls the other eye is sleeping!

Here are some great truths about life that children have learned:

1. Never hold a Dust-Buster and a cat at the same time.

2. You can't hide a piece of broccoli in a glass of milk.

3. When your mom is really angry with your Dad, don't let her brush your hair.

In fact it's not so much to protect the filling as to protect the soft tissue in your mouth such as your tongue and your cheeks. Eating with a numb mouth is dangerous. You are likely to mangle your tongue and cheeks as you chew because you can't feel a thing.

▶ You see, God gave us the ability to feel physical pain for our own protection.

If you had no ability to feel physical pain you would be a hopeless mass of scars within a matter of weeks.

Negative emotions perform this same function, but for your soul. Wouldn't it be great if you never felt depressed or anxious or angry? No, it wouldn't.

▶ You can think of negative emotions as being like that red warning light that comes on occasionally in your car. The light is there to alert you to a potentially serious problem in the engine.

Our natural reaction when a painful emotion appears can be to ignore it — but that's like taking a piece of tape to cover the warning light — "No problem, the light's gone away."

Consciously ignoring our feelings or choosing not to deal with them is unhealthy.

▶ It's like trying to bury a live mole. It will eventually tunnel its way to the surface . . . usually in some other unhealthy way — maybe in the form of an illness.

Another way of dealing with the red light is to pick up a hammer and smash it. In other words, we simply explode in an outburst of anger.

▶ "That's better. I just had to get that off my chest" — but it can be devastating for your spouse, children, or whoever else is within the perimeter of the explosion.

The most suitable response when that red light comes on, of course, is to stop and take a good look at the engine to see what the problem is. And that's the best way to handle negative emotions too. Their function is to alert you to a problem with what you believe.

If what you believe does not reflect what is actually true, then what you feel won't reflect reality.

Suppose your company is downsizing and people are being laid off. On Monday morning you get a message from your boss. He wants to see you at 10:30 a.m. on Friday morning. Maybe your first reaction is anger: "I've been here 20 years — they can't fire me." Then anxiety: "Yes, they can, the swines. How am I going to pay the bills?" By Thursday you've convinced yourself you're going to lose your job and there's nothing you can do about it, so you're depressed. You decide to resign, but your better half talks you out of it. So on Friday morning you are an emotional mess, haven't slept a wink. You knock on the boss's door: there's the sound of champagne corks popping and they say, "Congratulations, we're promoting you to the board." How do you feel now? You probably faint!

All week you've been going through a range of emotions — but none of them were based on reality. What you believed wasn't actually true.

There was a child street performer in Pakistan who had the ability to stick knives through his arms and walk on hot coals without feeling any pain. He and others in his family had genetic mutations that left them incapable of feeling pain. The lack of ability to feel pain has been much more of a curse than a blessing to the young performer and his family. According to one of the scientists who studied them, "They would walk awkwardly and bump into things as they didn't get hurt. They were covered in bruises. Life without pain sounds like a blessing, but it isn't." In fact the performer died on his 14th birthday after jumping from a roof, possibly made braver by the fact that he knew that, whatever happened, it would not hurt. [This story was reported in *The Times* on December 14, 2006.]

Let's look at a Biblical example. It's in Lamentations 3:1–11 and Jeremiah is in complete despair because he believes that God is the cause of all his problems.

▶ I am the man who has seen affliction by the rod of the LORD's wrath.

He has driven me away and made me walk in darkness rather than light;

indeed, he has turned his hand against me again and again, all day long.

He has made my skin and my flesh grow old and has broken my bones.

▶ He has besieged me and surrounded me with bitterness and hardship.

He has made me dwell in darkness like those long dead.

He has walled me in so I cannot escape; he has weighed me down with chains.

▶ Even when I call out or cry for help, he shuts out my prayer.

He has barred my way with blocks of stone; he has made my paths crooked.

Like a bear lying in wait, like a lion in hiding,

he dragged me from the path and mangled me and left me without help.

[Can you replace this story from Nancy Maldonado with one of your own?]

I can definitely relate to how Jeremiah was feeling. The last four years my family has been through circumstances that I wouldn't wish upon anyone. After 17 years living in Spain we felt led to move with our two teenage children to the US. Within a year it had all gone horribly wrong and we felt it right to move back to Spain, this time to a different city. Would you believe that ten months later, we then moved back to the US, to a different state? So, in the space of three years we uprooted ourselves three times to cross the Atlantic Ocean. Each move meant letting go, leaving behind, parting with . . . to start anew on the other side: different school, new language, another home, a different job. After the third move I broke down. It was too much. The desert of New Mexico where we had moved reflected how I felt — no life, no water,

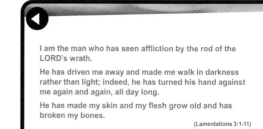

I am the man who has seen affliction by the rod of the LORD's wrath.

He has driven me away and made me walk in darkness rather than light; indeed, he has turned his hand against me again and again, all day long.

He has made my skin and my flesh grow old and has broken my bones.

(Lamentations 3:1-11)

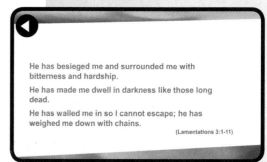

He has besieged me and surrounded me with bitterness and hardship.

He has made me dwell in darkness like those long dead.

He has walled me in so I cannot escape; he has weighed me down with chains.

(Lamentations 3:1-11)

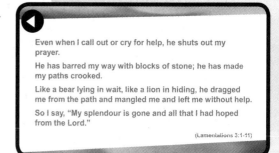

Even when I call out or cry for help, he shuts out my prayer.

He has barred my way with blocks of stone; he has made my paths crooked.

Like a bear lying in wait, like a lion in hiding, he dragged me from the path and mangled me and left me without help.

So I say, "My splendour is gone and all that I had hoped from the Lord."

(Lamentations 3:1-11)

isolated, exposed to the elements. I felt just like Jeremiah — "I am the woman who has seen affliction by the rod of God´s wrath." After all, if my life is in God's hand, then He must be behind my pain and hardship. My conclusion? "I must have done something wrong and God is punishing me." Or even worse, "There's something wrong with me."

But look again at what Jeremiah believed. Is it true? Would God really turn His hand against one of His servants again and again? Does He surround His people with bitterness and hardship? Does He shut out our prayers? Of course not!

What was the problem? Simply that what Jeremiah believed about God wasn't actually true! God hadn't walled him in. God wasn't like a wild animal who had mangled him. If your hope was in God and this was your belief about what He was like, you'd be depressed too!

Thankfully, Jeremiah doesn't leave it there. He thinks more about it. It's like he gets up and goes for a walk. And he has a change in perspective. The passage continues:

Lamentations 3:19–24:

▶   I remember my affliction and my wandering, the bitterness and the gall.

I well remember them, and my soul is downcast within me.

Yet this I call to mind and therefore I have hope:

▶   Because of the LORD's great love we are not consumed, for his compassions never fail.

They are new every morning; great is your faithfulness.

I say to myself, "The LORD is my portion; therefore I will wait for him."

What changed in his circumstances? Absolutely nothing. Did God change? No! The only thing that changed was in his mind: how he looked at his circumstances. Everything changed internally for him when he said, in essence, "Come on Jeremiah, get a grip. What's really true here?" Then he wrote, "This I call to mind and therefore, I have hope. Great is your faithfulness." And he had to talk truth to himself: "The LORD is my portion; therefore I will wait for him."

I had to do the same. With the support of a spiritual mentor, the next 6 months I held on to truth for dear life. To the truth

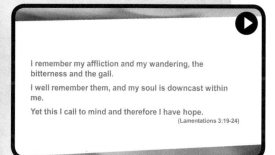

I remember my affliction and my wandering, the bitterness and the gall.
I well remember them, and my soul is downcast within me.
Yet this I call to mind and therefore I have hope.
(Lamentations 3:19-24)

Because of the Lord's great love we are not consumed, for his compassions never fail.
They are new every morning; great is your faithfulness.
I say to myself, "The Lord is my portion; therefore I will wait for him."
(Lamentations 3:19-24)

that my emotional pain was a normal and healthy result of accumulated loss. To the truth that God was not punishing or rejecting me, rather I was dealing with the consequences of other people's choices. To the truth that what Satan intended for my demise, God was using to strengthen me.

Have my circumstances changed? Not a bit. But now I know that God did not banish me to the desert to die. He carried me there in His arms to heal and get stronger.

PAUSE FOR THOUGHT 1

OBJECTIVE:

TO REINFORCE THE CONCEPT THAT GOD GAVE US EMOTIONS FOR OUR OWN PROTECTION.

▶ QUESTIONS:

Look at the example of Jesus in Matthew 26:37 and that of David in 2 Samuel 6:14. What can they teach us?

"God gave us the ability to feel emotional pain for our own protection." Do you agree? If so, how do you think that works in practice?

Discuss this statement: "If what you believe does not reflect what is actually true, then what you feel won't reflect reality."

Negative Emotions Can Help Us

Things like hormones or even the weather can play a part in producing negative emotions, but generally speaking they are a gift from God to help us uncover something we believe that isn't actually true. Let's consider two areas where they do that.

1. Faulty Life-Goals

Firstly they can help us uncover faulty life-goals. We've seen how God created us to be accepted, significant, and secure.

▶ Every day as we grew up, we saw our lives stretching out ahead of us and, whether we realized it or not, we got up and we worked toward whatever we thought would give us those things. Consciously or unconsciously we developed a set of "life-goals." But are those life-goals the same as the goals God has for us? Negative emotions can help us identify those that are not.

Anger Signals A Blocked Life-Goal

▶ If you are finding yourself feeling angry a lot, it's usually because someone or something is blocking a goal you have. I don't know about you but I have a strange knack of always choosing the wrong queue in the supermarket. No matter how short the queue, a problem develops. . . . If you are in a hurry to get to a meeting, that makes you angry because your goal is being blocked.

Suppose you have consciously or unconsciously developed a life-goal to have a loving, harmonious, happy Christian family. Is that a good thing? Well, who can block that goal? Every person in the family! At the end of the day, you can only do so much to influence how your family turns out but you can't control every factor. If you have a belief that achieving this goal is what's going to make you significant, you will go to pieces every time your spouse or children fail to live up to your image of family harmony.

A pastor might feel that in order to be significant or approved by God they have to reach the community for Jesus. That's a great thing to work toward — if it's for the right reason. But if they are doing it because their sense of worth and success as a pastor is dependent on that happening, they will experience tremendous problems in ministry. Why? Again, because it's dependent on other people acting in a certain way. Who can block that goal? Every person in the community (and a couple of members of their leadership team!) They will get angry and try to manipulate church members into evangelistic efforts and perhaps end up falling out with their church.

Anxiety Signals An Uncertain Life-Goal

▶ It's not just anger that highlights unhealthy life-goals: anxiety does too. Anxiety is signaling that achieving a goal feels uncertain. You are hoping something will happen, but you have no guarantee that it will. You can control some of the factors, but not all of them. For example, if you have come to believe that your sense of security depends on financial success and that has become a life-goal, you will probably suffer from anxiety. Why? Because you have no guarantee that you can ever get enough money or, even if you feel you have enough, that it won't be wiped out by a financial crisis.

Depression Signals An Impossible Life-Goal

Sometimes a life-goal that was already uncertain seems to slip even further away to the point where its fulfillment begins to appear impossible: "It's never going to happen." At that point anxiety turns to depression.

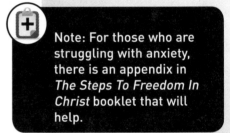

Note: For those who are struggling with anxiety, there is an appendix in *The Steps To Freedom In Christ* booklet that will help.

▶ Of course, the causes of depression are complex and our hormones and other things going on in our bodies can play a part. But if there is no overriding physical cause, then depression is usually rooted in a sense of hopelessness or helplessness. But no child of God is helpless and no child of God is hopeless, whatever their circumstances.

We will get rid of a great deal of anger, anxiety, and depression if we ensure that our life-goals are in line with God's goals for us.

And one thing we can be sure of is that any goal God has for us is one that will not be able to be blocked by other people or by circumstances that we have no right or ability to control. How can we be so sure? Because God loves us too much to set us a goal that we couldn't reach.

In our final session we will come back and work out what a

healthy life-goal for the parent and the pastor would be and, more importantly, what God's life-goal for you and me is.

2. Uncovering Lies That Past Experiences Have Taught Us To Believe

▶ The other area where negative emotions can help is in uncovering lies that past experiences have introduced into our belief system. All of us have had traumatic experiences that have scarred us in some way — a frightening experience, loss of a loved one, some form of abuse.

When you suffered that negative experience you mentally processed it at the time it happened. It almost certainly caused you to believe some things about God and yourself: "Those bullies told me I was rubbish — I guess I am"; "My Dad never has time for me — I'm not important." If you suffered some kind of sexual abuse as a child, at the time it happened you probably felt dirty. If you thought God wasn't there for you, then you probably question God's love and your salvation.

The beliefs that come as a result of those traumatic experiences stay with you and become deeply ingrained strongholds. We'll look at how to demolish them in Session 8 but for now let's just recognize this: we remain in bondage to the past, not because of the traumatic experience itself, but because of the lies it caused us to believe.

Children of God are not primarily products of their past. They are primarily products of Christ's work on the cross and His resurrection. Nobody can change our past, but we can choose to walk free of it. That's the whole point of the Gospel.

When Jesus was in the synagogue at Capernaum, He specifically turned to what we now know as Isaiah 61 and said "Today this is fulfilled in your presence." He was stating His mandate:

"The Spirit of the Lord is on me,

because he has anointed me

to proclaim good news to the poor.

He has sent me to proclaim freedom for the prisoners

and recovery of sight for the blind,

to set the oppressed free,

to proclaim the year of the Lord's favor."

(Luke 4:18–19)

▶ And He meant it. Every Christian needs the principles we are teaching but the wonderful thing is that they work for those with even the deepest hurts.

[You could either quote this example from Steve Goss or give your own example of someone whose testimony shows the truth that Jesus came to help us resolve even the deepest issues.]

I had the privilege of getting to know a lady by the name of Carolyn Bramhall who for years suffered the worst kind of abuse with Satanic rituals thrown in. As part of a team in my church, I worked with Carolyn using Freedom In Christ's discipleship tools, and over eight months saw her turn from a very needy person, who would go from church to church and do unpredictable things, into a fruitful disciple. Several years ago she started her own ministry, Heart For Truth, to equip churches to help others who have suffered similar things and they regularly see deeply wounded people coming into their freedom in the context of local churches. She once went to a conference and met the foremost secular expert on her condition (which is called "Dissociative Identity Disorder") and told the story of how she found her healing in Jesus. The expert said, "You know, Carolyn, that you aren't really healed don't you? People don't get better from this condition but sometimes the mind just deceives you into believing you're healed for a period of time." "Well," said Carolyn, "the deception's been working really well for ten years now!"

Jesus didn't just come to give you a way to cope with the effects of the past. He came to help you resolve those effects completely. It takes time and it's a struggle. But He is with you every step and He's already given you everything you need.

PAUSE FOR THOUGHT 2

OBJECTIVE:

TO HELP PEOPLE UNDERSTAND HOW EMOTIONS CAN HIGHLIGHT FAULTY BELIEFS WE MAY HOLD AND THAT WE CAN RESOLVE PAST ISSUES IN CHRIST.

▶ **QUESTIONS:**

Describe a life-goal you have had that you thought would make you feel significant, secure, and accepted that ended up being "blocked."

How can traumatic experiences lead us to believe a lie about ourselves, God, or Satan?

Discuss this statement: "Children of God are not primarily products of their past. They are primarily products of Christ's work on the cross and His resurrection. Nobody can change our past, but we can choose to walk free of it. That's the whole point of the Gospel. "

The Dangers

We saw in the last session how the emotion of anger can give the enemy a foothold in our lives if we don't quickly resolve an offense. Anxiety has similar dangers.

Here's a verse you probably know: "Cast all your anxiety on him because he cares for you." And here's another one: "Be alert and of sober mind. Your enemy the devil prowls around like a roaring lion looking for someone to devour."

▶ What you many not know is that these verses directly follow each other in 1 Peter 5:7–8. They are both part of the same idea. Peter is telling us to be self-controlled and not let anxiety take hold of us. If we don't, he warns that the devil, like a roaring lion, is prowling around looking to devour us.

Three Keys To Emotional Health

Let's look at three keys to being emotionally healthy:

▶ Know Who You Are In Christ

If you know your true identity in Christ — in your heart, not just your head — you won't go looking for acceptance, significance, and security in those faulty life-goals.

And those who have suffered trauma in the past, you can learn to re-evaluate your past experiences from the perspective of who you now are in Christ.

The truth is you are a complete, clean, holy child of God with unlimited potential in Him. You might be thinking, "But I had awful things done to me that make me feel dirty." That doesn't change who you are now. You may **feel** dirty but you are not actually dirty because you are a new creation in Christ. As you understand and believe this truth — and forgive those who have hurt you from your heart — you can walk in your freedom in Christ.

▶ What once might have seemed like a huge mountain that was impossible to move ▶ can become something that actually makes you stronger as you climb and conquer it in Jesus.

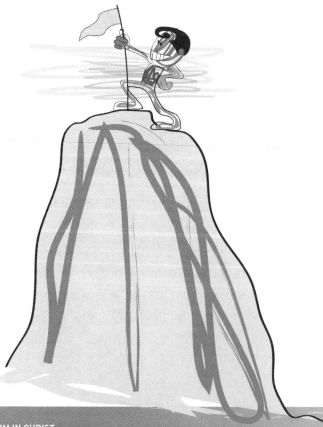

Be Honest

▶ The second thing we can do to guarantee that we are emotionally healthy is to be honest about how we feel, rather than try to bury our feelings or thoughtlessly express them. And that starts with being honest with God.

Let me read you a prayer from David who was described as a man after God's heart. Maybe you can use this passage as a model when you pray for people.

Psalm 109:6-15:

▶ Appoint someone evil to oppose my enemy; let an accuser stand at his right hand. When he is tried, let him be found guilty, and may his prayers condemn him. May his days be few; may another take his place of leadership. May his children be fatherless and his wife a widow. May his children be wandering beggars; may they be driven from their ruined homes. ▶ May a creditor seize all he has; may strangers plunder the fruits of his labor. May no one extend kindness to him or take pity on his fatherless children. May his descendants be cut off, their names blotted out from the next generation. ▶ May the iniquity of his fathers be remembered before the LORD; may the sin of his mother never be blotted out. May their sins always remain before the LORD that he may cut off the memory of them from the earth.

In the name of Jesus. Amen!

What on earth is that doing in the Bible? Well, have you ever felt like that? Have you ever prayed like that? Would it be right to pray like that?

Well, David prayed like that, and God inspired him to write it down.

Does God already know you feel that way? Of course He does. God knows the thoughts and intentions of our hearts. So the question is, if God already knows it, why can't we be honest with Him? Would He still love us if we were totally honest with Him about how we feel? Absolutely!

The problem with this Psalm is that it sounds like it's OK to ask God to wipe someone out. But finish the Psalm. Once David had his emotional eruption, after he has been honest with God about how he was really feeling, he returns to praising God.

Appoint someone evil to oppose my enemy; let an accuser stand at his right hand. When he is tried, let him be found guilty, and may his prayers condemn him. May his days be few; may another take his place of leadership. May his children be fatherless and his wife a widow. May his children be wandering beggars; may they be driven from their ruined homes.

(Psalm 109:6-15)

3 SLIDES IN TOTAL

ℹ

The idea here is to deliberately "ham up" the reading of this Psalm so that people gradually become aware of how extreme the language is.

It can be difficult to accept the concept that David prayed that God would harm someone else and some point out that this Psalm can legitimately be translated differently.

However, it is not the only example of psalms that contain prayers and wishes for the harm of the writer's enemies ("imprecatory psalms"). See Psalms 7, 35, 55, 58, 59, 69, 79, 137 and 139, for example, "Let death take my enemies by surprise" (Psalm 55:15) and "Happy is he who repays you for what you have done to us — he who seizes your infants and dashes them against the rocks." (Psalm 137:8-9)

Although shocking, psalms that ask God to harm people do exist and are not just a matter of translation. All we are saying here is that they show the psalmist being emotionally honest with God, telling Him how he really feels.

You can be completely honest with God. He is your closest friend. As a matter of fact, you can't be right with God without first being real with Him. God may use the circumstances of your life to make you real in order that you can be right with Him.

Commit To Believing The Truth

The third thing we need to do to guarantee that we are emotionally healthy is to embrace the truth. We've seen that behind those wrong life-goals are lies. And those traumatic experiences we had continue to affect us because they made us believe lies. Our freedom comes from knowing the truth.

[Do you have a personal illustration to replace this one from Daryl Fitzgerald concerning a lie you believed about God?]

My parents were really into sports and they pushed us to be the best we could be when we played. But when they pushed us, it didn't come out very affirming but actually very critical. That led me to believe that God was harsh, critical, and distant.

None of us have had perfect fathers — and we often have come to believe lies about our Heavenly Father because of our experiences with our earthly fathers.

To finish this session, we have another list of Biblical truths. It's the truth about our Heavenly Father.

Let's say these words together to our amazing and loving Father God to remind ourselves what is really true:

▶   I renounce the lie that You, Father God, are distant and uninterested in me.

I choose to believe the truth that You, Father God, are always personally present with me, have plans to give me a hope and a future, and have prepared works in advance specifically for me to do.

▶   I renounce the lie that You, Father God, are insensitive and don't know me or care for me.

I choose to believe the truth that You, Father God, are kind and compassionate and know every single thing about me.

I renounce the lie that You, Father God, are stern and have placed unrealistic expectations on me.

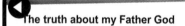

The truth about my Father God

I renounce the lie that You, Father God, are distant and uninterested in me.

I choose to believe the truth that You, Father God, are always personally present with me, have plans to give me a hope and a future, and have prepared works in advance specifically for me to do.

I renounce the lie that You, Father God, are insensitive and don't know me or care for me.

I choose to believe the truth that You, Father God, are kind and compassionate and know every single thing about me.

I renounce the lie that You, Father God, are stern and have placed unrealistic expectations on me.

I choose to believe the truth that You, Father God, have accepted me and are joyfully supportive of me.

I choose to believe the truth that You, Father God, have accepted me and are joyfully supportive of me.

▶   I renounce the lie that You, Father God, are passive and cold toward me.

I choose to believe the truth that You, Father God, are warm and affectionate toward me.

I renounce the lie that You, Father God, are absent or too busy for me.

I choose to believe the truth that You, Father God, are always present and eager to be with me and enable me to be all that You created me to be.

▶   I renounce the lie that You, Father God, are impatient or angry with me or have rejected me.

I choose to believe the truth that You, Father God, are patient and slow to anger, and that when You discipline me, it is a proof of Your love, and not rejection.

I renounce the lie that You, Father God, have been mean, cruel, or abusive to me.

I choose to believe the truth that Satan is mean, cruel, and abusive, but You, Father God, are loving, gentle, and protective.

▶   I renounce the lie that You, Father God, are denying me the pleasures of life.

I choose to believe the truth that You, Father God, are the author of life and will lead me into love, joy, and peace when I choose to be filled with Your Spirit.

I renounce the lie that You, Father God, are trying to control and manipulate me.

I choose to believe the truth that You, Father God, set me free and gave me the freedom to make choices and grow in Your grace.

▶   I renounce the lie that You, Father God, have condemned me and no longer forgive me.

I choose to believe the truth that You, Father God, have forgiven all my sins and will never use them against me in the future.

I renounce the lie that You, Father God, are passive and cold towards me.

I choose to believe the truth that You, Father God, are warm and affectionate towards me.

I renounce the lie that You, Father God, are absent or too busy for me.

I choose to believe the truth that You, Father God, are always present and eager to be with me and enable me to be all that You created me to be.

I renounce the lie that You, Father God, are impatient or angry with me, or have rejected me.

I choose to believe the truth that You, Father God, are patient and slow to anger, and that when You discipline me, it is a proof of Your love, and not rejection.

I renounce the lie that You, Father God, have been mean, cruel, or abusive to me.

I choose to believe the truth that Satan is mean, cruel, and abusive, but You, Father God, are loving, gentle, and protective.

I renounce the lie that You, Father God, are denying me the pleasures of life.

I choose to believe the truth that You, Father God, are the author of life and will lead me into love, joy, and peace when I choose to be filled with Your Spirit.

I renounce the lie that You, Father God, are trying to control and manipulate me.

I choose to believe the truth that You, Father God, have set me free, and give me the freedom to make choices and grow in Your grace.

I renounce the lie that You, Father God, have condemned me, and no longer forgive me.

I choose to believe the truth that You, Father God, have forgiven all my sins and will never use them against me in the future.

I renounce the lie that You, Father God, reject me when I fail to live a perfect or sinless life.

I choose to believe the truth that You, Father God are patient towards me and cleanse me when I fail.

I AM THE APPLE OF YOUR EYE!

I renounce the lie that You, Father God, reject me when I fail to live a perfect or sinless life.

I choose to believe the truth that You, Father God, are patient toward me and cleanse me when I fail.

I AM THE APPLE OF YOUR EYE!

If you realize that you have had a faulty understanding of God, reading this list out loud every day for six weeks or so can dramatically help heal your emotional pain.

REFLECTION

OBJECTIVE:
TO GIVE OPPORTUNITY TO TAKE THE "MY FATHER GOD" TRUTH STATEMENTS TO A DEEPER LEVEL.

LEADER'S NOTES:
THIS IS BEST DONE INDIVIDUALLY RATHER THAN IN A GROUP WITH SOME INSTRUMENTAL MUSIC PLAYING SOFTLY IN THE BACKGROUND.

▶ REFLECTION

How easy do you find it to tell God exactly how you feel?

Read the "My Father God" truth statements one at a time and pause after each one to let it sink in.

How does understanding the truth about Him make it easier to be emotionally honest with Him?

WITNESS

If you are feeling angry, anxious, or depressed, do you think it would be better not to let that show to not-yet-Christians around you? Why? Why not?

IN THE COMING WEEK

Consider the emotional nature of the Apostle Peter. First, have a look at some occasions where he let his emotions run away with him and acted or spoke too hastily: Matthew 16:21–23; Matthew 17:1–5; John 18:1–11. Second, look at how Jesus was able to look beyond these emotional outbursts and see his potential: Matthew 16:17–19. Finally, see how that came true when Peter, under the power of the Holy Spirit, became the spokesperson of the early church: Acts 2:14–41. Nothing in your character is so difficult that God cannot make something good out of it!

My Father God

I renounce the lie that You, Father God, are distant and uninterested in me.

I choose to believe the truth that You, Father God, are always personally present with me, have plans to give me a hope and a future, and have prepared works in advance specifically for me to do. (Psalm 139:1–18; Matthew 28:20, Jeremiah 29:11, Ephesians 2:10)

I renounce the lie that You, Father God, are insensitive and don't know me or care for me.

I choose to believe the truth that You, Father God, are kind and compassionate and know every single thing about me. (Psalm 103:8–14; 1 John 3:1–3; Hebrews 4:12–13)

I renounce the lie that You, Father God, are stern and have placed unrealistic expectations on me.

I choose to believe the truth that You, Father God, have accepted me and are joyfully supportive of me. (Romans 5:8–11; 15:17)

I renounce the lie that You, Father God, are passive and cold toward me.

I choose to believe the truth that You, Father God, are warm and affectionate toward me. (Isaiah 40:11; Hosea 11:3–4)

I renounce the lie that You, Father God, are absent or too busy for me.

I choose to believe the truth that You, Father God, are always present and eager to be with me and enable me to be all that You created me to be. (Philippians 1:6; Hebrews 13:5)

I renounce the lie that You, Father God, are impatient or angry with me or have rejected me.

I choose to believe the truth that You, Father God, are patient and slow to anger, and that when You discipline me, it is a proof of Your love, and not rejection. (Exodus 34:6; Romans 2:4; Hebrews 12:5–11)

I renounce the lie that You, Father God, have been mean, cruel, or abusive to me.

I choose to believe the truth that Satan is mean, cruel, and abusive, but You, Father God, are loving, gentle, and protective. (Psalm 18:2; Matthew 11:28–30; Ephesians 6:10–18)

I renounce the lie that You, Father God, are denying me the pleasures of life.

I choose to believe the truth that You, Father God, are the author of life and will lead me into love, joy, and peace when I choose to be filled with Your Spirit. (Lamentations 3:22–23; Galatians 5:22–24)

I renounce the lie that You, Father God, are trying to control and manipulate me.

I choose to believe the truth that You, Father God, set me free and gave me the freedom to make choices and grow in Your grace. (Galatians 5:1; Hebrews 4:15–16)

I renounce the lie that You, Father God, have condemned me and no longer forgive me.

I choose to believe the truth that You, Father God, have forgiven all my sins and will never use them against me in the future. (Jeremiah 31:31–34; Romans 8:1)

I renounce the lie that You, Father God, reject me when I fail to live a perfect or sinless life.

I choose to believe the truth that You, Father God, are patient toward me and cleanse me when I fail. (Proverbs 24:16; 1 John 1:7–2:2)

I AM THE APPLE OF YOUR EYE! (Deuteronomy 32:9–10)

Forgiving From The Heart

Session 7:
Forgiving From The Heart

FOCUS VERSE:

Matthew 18:34–35: In anger his master turned him over to the jailers to be tortured, until he should pay back all he owed. This is how my heavenly Father will treat each of you unless you forgive your brother from your heart.

OBJECTIVE:

To recognize what forgiveness is and what it is not, and to learn how to forgive from the heart.

FOCUS TRUTH:

In order to experience our freedom in Christ, we need to relate to other people in the same way that God relates to us — on the basis of complete forgiveness and acceptance.

POINTERS FOR LEADERS:

This is a critical part of the course. Most Christians know they should forgive but, in our experience, most still have some unforgiveness. Some feel that what they have suffered is a "special case." Some are deceived into thinking that they have forgiven when, in reality, all they have done is pressed the problem down and tried to ignore it. Some believe wrongly that they simply cannot forgive, or that they shouldn't forgive.

Most don't understand what forgiveness actually is and why we are instructed to do it. When this is properly explained, most choose to forgive from their hearts for the sake of their own freedom and relationship with God. Some believe the lie that they can't forgive. You may need to help them understand that this is a lie by showing them verses such as Philippians 4:13 and asking a question such as, "Would God tell you to do something that is impossible?"

We recommend that at the end of this session you give people the opportunity to allow the Holy Spirit to show them if there are people they need to forgive and to indicate to God that they are willing to do so during *The Steps To Freedom In Christ*. This is very helpful for many — but do not make it a long-drawn-out time. If you are using this session as part of an away day combined with going through The Steps, run the session after Step 2 of *The Steps To Freedom In Christ* so that participants can go straight into Step 3, Forgiveness. There is a Steps To Forgiveness section at the end of the notes for this session in the Leader's Guide (pages 190–191) which is also in the Participant's Guide (pages 122–125).

Remember to run through the logistical information for your away day if you are running one between this session and the next.

SMALL GROUP TIMINGS:

Welcome . . . . 15 minutes 15

Worship . . . . 12 minutes 27

Word part 1 . . . . 15 minutes 42

Pause For Thought 1 . . . . . . 18 minutes 60

Word part 2 . . . . 10 minutes 70

Pause For Thought 2 . . . . 20 minutes 90

Word part 3 . . . . 16 minutes 106

Reflection . . . . 14 minutes 120

Registered users of the course can download a spreadsheet with these timings. Simply enter your own start time, adjust the length of the various components as desired, and you will have a timed plan of your session.

SONGS:

The song from *Worship In Spirit And Truth* (see page 26) that has been written to accompany this session is *Freely Forgive*. See page 219 of the Participant's Guide for the lyrics and background info.

 WELCOME

Read Matthew 18:21–35 or act it out using the script on pages 126–127 of the Participant's Guide (and page 192 of this Leader's Guide). Then try to put yourself in the place of one of the characters and say what strikes you most about the story.

 WORSHIP

Suggested theme: His complete forgiveness of us.

Read aloud the following passages:

"Let us then approach the throne of grace with confidence, so that we may receive mercy and find grace to help us in our time of need." (Hebrews 4:16)

"In him and through faith in him we may approach God with freedom and confidence." (Ephesians 3:12)

"Out of the depths I cry to you, Lord; Lord, hear my voice. Let your ears be attentive to my cry for mercy. If you, Lord, kept a record of sins, Lord, who could stand? But with you there is forgiveness, so that we can, with reverence, serve you. I wait for the Lord, my whole being waits, and in his word I put my hope." (Psalm 130:1–5)

After each one, reassure people that these passages apply not just to other people but to them! You could then personalize the passages, for example, "Jane, you can now approach the throne of grace with confidence." Invite people to thank God that these verses do indeed apply to them.

 **WORD**

Why Forgive?

Forgiving From The Heart

SESSION 7

The third book in the FREEDOM IN CHRIST DISCIPLESHIP SERIES, *Break Free, Stay Free*, corresponds to Part C of the course. Pages 56–98 relate to *The Steps To Freedom In Christ* including forgiveness, the subject of this session (read pages 63–75 in the book for the specific material on forgiveness).

What, in your opinion, gives Satan the greatest opportunity to defeat Christians? Occult activity? Sexual immorality? Cults and sects?

It may surprise you but, in our experience, the biggest issue is an unwillingness to forgive. Nothing gives Satan greater opportunity to stop a church growing than bitterness and division.

A staggering number of Christians are walking around with unforgiveness. And it's usually because we haven't understood what forgiveness is, why we should do it, and how to do it.

Let's remember what Paul says in 2 Corinthians 2:10–11:

> Anyone you forgive, I also forgive. And what I have forgiven . . . I have forgiven in the sight of Christ for your sake, in order that Satan might not outwit us. For we are not unaware of his schemes.

> The word "schemes" in 2 Corinthians 2:11 is the Greek word "noema" which is translated elsewhere as "mind" (2 Corinthians 4:4, 11:3) and "thought" (2 Corinthians 10:5). It is interesting to note that this verse could just as well be translated "we are not unaware of his thoughts."

What is the worst thing anybody ever did to you? [Pause and look around]. Have you got it in your mind? Here's the big question: why should you forgive that? That's the issue we're addressing today.

It Is Required By God (Matthew 6:9–15)

The first reason is simply because God tells you to.

> This, then, is how you should pray: "Our Father in heaven, hallowed be your name, your kingdom come, your will be done on earth as it is in heaven. Give us today our daily bread. Forgive us our sins, as we also have forgiven those who have sinned against us." (Matthew 6:9–12 our own translation)

When you pray, "Forgive us our sins, as we also have forgiven those who have sinned against us," if you think about it, you might not be asking for much.

▶ Your relationship with God is tied to your relationship with other people. You really can't have a righteous relationship with God in isolation from your relationships with other people. As John says,

> Whoever claims to love God yet hates a brother or sister is a liar. For whoever does not love their brother and sister, whom they have seen, cannot love God, whom they have not seen. (1 John 4:20)

God wants us to learn to relate to others on the same basis that He relates to us.

Jesus continues in Matthew 6:14–15:

> For if you forgive other people when they sin against you, your heavenly Father will also forgive you. But if you do not forgive others their sins, your Father will not forgive your sins.

We need to be careful not to apply this wrongly. God relates to us in two ways: as a judge and as a Father. Because you are in Christ, your sins are forgiven, you are saved, and there is no longer any issue with God as judge. What's at stake, however, is your relationship with God as Father. If you have not forgiven someone, God won't let you be comfortable until you do. You will not move on. You will not bear fruit. Your final destiny is secure, but what's at stake are your daily victories and the potential fruit from your life.

▶ It Is Essential For Our Freedom

The most definitive teaching on forgiveness is in Matthew 18:21–35.

> Then Peter came to Jesus and asked, "Lord, how many times shall I forgive my brother when he sins against me? Up to seven times?" Jesus answered, "I tell you, not seven times, but seventy-seven times."

Now, Jesus isn't suggesting here that you keep tabs of each time you are offended until you reach 78, then get a gun and blow his brains out! He's saying that you just continue to forgive for your own sake. God doesn't want His children to languish in bitterness and be bound to the past.

The Extent Of Our Own Debt

In order to forgive this freely we need to understand, first of all, the extent of our own debt to God. There's a story in Luke 7:36–50 where a Pharisee by the name of Simon threw a party and invited a lot of people including Jesus. A woman who had lived a sinful life slipped in uninvited.

▶ She began to wash Jesus' feet with her tears, wipe them with her hair, anoint His feet with oil and kiss them repeatedly. This irritated Simon who said, "Well, if he were a prophet he would know what sort of woman she is." Jesus said, "Simon, I have something to say to you. Suppose someone had been forgiven a debt of 50 denarii and someone else 500 denarii, which one would love more?" He said, "Well I suppose the one who'd been forgiven 500 denarii." Jesus said, "That's right. You see this woman. When I came to this house you didn't greet me with a kiss. She hasn't stopped kissing my feet since I came. You didn't wash my feet, she's done it with her tears. You didn't anoint my feet with oil, but she has."

Then He says, "Those who have been forgiven much love much. Those who have been forgiven little love little."

How much have you been forgiven? Little or much?

No matter how well we may think we've done, the truth is our best is like a dirty rag before God (Isaiah 64:6). Without Christ, we all stand condemned. We've all been forgiven much though we may not realize it. But if we do realize it, we'll find that our capacity for loving others will increase.

Repayment Is Impossible

Jesus continues in Matthew 18:

> Therefore, the kingdom of heaven is like a king who wanted to settle accounts with his servants. As he began the settlement, a man who owed him ten thousand [talents] was brought to him. Since he was not able to pay, the master ordered that he and his wife and his children and all that he had be sold to repay the debt.

> At this the servant fell on his knees before him. "Be patient with me," he begged, "and I will pay back everything."

▶ Do you know what it's like to have a debt that you can't pay? [Do you have an example you can give here?]

Ten thousand talents was a huge sum, way beyond a lifetime's earnings — a seven figure sum in today's terms. What Jesus is trying to show by using such a large amount is that repayment is not an option. There was no way the servant could possibly repay the debt!

How big was your debt to God? Far too large for you ever to repay.

So if the servant is to sort this issue out, another way has to be found.

Mercy Is Required

And here's what happened (verse 27):

> The servant's master took pity on him, canceled the debt and let him go.

And that's what God has done for you.

Let's define some important terms — justice, mercy, and grace.

Justice is rightness or fairness. In other words ▶ it is *giving people what they deserve*. God is just, it's part of His character. If He gave us what we deserve, we would all get hell.

Thankfully God is also merciful and He found a way to forgive and accept us without compromising justice. The punishment we deserved fell at unimaginable cost on Christ.

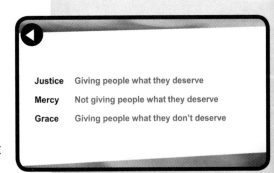

Justice	Giving people what they deserve
Mercy	Not giving people what they deserve
Grace	Giving people what they don't deserve

▶ **Mercy** is *not giving people what they deserve*. We are told to be merciful to others as God has been merciful to us (Luke 6:36).

But our generous God goes even further than that. He didn't just take our punishment on Himself so that we could go free. He actually showers us with good gifts that we don't deserve.

▶ **Grace** is *giving people what they don't deserve*.

God set the standard by His own example. So He expects us to relate to other people in exactly the same way. We are not to give people the retribution they deserve. In fact we are to give them the forgiveness and blessings they don't deserve, which is what the master did for the servant and what Jesus has done for us.

It all begins with the relationship that God has established with us: "Freely you have received, freely give" (Matthew 10:8).

PAUSE FOR THOUGHT 1

OBJECTIVE:

TO UNDERSTAND THAT IN COMMANDING US TO FORGIVE OTHERS, GOD IS ONLY ASKING US TO DO WHAT HE HAS ALREADY DONE FOR US.

▶ **QUESTIONS:**

Why are people (including Christians) often unwilling to forgive?

In order to understand how important it is to forgive others, we need to understand how much we ourselves have been forgiven. Discuss this idea.

Look at the definitions of justice, mercy, and grace. How does God come to us when we go wrong? How can we go to other people in the same way?

So That No Advantage Can Be Taken Of You
(2 Corinthians 2:10–11)

So the master took pity on the servant who owed the huge debt. He canceled the debt and let him go. Jesus continues:

> But when that servant went out, he found one of his fellow servants who owed him a hundred [denarii].

A denarius is a day's wages — so one hundred denarii is about three months' worth of income. That's not a small debt, but it was a lot less than the one he had been let off.

> He grabbed him and began to choke him. "Pay back what you owe me!" he demanded. His fellow-servant fell to his knees and begged him, "Be patient with me, and I will pay everything back."

> ▶ But he refused. Instead, he went off and had the man thrown into prison until he could pay the debt. When the other servants saw what had happened, they were outraged and went and told their master everything that had happened. Then the master called the servant in. "You wicked servant," he said, "I canceled all that debt of yours because you begged me to. Shouldn't you have had mercy on your fellow servant just as I had on you?"

> ▶ In anger his master turned him over to the jailers to be tortured, until he should pay back all he owed.

The word used for "torture" usually refers to spiritual torment in the New Testament. It is the same word the demon used in Mark 5:7 when the demon said to Jesus, "Swear to God that you won't torture me!"

Jesus finished the story by saying perhaps one of the most scary things in the New Testament:

> This is how my heavenly Father will treat each of you unless you forgive your brother from your heart.

Jesus warns us that if we don't forgive others from our heart, we will suffer some kind of spiritual torment. In other words, we are opening a door to bring the enemy's influence or spiritual attack into our life.

Forgiving From The Heart

To forgive someone from the heart means we have to be emotionally honest with God and ourselves and face the hurt and pain we feel.

In *The Steps To Freedom In Christ* we use a simple but effective formula. You go to God and choose to be emotionally honest with Him by saying:

"Lord I choose to forgive [the person] for [say what they did or failed to do] because it made me feel [then tell God every hurt and pain you felt]."

We encourage people to stay with this process until every hurt that is uncovered has been put on the table. We have to let God lead us to the emotional core where healing is going to take place.

I'm not pretending that this is easy or that it is not painful. But it's not a meaningless exercise. We do this in order to completely resolve the pain that we have been carrying around. We can't move on from the past until we choose to forgive.

One of the key points we need to understand when it comes to forgiveness is that the real issue is not so much between us and the other person but between us and God because He is the one who commands us to forgive. We don't even have to go to the other person in order to forgive them. In fact, the process of forgiveness doesn't involve them at all — it is between us and God alone.

Yes, Jesus did say that if we go to church and remember that somebody has something against us, we should leave our offering and go and be reconciled with that person. If you have offended someone else, go to that person, ask for forgiveness and put things right as far as you are able. But if someone has offended you, don't go to them, go to God. Your need to forgive others is first and foremost an issue between you and God. If you think about it, there is logic in it: because your freedom cannot be dependent on other people — otherwise it could not be guaranteed.

After you have forgiven, you may or may not be reconciled to the other person. That doesn't depend just on you. But whether you are reconciled or not, you will have removed the enemy's ability to hold you back.

We Forgive To Stop The Pain

When you forgive, it is for your sake. You might be thinking, "But you don't know how much they hurt me." But don't you see that they are still hurting you? How do you stop the pain? By forgiving.

▶ If you went fishing and someone accidentally hooked your cheek when they cast the line, what would you do to get rid of the pain? Would you leave the hook in your cheek and go around shouting, "Look what they did to me . . . this hook is in my cheek . . . and it hurts . . . I will never forgive them"? That night you go to sleep with the hook in your cheek and you get up the next morning and it's worse. You go out and tell others the same story — but you leave the hook in your cheek.

Would you do that? No, you wouldn't. You would take the hook out of your cheek to relieve the pain!

By choosing not to forgive someone for what they did, we stay hooked to the pain of what they did. We think that by forgiving someone, we let him or her off the hook — but, if we don't forgive, we're the ones with the hook in us.

Holding on to bitterness and unforgiveness is like swallowing poison and hoping the other person will die!

PAUSE FOR THOUGHT 2

OBJECTIVE:

TO PREPARE PEOPLE FOR THE FORGIVENESS STEP IN *THE STEPS TO FREEDOM IN CHRIST* BY HELPING THEM UNDERSTAND THAT WE MAKE THE CHOICE TO FORGIVE FOR OUR OWN SAKE.

▶ **QUESTIONS:**

What is your reaction to the idea that unforgiveness opens the door to the enemy's influence in your life?

"The longer you leave the hook in, the more pain it will cause you." Discuss.

What do you think about this statement: "When it comes to forgiveness, the real issue is not so much between us and the other person, it's between us and God"?

What Forgiveness Is And What It Isn't

▶ Do you still have in your mind the worst thing that anyone ever did to you? Let's get to the crux of the matter.

A major reason that people don't forgive is because they don't understand what forgiveness is — and what it isn't.

Not Forgetting

It's not forgetting. You can't get rid of a hurt simply by trying to forget it.

You might say, "Well, doesn't God forget our sins?" God is all-knowing — He couldn't forget if He wanted to. When God says "I will remember their sins no more" (Jeremiah 31:34), what He is saying is, "I won't take the past and use it against you. I will put it away from Me as far as the east is from the west."

If a husband says to a wife, "I've forgiven you but remember, on January 10, 2013, you did this . . . ," do you know what he's actually saying? "I haven't forgiven you. I am still taking the past and using it against you." So part of that commitment to forgive is about deciding not to bring up the past and use it against them ever again.

Not Tolerating Sin

Forgiveness does not mean that we tolerate sin. Does God forgive? He does. Does He tolerate sin. No, He can't.

This is most difficult when someone is in a situation where they are being sinned against continually, for example a wife who is being physically abused by her husband. In the past, some churches advised abused wives in effect, "Go home and be submissive." What if that man beat up another woman in the church — would they tolerate that? Was it all right to beat up his own wife? It's not only wrong, it is doubly wrong because she's not just getting beaten up, she is getting beaten up by the one who is there by God's instruction to provide for her and protect her.

The Bible certainly tells wives to be submissive but that's not all it says. 1 Peter 2:13–18 and Romans 13:1–7 instruct us to submit to the governing authorities whom God has placed over us. They have put laws in place to protect that wife. It is perfectly possible to forgive someone yet still decide to turn them over to the authorities to let the law take its course. The fact is that that kind of abuse tends to run in a cycle that simply goes on and on until someone puts a stop to it.

You have every right to put a stop to sin by laying down Biblical guidelines, or by removing yourself from a particular situation. That is not at all inconsistent with forgiveness.

[You could use this example from Steve Goss or replace it with one of your own if you have one.]

A lady rang our office and told me that her Christian husband kept having affairs. She continually forgave him and took him back but he kept having affairs. I advised her to forgive him but then draw a line in the sand and say that if he did it one more time, he must leave. That is not inconsistent with forgiving him. To be honest you feel a little nervous when you give that kind of advice. Well, it worked. I met them again when they came on a marriage course we were running. He thanked me and told me that the line in the sand was the wake-up call he needed to get his act together and sort his life out.

If you don't put an end to a cycle of abuse it will just continue.

Not Seeking Revenge

▶ The main difficulty we have with forgiveness is we remember that nasty thing that was done to us and understandably we want revenge, we want justice.

We somehow think that forgiving means we just have to sweep it under the carpet and say it didn't matter. But it did matter. Very much.

Listen carefully to what God says about this:

> Do not take revenge, my dear friends, but leave room for God's wrath, for it is written: "It is mine to avenge; I will repay," says the Lord. (Romans 12:19)

In no way is God asking you to sweep what was done under the carpet as if it did not matter. In fact quite the opposite.

▶ He promises that if you hand the matter over to Him, He will ensure that it is not swept under the carpet. When you forgive, although you are letting the person off your hook, you are not letting them off God's hook.

▶ "I will repay." When you choose to forgive, you are taking a step of faith to trust God to be the righteous judge who will weigh what was done on the scales of justice and will demand that the scales balance.

Nothing will be swept under the carpet. God really will demand full payment for everything done against you. Everyone who sinned against you will have to stand before God and explain it — either it will be paid for by the blood of Christ if the person is a Christian, or they will have to face the judgment of God if they are not. "I will repay" — God will settle every account some day.

You are choosing to take a step of faith and trust God with what happened, to hand all of that pain and those demands for justice and revenge over to Him safe in the knowledge that He will ensure that justice is done. In the meantime you can walk free of it.

Resolving To Live With The Consequences Of Another's Sin

And part of forgiveness is agreeing to live with the consequences of someone else's sin. You may say, "Well, that's not fair." No it's not — but you will have to do it anyway. Everybody is living with the consequences of somebody else's sin (we are all living with the consequences of Adam's sin for example).

▶ The only real choice we have is whether to do that in the bondage of bitterness or the freedom of forgiveness.

Conclusion

Forgiveness is to set a captive free and then realize that you were the captive. This is an issue between you and God. He commands you to forgive because He loves you. He knows that bitterness will defile you and others, and cause you to miss out on the abundant life that Jesus came to give you and not become a fruitful disciple.

You may agonize about whether what they did was actually wrong or you might think of reasons to justify what they did. Don't do any of that. The issue of forgiveness is not primarily about who was right and who was wrong. If you felt offended you need to forgive — regardless of any other circumstance. It's about clearing rubbish out of your life and walking away from it. It's for your sake and in some ways has little to do with the person who hurt you.

You will have an opportunity to deal with this issue when we go through *The Steps To Freedom In Christ*. There are some guidelines on pages 122–125 of your Participant's Guide that are well worth reading to prepare you for that.

Let's finish by asking the Holy Spirit to show us whether we have one or more people to forgive and resolving before God to do so.

Lord Jesus, will You please show us if there is someone that we need to forgive in order to walk in the freedom You have won for us.

If you have become aware that you have people to forgive and you want to say to God that you are prepared to do that, then simply raise a hand.

We recommend that you finish with a moment of silent reflection and then pray that the Holy Spirit will show the group if they still have people to forgive. Ask people to respond by standing up or raising their hand if they recognize that they have some issues and are prepared to do something about them when they go through *The Steps To Freedom In Christ*.

Lord God, we want to be free in Christ and we want to become fruitful disciples. We don't want the enemy to have any hold on us. So we say before You now, that we are resolving to forgive all those who have hurt us just as You have freely forgiven us. In the name of Jesus who died that we might be forgiven. Amen. ▶

REFLECTION

OBJECTIVE:

TO PREPARE FOR THE FORGIVENESS STEP IN *THE STEPS TO FREEDOM IN CHRIST*.

▶ **REFLECTION**

Spend some time praying together for those who have indicated they are ready and willing to forgive others when we go through *The Steps To Freedom In Christ*. (There is no need to share anything — just pray.)

Then discuss the following statements:
"Forgiving has little to do with the person who hurt you."
"Forgiving is not forgetting."
"God will ensure justice is done."

 # WITNESS

How might this question of forgiveness challenge someone who is not yet a Christian? Are there any ways you can demonstrate forgiveness to someone who does not yet know God?

 # IN THE COMING WEEK

Ask the Holy Spirit to prepare your heart by leading you into truth and starting to reveal to you the areas you will need to bring into the light when you go through *The Steps To Freedom In Christ*.

Steps To Forgiveness

1. Ask God to reveal to your mind the people you need to forgive

Make a list of everyone God brings to your mind. Ask the Holy Spirit to guide you and write the names on a separate piece of paper. Even if you think there is no one, just ask God to bring up all the right names. The two most overlooked names are yourself and God.

Forgiving yourself: Only God can forgive your sins — but for many people, especially perfectionists, the hardest person to forgive is themselves, for letting themselves down. You are in effect accepting God's forgiveness and refusing to listen to the devil's accusations. Some people are really helped by being able to say, "I forgive myself for [list everything you hold against yourself], and I let myself off my own hook."

Forgiving God: Forgiving God is harder to understand because God has done nothing wrong. He has always acted in your best interests. But because you have not understood God's larger plan, or because you have blamed God for something that other people or the devil have done, you may have felt that God has let you down.

Many people feel disappointed with God, even angry with Him, because He didn't answer their prayer; He didn't seem to be there for them. They cried out for help and nothing came. Usually they are embarrassed to admit it. But God knows anyway and He's big enough to handle it.

If you feel uncomfortable telling God you forgive Him, say something like, "I release the expectations, thoughts, and feelings I have had against You."

2. Acknowledge the hurt and the hate

Jesus instructed us to forgive from the heart. That's much more than simply saying "I forgive" and pretending we've dealt with it. To forgive from the heart we need to face the hurt and the hate. People try to suppress their emotional pain, but it is trying to surface so that we can let it go.

3. Understand the significance of the cross

The cross is what makes forgiveness legally and morally right. Jesus has already taken upon Himself your sins and the sins of the person who has hurt you. He died "once for all" (Hebrews 10:10). When your heart says, "It isn't fair," remember that the justice is in the cross.

4. Decide that you will bear the burden of each person's sin

You need to make a choice not to use the information you have against that person in the future.

"He who covers over an offense promotes love, but whoever repeats the matter separates close friends" (Proverbs 17:9). That doesn't mean that you never testify in a court of law — however, you do it not in the bitterness of unforgiveness but having first forgiven from your heart.

5. Decide to forgive

Forgiveness is a crisis of the will. If you wait until you feel like doing it, you probably never will. You may feel you can't do it — but would God really tell you to do something you couldn't do? When He says that you can do everything through Christ who gives you strength (Philippians 4:13), is that true or not? The reality is that you have a choice to make — are you going to remain in bitterness, hooked to the past, giving the enemy an entrance to your mind; or are you going to get rid of it once and for all?

You **choose** to forgive, and in making that choice you are agreeing to live with sin and its consequences. You are choosing to let God be the avenger, and trust Him to bring justice in the end. You choose to take it to the cross and leave it there.

The gates of hell can't prevail against the Kingdom of God. There is nobody out there keeping you from being the person that God created you to be. The only one that can do that is you. You need to forgive, be merciful, and love as Christ has loved you. Let that person go; get on with your life; walk away free in Christ.

6. Take your list to God

To forgive from your heart, say, for example, "Lord, I choose to forgive my father" and then specify what you are forgiving him for. Stay with the same person until you have told God every pain and hurt that has surfaced and be as specific as you can. It's then helpful to take it a step further and say how it made you feel: "I choose to forgive my father for leaving us, because it made me feel abandoned."

Tears will often come at this point, but this is not about trying to get somebody to cry. It's making sure that it's as thorough as possible. One lady said, "I can't forgive my mother. I hate her." Having recognized her real feelings of hatred, now for probably the first time she could forgive — if she didn't admit that she hated her mother, she wouldn't be able to forgive.

Pray as follows for each person you need to forgive: "Dear Heavenly Father, I choose to forgive [name the person] for [what they did or failed to do], because it made me feel [share the painful feelings, for example, rejected, dirty, worthless, inferior]."

Take careful note of what is said after the statement "because it made me feel." Usually the same word (for example, "abandoned," "stupid," "dirty") is repeated several times. That may well reveal a stronghold that your past experiences have led you to believe. You can tear down those strongholds by saying, for example: "I renounce the lie that I am stupid. I announce the truth that I have the mind of Christ" (1 Corinthians 2:16). "I renounce the lie that I am abandoned. I announce the truth that God has promised never to leave me nor forsake me" (Hebrews 13:5). Session 8 of the *Freedom In Christ Course* teaches a specific strategy ("stronghhold-busting") that will enable you to do this effectively and the Freedom In Christ app incorporates a "Stronghold-Buster Builder" that will be a great help.

7. Destroy the list

You are now free from those people and those events in the past.

8. Do not expect that forgiving others will result in changes in them

Forgiving others is primarily about you and your relationship with God. Pray for those you have forgiven, that they may be blessed and that they too may find the freedom of forgiveness (see Matthew 5:44; 2 Corinthians 2:7).

9. Try to understand the people you have forgiven

You may find it helpful to understand some of what the other person was going through, but don't go so far as to rationalize away the sin — this is not about saying "It didn't matter," because it did matter.

10. Expect positive results of forgiveness in you

Forgiveness is not about feeling good; it's about being free. However, good feelings will follow eventually. You will need to concentrate on renewing your mind so that negative ways of thinking are replaced by the truth.

11. Thank God for what you have learned and the maturity gained

You are now free to move on and grow as a Christian.

12. Accept your part of the blame for the offenses you suffered

Confess your part in any sin and know that you are forgiven. If you realize that someone has something against you, go to them and be reconciled. When you do that, be careful to simply confess your own wrongdoing rather than bringing up anything they did.

Dramatization

Matthew 18:21–35

Characters: Peter, Jesus, Servant 1, Servant 2, Master

Peter   Lord, how many times shall I forgive my brother when he sins against me? Up to seven times?

Jesus   I tell you, not seven times, but seventy-seven times.

Therefore, the kingdom of heaven is like a king who wanted to settle accounts with his servants. As he began the settlement, a man who owed him ten thousand talents was brought to him. Since he was not able to pay, the master ordered that he and his wife and his children and all that he had be sold to repay the debt.

The servant fell on his knees before him.

Servant 1   Be patient with me, and I will pay back everything.

Jesus   The servant's master took pity on him, canceled the debt, and let him go. But when that servant went out, he found one of his fellow servants who owed him a hundred denarii. He grabbed him and began to choke him.

Servant 1   Pay back what you owe me!

Jesus   His fellow servant fell to his knees and begged him:

Servant 2   Be patient with me, and I will pay you back.

Jesus   But he refused. Instead, he went off and had the man thrown into prison until he could pay the debt. When the other servants saw what had happened, they were greatly distressed and went and told their master everything that had happened.

Then the master called the servant in.

Master   You wicked servant, I canceled all that debt of yours because you begged me to. Shouldn't you have had mercy on your fellow servant just as I had on you?

Jesus   In anger his master turned him over to the jailers to be tortured, until he should pay back all he owed. This is how my heavenly Father will treat each of you unless you forgive your brother from your heart.

The Steps To Freedom In Christ

Leading People Through *The Steps To Freedom In Christ*

FOCUS VERSE:

James 4:7: Submit yourselves, then, to God. Resist the devil, and he will flee from you.

OBJECTIVE:

To lead participants through a process of repentance so that they can resolve their personal and spiritual conflicts by submitting to God and resisting the devil, and thereby experience their freedom in Christ.

To help them become aware of lies that they have been believing so that they can take steps to renew their mind.

FOCUS TRUTH:

Christ has set us free (Galatians 5:1), but we will not experience that freedom without genuine repentance.

Confession (admitting that we did wrong) is the first step to repentance, but on its own it is not enough.

We must both submit to God and resist the devil. We must also make a choice about what we believe and how we are living, and decide to change. If we want to grow in Christ we must choose to renounce the lies we have believed and any sin in our lives, and announce our choice to believe that what God says is true and start to live accordingly.

POINTERS FOR LEADERS:

The notes for this session are different from others in the course in that they consist of information for the leader of the session and are not a script to use. You might also like to read the section in the Participant's Guide to see what we are saying to participants about this session.

We recommend strongly that everyone who does this course goes through *The Steps To Freedom In Christ*, a kind and gentle way to resolve personal and spiritual conflicts. Resolving these conflicts will help participants connect with the truth that has been taught. Simply teaching truth is not enough because people may be unable to receive it because of personal and spiritual conflicts.

The process is straightforward: the participants ask the Holy Spirit to show them areas in their lives where they need to repent, and then choose to do so. The process may well help them become aware of lies they have been believing. They should be encouraged to write these down — we will give them a strategy for renewing their mind in the next session.

A slide presentation is available for this session. It features the prayers and declaration from *The Steps To Freedom In Christ* that a group will say out loud together, as well as a brief introductory slide for each Step. Each participant will need their own copy of *The Steps To Freedom In Christ*. You can either use *The Steps To*

Freedom In Christ video session (available on a separate DVD or in FreedomStream) to guide people through this session or guide them yourself.

We recommend that you read through the notes and instructions in *The Steps To Freedom In Christ* book before leading this session and also view *The Steps To Freedom In Christ* video which features Dr. Neil Anderson, the author of *The Steps To Freedom In Christ*, and Steve Goss.

Various different versions of the *The Steps To Freedom In Christ* have been published over the years. The notes for this session assume you are using the version published in 2017 by Bethany House in the USA and by Monarch in the UK (the page numbers in these two versions are identical).

Introduction

Seeing people go through *The Steps To Freedom In Christ* is exciting! It's a gentle, kind, undramatic process but it can make an enormous difference. Many Christians rank it second in importance only to their conversion experience.

There is no need to feel nervous about leading the process. You are simply facilitating an encounter between those seeking freedom and the One who is the Wonderful Counselor. The outcome does not depend on you.

In this section we will give you some general and practical information about leading *The Steps To Freedom In Christ* session.

Approaches To Taking People Through The Steps

Participants should be given an opportunity to go through *The Steps To Freedom In Christ* between Sessions 7 and 8. There are two different ways you can approach this and you need to decide which will suit your situation:

1. A Personal Freedom Appointment

This is the ideal. In this scenario each individual is led through the process by an "encourager," with a prayer partner in attendance, in a session that typically lasts three to six hours. It can be amazingly upbuilding when people in a church or small group are willing to confess their sins to one another and pray for each other (see James 5:16). Encouragers and prayer partners do not generally need any special skills other than a reasonable maturity in Christ and an understanding of the Biblical principles of freedom, but will benefit from having attended Freedom In Christ's training or having read *Discipleship Counseling* by Neil Anderson.

Please read the Three Key Principles section below and then the notes starting on page 200 for more information on using the personal Freedom Appointment approach.

2. As A Group On An Away Day

Taking your group away for a day (or even a weekend) to go through The Steps works well. It allows everyone to go through The Steps at the same time while ensuring that people have enough time to do business with any issues that the Holy Spirit brings to their mind. It is best to book a location away from your church and to include times of worship. You will need leaders to make themselves available to participants who may need help at various times. It also works well to include Session 7 (Forgiving From The Heart) in the away day directly before Step 3 rather than making it a separate weekly session. If you go away for a longer time, you could also cover Session 8 or even Sessions 8 to 10.

Please read the Three Key Principles notes below and then the notes starting on page 204 for more information on this approach.

Even if you are using the away day approach, you will need to make some provision for personal Freedom Appointments. We recommend that those leading the course have personal appointments, for example, and you will probably find that people with deeper issues will not be able to get everything done on the away day or will struggle and will need a personal appointment. Simply see how they get on and arrange a personal appointment afterward if needed.

Three Key Principles

When it comes to dealing with issues in the lives of Christians, the Church has tended to polarize into either a psychotherapeutic ministry that doesn't take into account the reality of the spiritual world, or some kind of deliverance ministry that doesn't take into account psychological issues and personal responsibility. Any lasting answer, however, must take all of reality into account.

The Steps To Freedom In Christ has the following benefits:

- The method is transferable because it doesn't require experts — it can be conducted by any reasonably mature Christian who is walking in freedom.

- It produces lasting results because the "freedom-seekers" are the ones making the decisions and assuming personal responsibility, rather than a pastor or counselor doing it for them.

- It doesn't bypass the person's mind.

- The focus is on Christ and repentance. The real issue isn't Satan, it is God and our walk with Him. The seven Steps are seven issues that are critical between ourselves and God.

There are three key principles that it is helpful to understand as you prepare to lead people through *The Steps To Freedom In Christ*.

1. This Is A Truth Encounter Not A Power Encounter

Before the cross, Satan was not a defeated foe, and the Church was not yet in existence. Believers were not born again. In that environment it took someone with specially endowed authority from God to confront the demonic. Jesus was one such person and clearly demonstrated His authority and power over the kingdom of darkness. He also conferred this onto the twelve disciples (Luke 9:1), and then the seventy (Luke 10).

We are now living in a completely different spiritual environment. Now every believer is a new creation in Christ and seated with Him in the heavenly realms.

Casting out demons is no longer the responsibility of an outside agent. Every Christian has the same standing in Christ, and we can't confess, repent, believe, renounce, forgive, or assume any responsibility for another person. That is why there are no instructions for casting out demons in the Epistles.

Some Christians have adopted their methodology from the Gospels, which, of course, deal with the spiritual environment that existed before the cross. They may attempt to call up demons, get their name and rank, and cast them out. With this approach, the pastor or counselor is the deliverer and he or she is getting information from a demon. We should never believe demons, however, because they are all liars: "When he lies, he speaks his native language, for he is a liar and the father of lies" (John 8:44).

If you were successful in casting a demon out of someone without his or her involvement, what is to keep the demon from coming back when you leave? Unless the individual assumes responsibility for their own freedom, they may end up being freed from one spirit only to be occupied by seven others who are worse than the first (Matthew 12:43–45).

The Epistles (which were written in the spiritual environment that existed after the cross) teach a different approach when the person seeking freedom is a Christian. First, the Deliverer is Christ and He has already come. Second, we should get our information from the Word of God and the Holy Spirit who will lead us into all truth and that truth will set us free. If we try to resist the devil without first submitting to God, the result will be a dogfight. On the other hand, we can submit to God without resisting the devil and stay in bondage, which sadly is where many Christians find themselves. They have come to Christ but have never been taught how to close the door to the enemy's influence in their lives through genuine repentance.

In order for a Christian to be set free, there is no need for a power encounter. The only power encounter needed took place 2,000 years ago when Jesus completely disarmed Satan (Colossians 2:15). There is not a verse in the Bible that instructs us to pursue power because believers already have all the power they need in Christ (Ephesians 1:18–19).

Satan's power is in his ability to deceive. His power is only effective in the dark. However, all the darkness in the world cannot extinguish the light of one candle. Knowing the truth is what will set us free. Christians are to pursue the truth because they already have the power and authority to do His will. Truth is what makes an encounter with Satan effective because his primary strategy is deception.

Satan fears detection more than anything else. Whenever the light of truth comes on, he and his demons head for the shadows like cockroaches. Demons are afraid of God and of being exposed to the truth.

2. Individuals Must Assume Responsibility

God has set the world up in a certain way. He has given us certain responsibilities while keeping others for Himself. Nothing will interfere more in the process of someone growing to maturity than if we try to play God's role in their life.

The Steps To Freedom In Christ process follows the principles in this verse: "Submit . . . to God. Resist the devil and he will flee from you" (James 4:7). Who is the one who has to do the submitting and resisting? The person seeking freedom.

Most defeated Christians are in effect hoping that God will change His ways to accommodate them. They want God or you to assume their responsibility. God will not do that and we cannot do it. We can't submit, resist, repent, forgive, or believe the truth for anyone else.

James 5:13–16 gives clear instructions on who is to do what if someone is in trouble or sick. Note that it is the struggling person that needs to take the initiative. The one who is in trouble is to pray. The one who is sick is to call the elders of the church.

Note also the order that things are to be done in verse 16: "Therefore confess your sins to each other and pray for each other so that you may be healed. The prayer of a righteous man is powerful and effective."

Confession comes first. If you prayed for someone and you later discovered that they were locked into sins of pride, bitterness, and rebellion, would you be surprised if God did not answer your prayer? Of course not. "If I had cherished sin in my heart, the Lord would not have listened" (Psalm 66:18). It's essential that they first take on board their responsibility to confess their sins.

Confession is simply agreeing with God — being honest. All secular counselors will tell you that healing starts with honesty — facing up to the truth.

They also need to repent which includes actively shutting the door on the sin and taking back any ground given to the enemy. Again, we cannot do that for them.

We can take great encouragement from this: it's not our responsibility to work out what the problem is and "fix" someone. Our role is to encourage them to ask God to reveal any issues to them and to point them toward truth.

We can help them, however, and Paul indicates how in 2 Timothy 2:24–26:

> And the Lord's servant must not quarrel; instead, he must be kind to everyone, able to teach, not resentful. Opponents must be gently instructed, in the hope that God will grant them repentance leading them to a knowledge of the truth, and that they will come to their senses and escape from the trap of the devil, who has taken them captive to do his will.

This passage teaches that truth sets people free and that God is the One who grants repentance. True Christian counseling is an encounter with God. He is the Wonderful Counselor. Only God can bind up the broken-hearted and set the captive free. God does, however, work through His servants who are dependent upon Him. But our role is to point them always to the Wonderful Counselor rather than try and "fix" them ourselves.

According to 2 Timothy 2:24–26, our primary qualification as the one leading is to be "the Lord's servant." To be an instrument in God's hand we have to be totally dependent upon Him. Beyond that requirement, the Lord's servant must be kind, patient, gentle, and able to teach. In other words, we need to know and speak the truth in love, because the truth sets us free. Christians are not in bondage to past traumas. They are in bondage to the lies they came to believe as a result of past traumas. We can help them by pointing to the truth.

3. We Are Teaching A Way Of Life

The Steps To Freedom In Christ doesn't set anyone free! **Who** sets them free is Christ. **What** sets them free is their response to Him in repentance and faith.

The last thing we want is for people to think they have "done" *The Steps To Freedom In Christ* as if it were a one-off experience or a box that they have now ticked. The objective is to help them become fruitful disciples of Jesus and, in order to do that, we don't want to give them a one-off experience of freedom but to equip them for the future.

If people go through The Steps in a group on an away day, encourage them also to have their own individual Freedom Appointment where they speak out loud in front of another person. This could be as simple as doing it together with a trusted friend. Encourage them to revisit the process on a regular basis, perhaps annually. They won't, of course, need to deal with issues again if they have not fallen back into that particular sin but it's amazing what rubbish we can accumulate in a year.

Note too that there is a great difference between freedom and maturity. Taking hold of freedom through The Steps process is no guarantee that people will remain in that freedom. They will now, however, be able to make a free choice to renew their mind (the only way to be transformed — see Romans 12:2), perhaps for the first time.

Taking An Individual Through The Steps

1. Start By Gathering Background Information

The individual going through the appointment (the "freedom-seeker") should have completed a Confidential Personal Inventory before the appointment. You can find this in the appendix of *Discipleship Counseling* or obtain it from Freedom In Christ Ministries. You have permission to copy the inventory or adapt it for your own use. Bear in mind, however, that many people will not disclose certain confidential information in writing so there may well be more to come out.

Choose a comfortable room and allow for several hours should the case be difficult. Have a box of tissues available, and some water. We strongly recommend that you get the freedom-seeker to complete a Statement of Understanding which confirms for legal reasons their understanding that the encourager is not functioning as a trained counselor — a version is available from Freedom In Christ.

First, get a brief history of their family. What were the religious experiences of their parents or grandparents? Were they involved in the occult or a counterfeit religion? Was there harmony in the home? Have there been any divorces or affairs in the family history? Dysfunctional families breed false beliefs. For example, many children wrongly blame themselves for their parents' divorce. Others harbor bitterness toward their parents for years because of something that happened in their home.

You will want to know if their family has any history of alcoholism, drug abuse, sexual sin, or mental illness. What type of exercise and eating habits characterised the family? What was the moral climate in the home? Ask them to share their early childhood and school experiences.

Note that you are not trying to resolve anything by hearing their personal and family history. The purpose is to understand what happened to them and what may have caused them to have certain beliefs. The intimate details will come out when you take them through The Steps.

The Confidential Personal Inventory also provides important information concerning their physical, mental, emotional, and spiritual life.

2. Lead Them Through The Steps

The primary focus of The Steps is their relationship with God. The process is different from most counseling approaches, because the one who is praying is the one who needs the help, and they are praying to the only One who can help them.

It is recommended that as well as the leader ("the encourager") and the freedom-seeker, a prayer partner is also present.

Explain to the freedom-seeker what they are doing and why they are doing it. Try to go through all seven steps in one session. They may not need every Step but you want to be thorough for their sake. Have them read every prayer and doctrinal affirmation aloud. Encourage them to share any mental opposition or physical discomfort. When they do, thank them for sharing it with you. Once it is acknowledged, simply go on. In most cases there is very little opposition. Spiritual opposition usually shows up only in the first two Steps.

Unforgiveness (Step 3) is the most critical Step. Every person has at least one person and usually several people to forgive. Unforgiveness affords the biggest door into the Church for Satan. If we can't help a person forgive from the heart, we can't help them be free from their past.

When they pray and ask God whom they need to forgive, rest assured that God does reveal names to their mind. If they say, "Well there is no one," then respond by saying, "Would you just share the names that are coming to your mind right now?" Inevitably, several names will surface, and you should record them on a sheet of paper. It is not uncommon for freedom-seekers to have names come to mind that surprise them. And it is not uncommon for them to recall forgotten painful memories while in the process of forgiving.

Explain what forgiveness is and how to do it. The key issues are highlighted in The Steps book. Then hand the list back to them and ask if they would be willing to forgive those people for their own sake. Forgiving others is primarily an issue between them and their Heavenly Father. Reconciliation may or may not follow.

Very little opposition occurs during Steps 4 to 6. In Step 6, deal with sexual sins separately. It is amazing how much sex plays a part in human bondage. There are several prayers that they could pray in Step 6 for specific issues. Ask if any are pertinent to them.

In most cases complete freedom isn't realized until after the final declaration and prayer in Step 7. When they have finished, ask the freedom-seeker to sit comfortably and close their eyes. Then ask, "What do you hear in your mind? Is it quiet?" After a pause they usually respond with a relieved smile and say, "Nothing. It's finally quiet in my mind." If they had difficulty reading the doctrinal affirmation in Step 2, have them read it again. They can hardly believe the ease with which they can now read and understand the truth. The whole demeanor of many freedom-seekers often changes so dramatically that you may want them to look at themselves in a mirror.

Getting free in Christ is one thing; staying free is another. Paul says in Galatians 5:1, "It is for freedom that Christ has set us free; therefore keep standing firm and do not be subject again to a yoke of slavery." The Steps include several aftercare suggestions that will help them maintain their freedom in Christ. Freedom in Christ Ministries has prepared a 21-day devotional book entitled *Walking In Freedom*, which we encourage everyone to work through. Every third day they repeat one of The Steps. This helps reinforce what they have done.

We will introduce further strategies for maintaining freedom in Session 8.

3. Keep Pointing People Toward Truth

Most people caught in a spiritual conflict have a distorted concept of God and themselves, and it will help you if you can determine what those false beliefs are. Listen carefully to what is said. It may be helpful in some cases to review from previous sessions the truth about God and who we are in Christ. Defeated Christians don't know who they are in Christ, or understand what it means to be a child of God. Consequently, they question their salvation. Many think they are different from other people. The Christian life doesn't seem to work for them as it does for others. Some fear a mental breakdown and are filled with anxiety. Almost all feel unloved, worthless, and rejected. They have tried everything they can think of to improve their self-image, but nothing works. Some even suspect that their problem is spiritual, but they don't know how to resolve their conflicts.

Defeated Christians often have a distorted concept of the two kingdoms. They think they are caught between two equal but opposite powers. Bad old Satan is on one side, good old God is on the other, and poor old me is caught in the middle. That of course is not true, and they are defeated if that is what they believe. The truth is; God is omnipresent, omnipotent, and omniscient. Satan is a defeated foe and we are alive in Christ, and seated with Him at the right hand of the Father, the ultimate seat of power and authority in the universe.

4. When There Is A Major Battle For The Mind

The Steps process is for every Christian, not just those with obvious problems. However, the process can be highly effective for those with deep issues.

To some people Satan seems to be more present, real, and powerful than God. This type of person faces a major battle for their mind and usually hears opposing arguments in their head. They are constantly confronted with lies, told to get out of the Freedom Appointment, or threatened with harm or embarrassment.

Such mental interference is not uncommon. Explain that the mind is the control center; you could use the illustration of an air traffic controller deciding which planes are permitted to land and which are turned away. In the same way they are in control of their mind and can choose which thoughts they allow to land and which they turn away. If they don't lose control in their minds, then you will not lose control in the Freedom Appointment. In one sense it doesn't matter whether the negative or condemning thoughts are coming from a loudspeaker on the wall, from their own memory, or from a demonic spirit. The only way those thoughts can have any control over them is if they believe them. To help them maintain mental control, ask them regularly to share what is going on in their minds. You want them to bring those deceptive thoughts into the light. As soon as the lie is exposed, the power is broken.

They may be reluctant to share with you for two reasons. First, if they sense that you won't believe them, they won't tell you. If the freedom-seeker is hearing voices, secular counselors and many Christian counselors would not consider the voices to be demonic. They will be given a psychological label and a prescription for medication. Realizing this, the troubled person may share what has happened to them, but would be very reluctant to share the mental battle that is going on inside. Second, if they are hearing demonic voices, those voices can be very intimidating. They could be threatening harm to the freedom-seeker, the encourager, or family and friends of the freedom-seeker.

Watch their eyes very carefully. If they start to become dizzy or glassy-eyed, or start looking around the room, stop what you are doing and ask them to share what is going on inside. If you aren't paying attention, you could lose control of the session. If they are really struggling mentally, encourage them to get up and go for a walk. You want them to know that they have a choice and that they can exercise their will.

Highly subjective people are the hardest to help because they have never really assumed responsibility for their own thoughts; they have a thought and they act on it. They don't seem to realize they have a will or can say no to negative thoughts. Instruct them by saying, "If you have a thought, don't just do what it says. Share it with me." Help them understand that not every thought that comes into their mind is necessarily their own. It is revolutionary for some people to understand that their mind is their own and that they can decide which thoughts they will allow to "come in to land" and which to turn away.

To help maintain control, The Steps begin with a very specific prayer and declaration. If they have made a declaration of faith in God, Satan cannot harm them, because he has no authority over them.

Don't touch the person during a Freedom Appointment — if the person has been abused in the past, they may feel as if they have been violated. People still under demonic oppression will recoil, and move away from you. After they are free, however, just the opposite happens. They move toward you. Opposite spirits repel, but the Holy Spirit unites.

Never try to restrain anyone physically, because the weapons of our warfare are not of the flesh (2 Corinthians 10:3–4). If they run out of the room, let them go. Wait and pray, and invariably they come back, usually within five minutes. We should never violate their mind or try to control them. They are free to leave or stay.

If the person you are trying to help has been actively involved in Satanism, be prepared for major opposition. Step 1 contains a page of special renunciations for those who have worshiped Satan or been subjected to satanic ritual abuse. Everything they do is an antithesis of Christianity, because Satan is the Antichrist. It could take you several hours to work through those renunciations. Paul wrote, "Let us purify ourselves from everything that contaminates body and spirit, perfecting holiness out of reverence for God" (2 Corinthians 7:1). Rebuilding their fractured God-concept and self-concept takes time, lots of love and acceptance, and the support of an understanding Christian community. Paul summarizes this ministry in 2 Corinthians 4:1–4:

> Therefore, since through God's mercy we have this ministry, we do not lose heart. Rather, we have renounced secret and shameful ways; we do not use deception, nor do we distort the word of God. On the contrary, by setting forth the truth plainly we commend ourselves to every man's conscience in the sight of God. And even if our gospel is veiled, it is veiled to those who are perishing. The god of this age has blinded the minds of unbelievers, so that they cannot see the light of the gospel of the glory of Christ, who is the image of God.

Freedom In Christ Ministries runs regular training courses that explain more about taking individuals through *The Steps To Freedom In Christ*.

Running An Away Day

It is recommended that you hold the away day in pleasant surroundings, away from your church if possible. Aim to provide lunch or make sure that people bring packed lunches — it is recommended that you maintain a quiet atmosphere over lunchtime and suggest that people remain on the premises. You will find a suggested timetable on page 211.

The room you use should be large enough for participants to have some degree of privacy. It is helpful if people can spread out. It may help to have some music playing in the background during The Steps so that people can pray out loud without feeling that others are listening. Instrumental music works best as it is less distracting.

Each participant will need a copy of *The Steps To Freedom In Christ*, their Participant's Guide, and a pencil. The group will be praying several prayers together out loud. Then they will spend some time alone with God. Nobody will be embarrassed or asked to share anything with the group or another person. It is solely an encounter with God. Explain to the group that some will get in touch with real pain, and tears are understandable and acceptable.

People will at times benefit from individual attention during the steps that they find difficult (most usually Steps 1, 3, and 6). Plan to have a reasonable number of people whose role is to walk around and help those who are struggling (one for every ten people would be a good starting point). These should be mature Christians who have had their own Freedom Appointment and are well acquainted with freedom principles.

Some people will have very little to deal with on some steps, whereas others may have a lot. Suggest that those who do not have much on a particular step spend time praying for those who do: that the Holy Spirit will reveal everything that needs to be revealed; and that Satan's attempts to interfere in the process will be ineffective. If people have too much to deal with in the time available, reassure them that this is not a one-off opportunity and that they will be able to catch up in due course, ideally by having their own personal Freedom Appointment.

Most use The Steps video to guide people through the process because it does most of the work for you. The DVD version stops automatically in the right place. Start with prayer, and then explain how the session will work. Start The Steps video, which begins with some explanatory remarks about The Steps and the process they will be going through. Each Step will be explained and begun with group prayer. When the prayer and final instructions for the Step have finished, send people away to complete that section on their own. Wait until everybody has finished and has come back together and then continue.

You can also use the PowerPoint® presentation which has slides for all the prayers and declarations that are said together as well as an introduction to each Step. Start each Step with a brief explanation of what it is about, get everyone to say the opening prayers together and then allow them time alone with God to deal with the issues the Holy Spirit shows them. Below are some notes to guide you if you are leading without the video.

Notes For Taking A Group Through The Steps

These notes are written from the point of view of a group leader speaking to their group, and are meant to prompt you as you introduce each part of the process. They link to the slide presentation (images from the presentation are not shown — it will be obvious to you when to move the presentation on). You will find useful additional explanatory information in The Steps booklet itself.

If you are leading a group through The Steps yourself, it would be very helpful to watch The Steps video session first. Simply do what is modeled. Explain The Steps and then have the group pray together and out loud the prayer that begins each step. Then allow them to have time alone with God. The Steps are self-explanatory.

There is a useful summary of the things you will need to do starting on page 209.

Introduction

The third book in the FREEDOM IN CHRIST DISCIPLESHIP SERIES, *Break Free, Stay Free*, corresponds to Part C of the course. Read pages 56–98 for the material that relates to *The Steps To Freedom In Christ*.

The process is based on James 4:7: "Submit . . . to God, resist the devil, and he will flee from you." You will be asking the Holy Spirit to show you any footholds that the enemy has in your life through past sin. As he shows you, you will simply repent and renounce in order to take away the enemy's right to influence you.

Having submitted to God, at the end of the process you will command the enemy to leave your presence. Because you have dealt with the issues that the Holy Spirit has revealed to you, the enemy will have no option but to flee from you.

This is a kind and gentle process. You are in control and the outcome is in your hands. It's just between you and God. If you deal with everything the Holy Spirit shows you, at the end of the process you will be free in Christ.

Be aware, however, that the enemy will try to deceive you by giving you thoughts such as "This is not working," "I can't do this," or even "I've got to get out of here." If that happens to you, simply work out where the thought is coming from and tell the enemy to leave your presence. Ask for help if you need it.

On some steps you might have a lot to deal with; on others, not very much. It will be different for each person depending on their background. If you find that you have time left over, please spend that time praying for those who have a lot on that particular step: ask the Holy Spirit to keep revealing truth and ask God to prevent the enemy from interfering in the process. If on the other hand you find that you do not have enough time to complete a particular step, you can always come back to it later, either at home or in an individual Freedom Appointment. This is not a one-off process; you can come back to it at any time should you discover something else that needs to be dealt with. In fact we suggest that you consider going through The Steps regularly (perhaps once a year) as a form of spiritual check-up.

Step 1 — Counterfeit Versus Real

This step deals with false guidance you may have sought from occult practices, cults, non-Christian religions and any spiritual experience that was not of God.

You will simply say the prayer asking God to show you where there have been issues and then look through the lists provided and answer the questions to work out where you need to repent and renounce. The lists are not meant to be exhaustive but are simply a starting point.

Then say the prayer of renunciation for every item that the Lord has brought to mind — it is good to renounce out loud because the enemy cannot read your mind. You can mutter so that others do not hear.

If you are not sure whether you have already dealt with a particular issue, or if something comes to mind that you think has already been dealt with, then our advice is to deal with it now anyway. If it is not an issue, then you do no harm by renouncing it, but if it is an issue and you do not deal with it, you are leaving a potential foothold for the enemy.

Then consider the list of questions and specifically renounce any issue that you need to deal with. To renounce something is to turn your back on it, to refuse to have anything to do with it any longer, to say "no" to it.

Note Appendix A "Renouncing Satanic Worship" for those who have been involved — willingly or unwillingly — in Satanic rituals. We do not recommend that you go through this appendix in a group but only in a personal appointment.

Step 2 — Deception Versus Truth

In this step we are looking at ways in which we can be deceived in three areas:

- by the world

- by ourselves

- in defending ourselves wrongly

Remember that deception, by definition, feels like truth. As we go through this step, commit yourself to believe God's Word whether it feels true or not.

Step 3 — Bitterness Versus Forgiveness

Unforgiveness is Satan's primary scheme against us. It's important to spend time on this area to make sure that you have forgiven from the heart.

Remember that it is for your sake that you forgive, so that you can walk in freedom. By choosing to forgive you are not saying that what was done did not matter — it did — but you are simply handing the situation over to God and trusting Him to be the righteous judge who will avenge all wrongs.

Forgiving from the heart means being honest with God and yourself about how you feel. You will tell God how what was done to you made you feel. As you do that, keep a note of those feelings — they will probably reveal strongholds that you will need to do some work on later to ensure that Satan cannot get you to fall back into the same old ways of thinking.

We will say the Father God declaration together. This is really helpful to those whose own fathers have not been all they might have been, and merits ongoing study in future days and weeks.

Note Appendix B which contains some very useful guidelines for seeking the forgiveness of others.

[**Note to leaders:** One of the benefits of this process is that the Holy Spirit will make people aware of thought processes that are not in line with truth. In order for participants to stand in their freedom, it is essential that they commit themselves to believing what God says is true. We will come back to exactly how they can do that in Session 8 but the first step is helping them uncover their faulty thinking as they go through The Steps.

As the Holy Spirit brings them to mind during the session, encourage each person to write down ways they have been thinking that are not in line with truth. Use Step 3 (Forgiveness) in particular for this — as people use the formula, "I choose to forgive [name the person] for [what they did or failed to do], because it made me feel [share the painful feelings, for example, rejected, dirty, worthless, inferior]," suggest that they make a list of the things that they mention after "because it made me feel." These will often reveal strongholds and schemes that the enemy uses against them.

In the next session you will give participants a strategy for working on these strongholds. For many this is life-changing.

Step 4 — Rebellion Versus Submission

God sets up authorities for our protection and rebelling against them falls into the same category as witchcraft in terms of its seriousness (1 Samuel 15:23). Although this step does not usually take that long, it is important.

Being under authority is an act of faith. However, those that overstep the bounds of their authority do not have to be obeyed — you need only repent where you rebelled against authorities that were acting within their God-given boundaries.

Step 5 — Pride Versus Humility

This is another step that does not take very long but deals with a crucial issue.

Step 6 — Bondage Versus Freedom

This Step falls into three parts.

In the first part you will deal with sin-confess cycles. Saying sorry is not enough to end these. You need to confess what you did, submit to God, and then resist the devil.

In the second part you will deal with sexual sins: any sexual act outside marriage whether it was done willingly by you or not. You will ask God to break any sinful bond formed between you and other people.

The third part contains prayers for specific issues. Consider each one carefully — they may be more relevant to you than they appear at first sight. For example, if men have led a promiscuous life in the past, they might consider doing the Abortion Prayer simply to recognize the possible results of their lack of responsible behavior.

Note Appendices C and D for fear and anxiety. We recommend that most people do the appendix on fear, which is like a step in itself. It will help you uncover the lies behind the fears that you have, which you can then work on replacing with truth. The anxiety appendix is also very helpful — you can do these as "homework."

Step 7 — Curses Versus Blessings

In this step we are renouncing the sins of our ancestors. We are not guilty of their sins but if we do not choose to deal with them, they can have a negative effect on us.

The Holy Spirit may reveal things that we are totally unaware of — for example occult activity or adultery — or we may be prompted about family traits such as anger.

We will also take our stand against any satanic attacks that are directed toward us and our ministries.

Concluding Remarks

Close your eyes and be quiet for a minute [pause].

In your mind is it quiet? Is there a sense of peace?

You might feel on cloud nine right now — or you might just feel tired! Remember that the point of this process was not to get a good feeling but to claim your freedom in Christ. If you have honestly dealt with everything the Holy Spirit has shown you today, then you have claimed your freedom. Now you need to concentrate on walking in it.

The Holy Spirit may well show you more areas you need to deal with in the next few days, weeks, months, and years — but you now know what to do. Wherever you are, it's easy simply to renounce wrong things and move on.

Session 8 will equip you with strategies for walking in freedom and renewing your mind. In the meantime be prepared to put some effort into maintaining the freedom you have gained.

A really useful thing to do would be to make a list of the lies that you now realize that you have been believing. There is space in your Participant's Guide for this (on pages 201–204). These may have come out at any point during The Steps but Step 3 is often the main place: as you look at the things you wrote after "because it made me feel" you may well come across some lies. Look for repeated occurrences of the same word (but note that not everything you wrote there is necessarily a lie). You are looking for things such as "inadequate," "inferior," "useless," "dirty," "helpless," "hopeless," "evil" — none of those things is true of a child of the Living God.

Between now and the next session we recommend that you read out the list of Who I Am In Christ every day. You might also find the My Father God and the Twenty "Cans" Of Success lists helpful. In your Steps book there are some daily prayers to say (pages 24–25). You would also benefit from going through *Walking In Freedom*, a 21-day devotional book by Neil Anderson and Rich Miller specifically designed to help you renew your mind after going through The Steps.

We also recommend that you work through the two appendices in The Steps on overcoming fear (page 28) and overcoming anxiety (page 30). The appendix on fear will help you identify lies that you have been believing. We will look at how you can replace these with truth in the next session.

Please try not to miss the next session, which will help you consolidate your freedom and stand against Satan's schemes to get you back into bondage.

Outline For Taking A Group Through The Steps

The following outline is intended as a guide to help you lead a group through The Steps. It is essentially a checklist of the various things you will need to do so that you can keep track of the process rather than instructions on how to do them. You will not need it if you are using the video. The page numbers refer to *The Steps To Freedom In Christ* book published in 2017 by Bethany House in the USA and by Monarch in the UK.

Introduction

Explain the process and read together the prayer and declaration on page 4 of *The Steps To Freedom In Christ* booklet.

Introduce Step 1: Counterfeit Versus Real

Read the opening prayer on page 5 together.

Read the closing prayer on page 6 together ("Dear Heavenly Father, I confess that I have participated in . . .").

Go through the additional questions on page 6.

Point out Appendix A (page 26) on Renouncing Satanic Worship and suggest that people seek a personal Freedom Appointment if this is an issue that has affected them.

Introduce Step 2: Deception Versus Truth

Read the opening prayer on page 7 together.

Read together the Statements Of Truth (page 10).

Introduce Step 3: Bitterness Versus Forgiveness

Say together the opening prayer (page 11) and ask people to spend time simply writing a list of people that the Holy Spirit brings to mind — at this point they don't need to worry about why the people need forgiving; they should simply make a list of names that come to mind.

Emphasize briefly:

- **This is between you and God, not you and the person who hurt you.**

- **It is for your sake that you forgive.**

Explain the forgiveness prayer (page 12) and suggest that people keep a list of the "because it made me feel" items because these are likely to reveal strongholds that they can work on later.

Allow people to work through their list of names. If the time allotted is not long enough, emphasize that they can do more in their own time or when they have their own individual appointment.

Read together the My Father God statements on page 13.

Draw attention to Appendix B (page 27) on how to seek the forgiveness of others.

Introduce Step 4: Rebellion Versus Submission

Read the opening prayer on page 14 together.

Introduce Step 5: Pride Versus Humility

Read the opening prayer on page 15 together.

Introduce Step 6: Bondage Versus Freedom

Read the opening prayer together (page 16), explain that this step has three parts, and let people work through the first part.

Read the sexual sins prayer together at the top of page 17 and let people work through the second part of this step. Point out the prayer for those who have used pornography.

Read the prayer at the bottom of page 17 together to finish the second part of this step.

Point out the Special Prayers And Decisions For Specific Situations (pages 18–20) and allow people time to use the ones that they feel are appropriate to them.

Say the closing prayer together at the bottom of page 17.

Point out Appendices C and D (pages 28–31) on fear and anxiety and suggest people do them in their own time.

Introduce Step 7: Curses Versus Blessings

Say the opening prayer together (page 21).

Have people renounce out loud the things that the Holy Spirit has brought to mind.

Read together the Declaration (page 21) and the concluding prayer (page 22).

Ask people to be quiet for a minute and remain in an attitude of prayer. Then ask, "In your mind is it quiet? Is there a sense of peace?"

Make your concluding remarks. You will particularly want to let people know that they will learn a strategy for replacing lies with truth in Session 8.

Suggested Timetable For An Away Day

This is a suggested timetable for taking a group through Session 7 and *The Steps To Freedom In Christ* on an away day:

9:45	Welcome And Worship
10:10	The Steps To Freedom In Christ
	Introduction (15 minutes)
	Step 1 (30 minutes)
	Step 2 (30 minutes)
11:25	Break
11:40	Session 7: Forgiving From The Heart (Word section only)
12:20	The Steps To Freedom In Christ
	Step 3 (40 minutes — but can expand into lunchtime if required)
1:00	Lunch Break
2:00	The Steps To Freedom In Christ
	Step 4 (15 minutes)
	Step 5 (15 minutes)
	Step 6 (40 minutes)
	Step 7 (10 minutes)
3:20	Break
3:40	Worship
4:00	Concluding Remarks
4:15	Finish

Session 8

Renewing The Mind

Session 8: Renewing The Mind

FOCUS VERSE:

Romans 12:2: Do not conform to the pattern of this world, but be transformed by the renewing of your mind. Then you will be able to test and approve what God's will is — his good, pleasing and perfect will.

OBJECTIVE:

To understand that taking hold of — and living in — your freedom in Christ is not a one-off experience but needs to become a way of life, and to provide you with a strategy to continually renew your mind.

FOCUS TRUTH:

All of us have mental strongholds, ways of thinking that are not in line with God's truth. Our success in continuing to walk in freedom and grow in maturity depends on the extent to which we continue to renew our minds and train ourselves to distinguish good from evil.

POINTERS FOR LEADERS:

This is a very practical session designed to help people take personal responsibility to continue to walk in the freedom that they entered through *The Steps To Freedom In Christ*.

If you are doing this in small groups make sure you are able to spend significant time on the Reflection section at the end of the session. This consists of an exercise in which participants develop a "stronghold-buster." In our experience, those who really get the concept of stronghold-busting and make a commitment to do it, start to grow quickly as disciples whereas those who don't tend not to. It will be extremely useful if you can talk about stronghold-busting from personal experience. We encourage you to work one out for yourself and start it before you lead this session.

We suggest that, from this point on, you emphasise stronghold-busting and take every opportunity to encourage people to do it (without, of course, making it seem like a burden).

Throughout the session it is helpful to remind people that all Christians already have everything they need to live a godly life (2 Peter 1:3) and that we all need to learn to use what God has given us. Often this will take some effort and some determination.

The second question in Pause For Thought 2 contains a list of common lies people believe and asks participants to find Bible verses that show what is really true. Here are some that we found:

Unloved: Jeremiah 31:3; John 3:16; 1 John 4:10

Rejected: John 1:12; Romans 8:1; 1 Corinthians 9:19–20; Ephesians 1:11; 1 Thessalonians 1:4

Inadequate: Jeremiah 1:6–7; John 15:16; 2 Corinthians 12:9, Philippians 4:13

Hopeless: Ephesians 1:10–13; 1 Thessalonians 5:18; 1 Timothy 4:10

Stupid: Romans 12:2; 1 Corinthians 1:26–29, 1 Corinthians 2:16, James 1:5

THE APP:

There is a powerful Stronghold-Buster Builder on the app that enables people to construct their stronghold-buster and then set when they would like the app to alert them to do it.

SMALL GROUP TIMINGS:

Registered users of the course can download a spreadsheet with these timings. Simply enter your own start time, adjust the length of the various components as desired, and you will have a timed plan of your session.

SONGS:

The song from *Worship In Spirit And Truth* (see page 26) that has been written to accompany this session is *Butterfly* which expresses very well the struggle that we need to engage in if we want to see genuine transformation. See page 220 of the Participant's Guide for the lyrics and background info.

 # WELCOME

How did you find *The Steps To Freedom In Christ* process?

 # WORSHIP

Suggested theme: He has set me free!

Read the following passages:

"So Christ has truly set us free. Now make sure that you stay free, and don't get tied up again." (Galatians 5:1 NLT)

"I will walk in freedom, for I have devoted myself to Your commandments." (Psalm 119:45 NLT)

Suggest that each person spends a few minutes committing themselves to walk in the light of God's truth, and then personalizes these passages and reads them aloud to the person next to them: "Andy, Christ has truly set you free. . . ."

 # WORD

Ongoing Transformation

The accompanying material for this session is at the end of the third book in the FREEDOM IN CHRIST DISCIPLESHIP SERIES, *Break Free, Stay Free*, on pages 99–110.

We started the course by looking at who you now are: a holy one. We looked at the fact that faith is simply finding out from God's Word what is already true and then making a choice to believe it. We then considered the three enemies that try to keep us from knowing the truth — the world, the flesh, and the devil. Finally, if you did business with God during *The Steps To Freedom In Christ*, you've taken hold of the freedom that Jesus won for you.

▶ You became a brand new creation when you first turned to Jesus. But now the stage is set for you to be transformed further. When that word is used in the Bible it refers to the process through which a crawly, wormy caterpillar becomes a beautiful butterfly. It doesn't mean changed just a little bit — it means a really dramatic change.

How do you think that ongoing transformation happens? What do you need to do to experience it?

> Do not conform to the pattern of this world, but be transformed by the renewing of your mind. (Romans 12:2a).

Remember, the battle is for our minds. Our minds have been conditioned by the world, influenced by Satan the puppet master behind it. So we've developed a whole host of default beliefs and thought patterns that don't match up with God's Word. In other words, they are not actually true.

This dialogue takes place at a 50-year high school reunion:

▶ You were always the pretty one in class, Jane.

You thought I was pretty? You always ignored me!

▶ We weren't ignoring you. We were just too intimidated to speak to you!

▶ I've spent 50 years struggling with low self-esteem because I thought you were ignoring me!!

Ha ha! Isn't that silly!

▶ My entire personality has been formed around the wrong information!

Think about it — "My entire personality has been formed around the wrong information!" To a greater or lesser extent, that statement is true of every single one of us.

For much of our lives, our belief system has been shaped by our enemies. Isn't that sad? In other words, we've absorbed a whole load of lies and half-truths that really affect us. When we became Christians no one pressed a delete button up here [point to head]. We still have the same old default programming, those same old thought patterns, or what the Bible calls the flesh.

Taking hold of our freedom is essential, but is not enough. Now, we need to change that default thinking if we want to grow as disciples. We need to replace it with what is actually true. And the key to that is renewing our minds.

Strongholds

We touched briefly in Session 4 on the concept of a "stronghold." Let's look at the only place in the New Testament that the word appears, 2 Corinthians 10:3–5:

> For though we live in the world we do not wage war as the world does. The weapons we fight with are not the weapons of the world. On the contrary, they have divine power to demolish strongholds. We demolish arguments and every pretension that sets itself up against the knowledge of God, and we take every thought captive to make it obedient to Christ.

In the passage, Paul is clearly talking of something in the area of our thinking. He mentions **arguments** and every **pretension** that sets itself up against the true **knowledge** of God. He talks about taking every **thought** captive to make it obedient to Christ.

▶ The literal meaning of the word "stronghold" is a fortress, a strong defensive building. Have you ever seen a medieval castle up close? Not a Disney castle but the real thing. Now those are fortresses — solid rock buildings with few and small windows; surrounded by thicker walls, sometimes layers of wall after wall. The outer walls can be so thick you can drive a car on them! Impressive.

In this context a stronghold is a faulty belief that has been reinforced many times over a long period. It prevents you from knowing God and His ways. It's sitting there in your mind apparently strong and impenetrable — like a thick castle wall.

▶ Perhaps it started out right back in childhood when a little thought was planted in your mind by something that happened to you — maybe you were bullied, or worse — or someone said something negative about you: "You're useless," "You're a failure," "You're ugly," "It's all your fault."

Maybe the enemy lined up someone else at a different time who said or did the same thing. Since he knows your particular vulnerabilities, he ruthlessly tries to exploit them by lining up people or circumstances one after the other to give you the same wrong message.

The world then adds insult to injury with its constant bombardment of lies about what it means to be successful or happy or loved.

As it gets stronger and stronger, it becomes part of our default thinking and works itself out in our behavior. Then, whenever someone suggests we could go for a particular job or lead a small group at church, a tape plays in our mind, "I couldn't do that. I'm useless at that." We've believed it for so long it becomes part of our lives and we can't imagine it ever being any different.

A good definition of a stronghold is "a belief or habitual pattern of thinking that is not consistent with what God tells us is true."

▶ Feelings of inferiority, insecurity, and inadequacy are all strongholds. Because no child of God is inferior, insecure, or inadequate.

Is any child of God dirty or ugly? Absolutely not. It isn't true. It just **feels** true. It's a lie that's been reinforced so many times that it literally has a strong hold on you and causes you to think and act in ways that contradict God's Word.

Strongholds can have two faces: when we know what we should do but don't seem able to do it; and when we know we shouldn't do something but don't seem able to stop. So if that's how it feels, we're talking about strongholds getting in the way.

A little later we will introduce you to "stronghold-busting" which is a structured way of demolishing a stronghold.

Let me first share my experiences of using it.

[We hope that you might have your own story to share here. Failing that you could reference Nancy Maldonado's story below or show it on the video.]

I shared with you earlier my desert journey. My perspective on my circumstances was definitely changing, but as the weeks and months of tears went by my outlook on life continued to be gray — sometimes dark gray. So I asked God to show me what was behind it. And He did. He showed me that my outlook on life, since I was a girl, had always been some shade of gray, sometimes lighter, sometimes darker. And he called it discontent. So I set off with my stronghold-buster, which included Psalm 103:1–5:

> Praise the Lord, my soul; all my inmost being, praise his holy name.
>
> Praise the Lord, my soul, and forget not all his benefits —
>
> who forgives all your sins and heals all your diseases,
>
> who redeems your life from the pit
>
> and crowns you with love and compassion,
>
> who satisfies your desires with good things
>
> so that your youth is renewed like the eagle's.

Day after day I repeated it as soon as I woke up, before getting out of bed. Then again at night. On hard days I repeated it throughout the day. Some days I confess it felt phoney, "Yeah, right, remember all His benefits." Some days it was heartfelt. I stuck with it, and after six weeks or so, the gray cloud began to lift. Truly, "He satisfies my desires with good things." Life is now in color!

PAUSE FOR THOUGHT 1

OBJECTIVE:

TO UNDERSTAND THE CONCEPT OF "STRONGHOLDS."

▶ **QUESTIONS:**

"My entire personality has been formed around the wrong information." What do you think about the idea that for much of our lives, our belief system and how we think have been influenced and shaped by many lies and half-truths said over us?

"No child of God is inferior or inadequate." Discuss.

What practical ways can we consider to make us more aware of strongholds, and how they affect our lives?

How Strongholds Are Established

There are three ways that strongholds can be established in our minds:

YOU ARE HOPELESS!!!!

▶ **Our Environment**

We have already seen how we learn values and beliefs from the world we live in. It also can work at the micro-level in our home, school, or work environment.

Imagine you were raised in the home of an alcoholic and there are three boys in the family. As the father's problem continues to develop, it turns into domestic violence. When their father comes home drunk, the three boys develop different ways of coping. The oldest one feels he can stand up to his dad: "If you lay a hand on me, you'll regret it." The middle one learns a different way of coping with it: "Hi dad, can I get you something?" The third runs away and hides in his room. Twenty years later, the father is long gone and the three boys are adults. When each of them is confronted with a hostile situation, how do you think they will respond? The

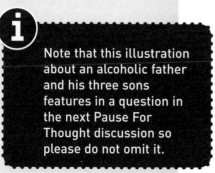

Note that this illustration about an alcoholic father and his three sons features in a question in the next Pause For Thought discussion so please do not omit it.

chances are the oldest one will fight, the middle one will accommodate, and the youngest one will run away.

We call them "strongholds" but psychologists might call them "defense mechanisms." They are ways of thinking and acting that have become deeply ingrained in the mind.

Traumatic Experiences

▶ It doesn't necessarily take something to be repeated over a long period of time to set up a stronghold. A one-time powerful traumatic experience can do it because of its intensity: a divorce, a rape, or a death in the home.

For example, if you were abused, you may come to see yourself as a victim: helpless; never able to stand up for yourself. At one time that may have been true but that's not true any more if you are a child of God.

Remember, it's not the traumatic experience itself that produces the stronghold. It's the lie we believe as a result of that traumatic experience. If one person is violently attacked, they may be able to shrug if off as an isolated incident. But for someone else, it might set up a lie in their mind that all men are dangerous. It's totally understandable but it's not true.

Whatever has happened to you in the past, you can go back to that traumatic event and process it again from the position of who you are now: a holy child of God.

No Christian, no matter how bad their past experiences, has to remain a victim. God doesn't change our past, He sets us free from it!

Giving In To Temptation

▶ Tempting thoughts that are not dealt with will immediately lead on to actions. Repeating the action will lead to a habit. Exercising the habit long enough will produce a stronghold.

Satan is actively trying to tempt you into the same sin time and time again, because he wants to set up strongholds in your life so that he can keep you going round in circles feeling hopeless.

The Bible is clear that there is a way out of every temptation. There is a short extra teaching film on the app to help you understand this and I recommend you take a look.

▶ If you drive a truck across a muddy field, it will create some ruts (grooves) in the field. If you drive the same way every day over a period of time, the ruts will get deeper and deeper and more noticeable. Eventually they will be so well established that you could let go of the steering wheel and the truck would drive itself.

That's fine as long as the ruts are going in the right direction. Strongholds are like ruts that are heading in the wrong direction.

If you don't intentionally change the direction, you are taking your hands off the steering wheel of your life and you are likely to end up somewhere you don't want to go.

The problem with strongholds is that they lead us to act on lies — false information — and cause our feelings to be out of line with reality. You may feel rejection when you are not actually being rejected. You may feel helpless to change when you are not helpless at all. For example, you may feel that you will never get out of a particular sin when in fact you have everything you need to walk away from it. If you live like this there's no way you can become a mature fruitful disciple.

Freedom And Maturity Are Not The Same

▶ The moment you turn to Jesus you are not expected to be instantly mature. When babies are born they drink milk for a while before they move on to solid food.

▶ But if babies keep acting like babies as they get older, they become less attractive!

Any Christian can become an old Christian — all it takes is time!

Any Christian can become a mature Christian — but many don't because they don't know how to deal with their strongholds.

But every Christian can tear these strongholds down.

PAUSE FOR THOUGHT 2

OBJECTIVE:

TO HELP PEOPLE BECOME AWARE OF STRONGHOLDS IN THEIR OWN LIFE AND TO REALIZE THAT THEY ARE BASED ON LIES.

▶ QUESTIONS:

Spend some time discussing the ways that strongholds are established. In what ways can you identify with the story of the alcoholic father and his three sons? Can you see any strongholds that have been established in your own life?

Look at this list of common lies that people come to believe about themselves: unloved, rejected, inadequate, hopeless, stupid. For each one, find a Bible verse to show that it cannot be true of any Christian.

"No Christian, no matter how bad their past experiences, has to remain a victim. God doesn't change our past, He sets us free from it!" Discuss.

Demolishing Strongholds

So how do you deal with these strongholds?

▶ Close Doors Open To The Enemy

In *The Steps To Freedom In Christ* you have taken away the footholds the enemy had in your life and that's a key reason that you can now demolish strongholds, even those that you may have tried time and again to deal with in the past but failed.

Take Personal Responsibility For The Whole Of Your Life

This is not about asking God or someone else to do something in order for us to get free or grow. You already have everything you need to live a godly life (2 Peter 1:3).

In the way God has set things up, some things are His responsibility and some things are our responsibility. If we don't do the things that He has given us to do, they simply won't get done.

▶ No one else can forgive for you. And no one else can choose to believe the truth for you.

In the passage we looked at, **we** fight, **we** demolish arguments and pretensions that set themselves up against truth, **we** take captive every thought. No one else can do it for us.

On the app you'll find a very useful extra teaching film about working out who is responsible for what.

Take Every Thought Captive

Paul tells us to "take every thought captive" (2 Corinthians 10:5). You can think of your mind as being like an airport and you are the air traffic controller. A lot of thoughts ask for permission to land. But you have complete control over which will land and which will be turned away.

We are in a battle between truth and lies. Every stronghold is an entrenched lie. The key to demolishing it is to uncover the lie behind it and then replace the lie with the truth.

[This story from Steve Goss is a good illustration of the need for "stronghold-busting" and is used throughout the next section. If you have a similar one of your own, that would be great. Otherwise you could simply relate Steve's story by way of illustration or show him telling the story on the video.]

When I first met Rachel, she was the epitome of a Christian who had lost all hope. She was covered in bandages from injuries that she had inflicted on herself. She had difficulty stringing two sentences together because of drug abuse. She had suffered from eating disorders for years. In fact it's a miracle she was alive at all. She had just been thrown out of a psychiatric hospital, a self-harm unit, for a week because she had self-harmed.

A local church took her in and wanted to work through this course and The Steps with her. At their request I was present when she went through The Steps. At the end, her face had completely changed. She had done real business with God and she broke into a beautiful smile and said "I'm free!"

But is that the end of the story? You see, it's a relatively quick straightforward process to take hold of your freedom. But staying free is another question.

Much as we encouraged you to do when you went through The Steps, I was keeping an ear open for faulty beliefs, lies that she believed. So at the end, I said to her, "It's great that you're free. Now it's important to ensure you stay free and to do that it's important to work out what lies you've been believing and take steps to renew your mind. It seems to me that the main thing you need to work on is the lie that you're dirty."

The big smile instantly vanished and she looked at me in anger and said, "That's not right at all!" "Oh," I said, "it's just that you seem to have mentioned feeling dirty a lot, especially in the forgiveness Step." "Yes," she said, "I am dirty. It's not a lie!"

Past abuse had taught Rachel to see herself and her body as dirty. Her subsequent anorexia, self-harm, and addictions were simply ways she used to try to cope with — blot out — those negative feelings.

Although by going through The Steps process she had kicked the enemy out of her life and was free, if she had been left at that point still believing the lie that she was dirty what would have happened? She would almost certainly have spiralled back down into her former coping mechanisms because the pain of feeling dirty would still be there.

I got her to have a look at some verses in the Bible, verses such as John 15:3: "You are already clean because of the word which I have spoken to you." And 1 Corinthians 6:11: "But you were washed, you were sanctified, you were justified in the name of the Lord Jesus Christ and by the Spirit of our God."

Then I said to Rachel, "So what are you going to choose to believe, what your past experiences are telling you or what God says about you?" She was quiet for a long time and then she said, "I suppose, what God says."

We then taught Rachel a tool we call "stronghold-busting," a way to renew your mind. We'll teach the same process to you in a minute but first let me tell you the end of Rachel's story. The next time they saw her at the hospital was a couple of months later when she walked in dressed in her nurse's uniform having been able to resume the career that she'd had to give up. She said "Hi!" and she looked so different, they had no idea who she was. She had been transformed through the renewing of her mind.

Be Transformed Through The Renewing Of Your Mind

So, what is "stronghold-busting"?

First of all, you need to determine the lie you have been believing (any way you are thinking that is not in line with what God says about you in the Bible). In doing this, ignore what you feel but commit yourself wholeheartedly to God's truth.

In Rachel's case the lie was "I am dirty."

It's helpful at this point to write down what effect believing the lie has had in your life. For Rachel, it led her to feeling bad about herself and then into anorexia and various addictions. Realizing the negative effects should spur us on to tear the stronghold down.

Then, find as many Bible verses as you can that state the truth and write them down. A good Bible app (or helpful pastor) will come in useful. If there are a lot of verses, pick the top seven or eight.

Write a declaration based on the formula:

> I renounce the lie that . . .

> I announce the truth that . . .

So Rachel would have said something like, "I renounce the lie that I am dirty. I announce the truth that I have been washed clean by Jesus, that I am a holy one."

Finally, read the Bible verses and say the declaration out loud every day for 40 days, all the time reminding yourself that God is truth and that if He has said it, it really is true for you.

Why 40 days? Psychologists tell us that it takes around six weeks to form or break a habit. Once you have dealt with any footholds of the enemy, a stronghold is simply a habitual way of thinking. Can you break a habit? Of course — but it takes some effort over a period of time.

Don't treat this as some kind of magic however! It's not the speaking out that will change you, and there's not some special formula that works for everyone. Don't get all religious either — if you miss a day or two, God still loves you! Just pick it up the next day and carry on.

Do persevere until you have completed a total of 40 days. In fact you may wish to go on longer and you will almost certainly want to come back and do it again at some point in the future.

It may sound easy but it's not — because the lie feels true to you. It's like watching a concrete wall being demolished. It withstands 10, then 15, then 30, then 35 blows with no visible sign of being weakened. That's how it can feel as you work through a stronghold-buster day after day. However, each day you renounce the lie and commit yourself to truth is making a difference.

4 SLIDES IN TOTAL

A wall might appear not to have been weakened right up to, say, ▶ 37 swings of a demolition ball. However, sooner or later, ▶ say on the 38th swing, a few small cracks will appear. On the next ▶ these cracks will get bigger until, finally, ▶ the wall completely collapses. Even though only the final three swings appear to have had an effect, without the previous 37, the wall would not have fallen.

There are some examples of completed stronghold-busters in your Participant's Guide. One of them is on comfort eating, another is on being drawn to internet porn. They are meant to help you get the idea, but if those issues are live ones for you it's much more effective if you work out your own stronghold-buster from scratch rather than taking a ready-made one.

Commit For The Long Term

▶ Forgetting what is behind and straining toward what is ahead, I press on toward the goal to win the prize for which God has called me heavenward in Christ Jesus. All of us, then, who are mature should take such a view of things (Philippians 3:13b–15a).

We need to take a long-term view. If we feel we have to do everything at once we are likely to start but not finish, to burn out and conclude that we have failed. If, however, we set out a long-term plan, we can deal with one area at a time and

make sure that we really have changed our thinking before moving on. In a year we could deal with eight or nine areas — and that would make a tremendous difference.

Every single one of us can leave here today knowing that absolutely nothing and no one can stop us becoming the people God wants us to be and accomplishing amazing things for Him. As long as we play our part and use the weapons He has already put in our hands.

REFLECTION

OBJECTIVE:

TO START WORK ON A STRONGHOLD-BUSTER.

LEADER'S NOTES: POINT OUT THAT THE APP HAS A VERY USEFUL "STRONGHOLD-BUSTER BUILDER."

▶ **REFLECTION**

Have you become aware of lies that you are prone to believe? What is the most significant one?

Use this time to create — or start to create — your very own stronghold-buster so that you can go on to demolish it. Use the guidelines on page 155 of your Participant's Guide and take note of the sample stronghold-busters on pages 159–161. There is space to create your own stronghold-busters on pages 162–167. You can also use the app.

 # WITNESS

Write down the two most important things you have learned in this course so far. How do you think you could explain them to a not-yet Christian?

 # IN THE COMING WEEK

Complete your stronghold-buster for the most significant lie you have uncovered and start going through it. You could use the Stronghold-Buster Builder on the app to create it and to alert you every day to go through it.

Stronghold-Busting

Work Out The Lie You Have Been Believing

This is any way you have learned to think that is not in line with what God says in the Bible. Ignore what you feel because, by definition, the lie will feel true.

Say What Effect Believing The Lie Has Had In Your Life

Imagine how different your life would be if you did not believe this. What would you be able to do that you currently don't do?

Find As Many Bible Verses As You Can That Say What Is Actually True And Write Them Down

If there are a lot of verses, pick the top seven or eight.

Write A Declaration

Base it on this formula: "I renounce the lie that . . . , I announce the truth that . . ."

If you prefer, you could use alternative language such as "I reject the lie that . . . , I embrace the truth that . . ." or "I say no to the lie that . . . , I say yes to the truth that . . ."

Read The Bible Verses And Say The Declaration Out Loud Every Day For 40 Days

Remember that for a long time, the verses and the declaration will not **feel** true. Remind yourself that God is the Truth and that if He has said it, it really is true. And it's not just true for other people, it's true for you!

You can use the app to remind you to make your declaration.

Stronghold-Buster Example 1

Taking Comfort In Food Rather Than God

The lie: that overeating brings lasting comfort.

Effects in my life: harmful to health; getting overweight; giving the enemy a foothold; stopping my growth to maturity.

Proverbs 25:28
Like a city whose walls are broken through is a person who lacks self-control.

Galatians 5:16
So I say, live by the Spirit, and you will not gratify the desires of the flesh.

Galatians 5:22–24
But the fruit of the Spirit is love, joy, peace, patience, kindness, goodness, faithfulness, gentleness and self-control. Against such things there is no law. Those who belong to Christ Jesus have crucified the flesh with its passions and desires.

2 Corinthians 1:3–4
Praise be to the God and Father of our Lord Jesus Christ, the Father of compassion and the God of all comfort, who comforts us in all our troubles, so that we can comfort those in any trouble with the comfort we ourselves have received from God.

Psalm 63:4–5
I will praise you as long as I live, and in your name I will lift up my hands. My soul will be satisfied as with the richest of foods; with singing lips my mouth will praise you.

Psalm 119:76
May your unfailing love be my comfort.

God, I renounce the lie that overeating brings lasting comfort. I announce the truth that You are the God of all comfort and that Your unfailing love is my only legitimate and real comfort. I affirm that I now live by the Spirit and do not have to gratify the desires of the flesh. Whenever I feel in need of comfort, instead of turning to foods I choose to praise You and be satisfied as with the richest of foods. Fill me afresh with Your Holy Spirit and live through me as I grow in self-control. Amen.

Tick off the days:

1	2	3	4	5	6	7	8	9	10	11	12
13	14	15	16	17	18	19	20	21	22	23	24
25	26	27	28	29	30	31	32	33	34	35	36
37	38	39	40								

Stronghold-Buster Example 2

Always Feeling Alone

The lie: that I am abandoned and forgotten.

Effects in my life: withdrawing from others; thinking people don't like me; seeming aloof; frightened.

Deuteronomy 31:6

Be strong and courageous. Do not be afraid or terrified because of them, for the LORD your God goes with you; he will never leave you nor forsake you.

Isaiah 46:4

Even to your old age and gray hairs I am he, I am he who will sustain you. I have made you and I will carry you; I will sustain you and I will rescue you.

Jeremiah 29:11

"For I know the plans I have for you," declares the LORD, "plans to prosper you and not to harm you, plans to give you hope and a future."

Romans 8:38–39

For I am convinced that neither death nor life, neither angels nor demons, neither the present nor the future, nor any powers, neither height nor depth, nor anything else in all creation, will be able to separate us from the love of God that is in Christ Jesus our Lord.

Dear Heavenly Father,

I say no to the lie that I am abandoned and forgotten and will be left on my own.

I say yes to the truth that You love me, that You have plans to give me a hope and a future and that absolutely nothing can separate me from Your love.

In Jesus' name. Amen.

Tick off the days:

1	2	3	4	5	6	7	8	9	10	11	12
13	14	15	16	17	18	19	20	21	22	23	24
25	26	27	28	29	30	31	32	33	34	35	36
37	38	39	40								

Stronghold-Buster Example 3

Feeling Irresistibly Drawn To Porn

The lie: that I cannot resist the temptation to look at porn.

Effects in my life: deep sense of shame; warped sexual feelings; unable to relate to other people as God intended; harmful to my marriage.

Romans 6:11–14
In the same way, count yourselves dead to sin but alive to God in Christ Jesus. Therefore do not let sin reign in your mortal body so that you obey its evil desires. Do not offer any part of yourself to sin as an instrument of wickedness, but rather offer yourselves to God as those who have been brought from death to life; and offer every part of yourself to him as an instrument of righteousness. For sin shall no longer be your master, because you are not under the law, but under grace.

1 Corinthians 6:19
Do you not know that your body is a temple of the Holy Spirit?

1 Corinthians 10:13
No temptation has overtaken you except what is common to mankind. And God is faithful; he will not let you be tempted beyond what you can bear. But when you are tempted, he will also provide a way out so that you can endure it.

Galatians 5:16
So I say, live by the Spirit, and you will not gratify the desires of the flesh.

Galatians 5:22–23a
But the fruit of the Spirit is love, joy, peace, patience, kindness, goodness, faithfulness, gentleness and self-control.

I reject the lie that I cannot resist the temptation to look at porn. I embrace the truth that God will always provide a way out when I am tempted and I will choose to take it. I announce the truth that if I live by the Spirit — and I choose to do that — I will not gratify the desires of the flesh and the fruit of the Spirit, including self-control, will grow in me. I count myself dead to sin and refuse to let sin reign in my body or be my master. Today and every day I give my body to God as a temple of the Holy Spirit to be used only for what honors Him. I declare that the power of sin is broken in me. I choose to submit completely to God and resist the devil who must flee from me now.

Tick off the days:

1	2	3	4	5	6	7	8	9	10	11	12
13	14	15	16	17	18	19	20	21	22	23	24
25	26	27	28	29	30	31	32	33	34	35	36
37	38	39	40								

Part D

GROWING AS DISCIPLES

Having taken hold of our freedom in Christ, we now need to concentrate on growing to maturity. In this final section we will learn the critical importance of relating well to others, and how to ensure that we stay on the path of becoming more and more like Jesus.

Session 9

Relating To Others

Session 9: Relating To Others

FOCUS VERSE:

Matthew 22:37–40: Jesus replied: "'Love the Lord your God with all your heart and with all your soul and with all your mind.' This is the first and greatest commandment. And the second is like it: 'Love your neighbor as yourself.' All the Law and the Prophets hang on these two commandments."

OBJECTIVE:

To understand our roles and responsibilities in relationships so that we can grow together in Christ and express true unity.

FOCUS TRUTH:

As disciples of Christ we will want to be part of the answer to Jesus' prayer that we will be one. In learning to relate well to others, we need to assume responsibility for our own character and seek to meet the needs of others, rather than the other way round.

POINTERS FOR LEADERS:

Jesus said we are to love the Lord our God with all our hearts, souls, and minds, and to love our neighbor as ourselves (Matthew 22:35–40). That sums up the whole Biblical message. We are called to fall in love with God and one another. The one thing He prayed for those who came after His original disciples is that we would be one so that the world may know that we are His disciples (John 17:20–21). This is a crucial topic.

We cannot have a righteous relationship with God if we do not have a righteous relationship with others. A right relationship with God should lead to a right relationship with our neighbors.

Satan often attacks our relationships. If we are to keep growing, it's essential that we understand how we are to relate to each other. Many will probably be laboring under misapprehensions about this. In this session we will help participants consider the balance between our rights and our responsibilities in relationships, the difference between judgment and discipline, accountability, and how we can meet the needs of others.

Remember to find a space to ask people how their stronghold-busters are going or to encourage them to get started if they have not already done so.

Note: At the end of this session, encourage people to complete the "What Do I Believe?" questionnaire on page 256 (page 184 of the Participant's Guide) before the next session. It takes just a couple of minutes and is important for the next session.

SMALL GROUP TIMINGS:

Welcome	9 minutes	9
Worship	12 minutes	21
Word part 1	11 minutes	32
Pause For Thought 1	20 minutes	52
Word part 2	13 minutes	65
Pause For Thought 2	20 minutes	85
Word part 3	20 minutes	105
Reflection	15 minutes	120

Registered users of the course can download a spreadsheet with these timings. Simply enter your own start time, adjust the length of the various components as desired and you will have a timed plan of your session.

SONGS:

The song from *Worship In Spirit And Truth* (see page 26) that has been written to accompany this session is *One*. See page 221 of the Participant's Guide for the lyrics and background info.

WELCOME

Have you ever done something that offended someone else without realizing at the time that you had caused offense? Tell the story briefly.

WORSHIP

Suggested theme: praising God for those people He has brought into our lives.

Read 1 John 3:16: "This is how we know what love is: Jesus Christ laid down his life for us. And we ought to lay down our lives for our brothers and sisters."

Invite people to say to each other or directly to Jesus what His love means to them. Then suggest that each person spends a short time committing all their relationships to God, making a commitment to love those people as Jesus loves us.

WORD

This session marks the start of the final section of the course in which we'll look at how we can set out into the rest of our lives as growing fruitful disciples who will make a real difference in the world. You'll find more information on this section in the fourth book in the FREEDOM IN CHRIST DISCIPLESHIP SERIES, *The You God Planned*. See pages 77–92 for the material that relates to this session.

Relating To Others

SESSION 9

Introduction

[Do you have a personal illustration of inadvertently causing offense to replace this one from Steve Goss?]

Habakkuk 3:17–18 has always been one of my favorite passages:

> Though the fig tree does not bud and there are no grapes on the vines, though the olive crop fails and the fields produce no food, though there are no sheep in the pen and no cattle in the stalls, yet I will rejoice in the LORD, I will be joyful in God my Savior.

When I was a teenager I used to quote this Bible reference in Christmas cards that I sent to other young people in my

Two women were talking. The first said, "My husband is like Moses. That man can wander about in the wilderness for 40 years, yet never once ask for directions!" The second replied, "Well, my husband is like God: I never see him and whenever he does anything, it's a miracle."

church group. My handwriting has never been a strong point and a lot of young people have never heard of a book of the Bible called "Habakkuk" so, I now know, my scrawled "Hab 3:17–18" was usually read as "Heb 3:17–18," slightly but significantly different.

Anyone who bothered looking up the passage they thought I was referring to in the book of Hebrews would find this:

> And with whom was he angry for forty years? Was it not with those who sinned, whose bodies fell in the desert? And to whom did God swear that they would never enter his rest if not to those who disobeyed? (Hebrews 3:17–18)

Apparently this had happened to a lot of people until one courageous young lady took me aside and asked me what sin I thought she had committed!

I have discovered that it's very easy to go through life giving offense to people and to be completely unaware of what you've done! In this session we're going to consider how God wants us to relate to other people and why that is so crucial.

The Importance Of Unity

Jesus' Prayer For You

If you could ask Jesus to go to the Father and ask Him one thing on your behalf, what would that one thing be?

▶   In the Gospels there is an occasion where Jesus prayed a prayer specifically for you and for me. It comes shortly before He went to the cross and He's been praying for His disciples. This is what He says next: "My prayer is not for them alone. I pray also for those who will believe in me through their message, [that's you and me — so what does He pray?] that all of them may be one, Father, just as you are in me and I am in you. May they also be in us so that the world may believe that you have sent me." (John 17:20–21)

So the one thing Jesus in His wisdom decided to pray for you and me and every other Christian is that we would be one, that we would be genuinely united at a heart level. The strange thing, if you think about it, is that it is not a prayer that God can answer. What, am I saying that God can't do anything He chooses?

Free Will Gives Us Responsibility

In His wisdom and humility God has given every human being personal responsibility for the choices we make.

▶ He could have chosen to make us like robots so that if we wanted to criticize what someone else believes or wanted to lash out against them in anger, we'd find that we just couldn't do it — the words wouldn't come out. But He hasn't done that.

▶ He gave us free will. We are completely free to choose not to be one and God does not overrule despite Jesus' prayer.

So why does Jesus pray this prayer at all? Surely He is sending a message to us. He is saying, "Look at this one thing I'm praying for you. This is absolutely the most important thing for you to focus on."

"But, Jesus, isn't preaching the Gospel more important than unity?" Look at why He says He wants us to be one: "So that the world may believe that you have sent me." It seems that our unity will in fact lead directly to people being saved.

Changing The "Spiritual Atmosphere"

How does this work? Well, why do you think more people in our community don't respond to the Gospel? You may rightly point out that techniques could be improved, that there aren't enough workers going into the harvest, or any number of other perfectly valid reasons.

▶ But with our Western worldview we tend to overlook clear verses like 2 Corinthians 4:4,

> The god of this age has blinded the minds of unbelievers, so that they cannot see the light of the gospel that displays the glory of Christ, who is the image of God.

Compare that with Psalm 133 which starts by saying: "How good and pleasant it is when God's people live together in unity!" and concludes, "For there the Lord bestows his blessing, even life forevermore."

There is more going on than each individual's response to God. Every community is a potential harvest field but the seeds need light in order to grow. Satan wants to keep it in darkness, but as the Church repents of its sin and works as

the one body that it actually is, he can't do that and light comes in. The result is that more people will respond to the Gospel as the workers go out into the harvest field.

It seems that repentance and unity can effect a positive change in what you might call "the spiritual atmosphere."

Let me give you a couple of illustrations.

▶   Imagine a scene of a huge field of wheat ready to harvested. In one corner is a man cutting the wheat with a scythe, a small hand-held blade. He works and works but makes hardly any impression. It's obvious that he can only harvest a tiny part of the potential of that field.

▶   Yet back in the farmyard is a brand new combine harvester, the sort that could do the whole job in a couple of hours. But it can't be used because it's in pieces — all the parts are scattered across the farmyard.

Here's the second illustration:

▶   Imagine a huge gushing waterfall coming over a cliff. A massive amount of water is flowing down.

▶   Yet the riverbed at the bottom is bone dry and, because no water is flowing out, the land at the bottom is a desert where nothing is growing. The reason there is no water is because there are deep fissures in the river bed and the water is simply disappearing down the cracks. If the cracks could be filled in, then the water would run down the riverbed and irrigate the land. And plants would begin to grow.

If God's people are not genuinely united we will only ever reach a tiny part of the harvest. And even though God is pouring out His Spirit upon us, the effects will be nowhere as great as they could be unless we are united. We can pray to the Lord to save people and pray for Him to send His Spirit upon us but He has **already** given us everything we need to do that. He is **already** pouring out His Spirit. But if we are not working together, in the way He has set things up there is nothing more He can do. He has given us specific responsibilities.

Paul's instruction to us is this:

> Make every effort to keep the unity of the Spirit through the bond of peace. There is one body and one Spirit, just as you were called to one hope when you were called; one Lord, one faith, one baptism; one God and Father of all, who is over all and through all and in all. (Ephesians 4:3–6)

This isn't easy! But it's crucial. In this session we want to look at how we can do our part to keep the unity of the Spirit whether that's in our own family, in our friendship group, in our own church fellowship, amongst the various ethnic groups in our area or in the wider church family where we live.

Understanding How God Comes To Us

"We love because he first loved us" (1 John 4:19). We give freely because we have received freely (Matthew 10:8). We are merciful because he has been merciful to us (Luke 6:36), and we forgive in the same way that Jesus has forgiven us (Ephesians 4:32).

If we truly understand how God comes to us and we go to others in the same way, we won't go far wrong.

Being Aware Of Our Own Weaknesses

When Isaiah was praying in the temple He saw a vision of God Himself "seated on a throne, high and exalted" (Isaiah 6:1). If that happened to you, would you immediately start thinking of the shortcomings of other people? No, you'd do what Isaiah did and cry out, "Woe to me! I am ruined! . . . For I am a man of unclean lips" (Isaiah 6:5).

In Luke 5 Peter has been fishing all night without success and Jesus says to him (verse 4), "Put out into deep water, and let down the nets for a catch." Peter obeys, goes back to the lake and starts pulling in fish after fish. He must have suddenly realized just who was in the boat with him. How did he respond? "Go away from me, Lord, I'm married to a sinful woman"? No! What Peter did say was, "I am a sinful man" (verse 8).

▶ When we see God for who He is, we don't become aware of the sin of others, but of our own sin. But when we are lukewarm in our relationship with God, we tend to overlook our own sin and see the sin of others and want to point it out to them.

PAUSE FOR THOUGHT 1

OBJECTIVE:

TO UNDERSTAND THE CRUCIAL IMPORTANCE OF GENUINE UNITY IN THE BODY OF CHRIST.

▶ **QUESTIONS:**

2 Corinthians 4:4 says that one reason people do not respond to the Gospel is that Satan has blinded their minds, and Psalm 133 says that where there is unity, God brings blessing. How do these verses help you understand why Jesus prayed that we would be one?

"If God's people are not genuinely united we will only ever reach a tiny part of the harvest." What are your thoughts on this statement?

"When we are lukewarm in our relationship with God, we tend to overlook our own sin and see the sin of others." Discuss this idea.

We Are Responsible For Our Own Character And Others' Needs

I don't know about you, but what comes naturally to me as a wife is to feel the responsibility to point out my husband's faults. With the best of intentions, of course, looking after his best interests. If I don't do it, who else will, right?

Is that the responsibility God has given me toward him and toward others?

> Who are you to judge someone else's servant? To their own master, servants stand or fall. And they will stand, for the Lord is able to make them stand. (Romans 14:4)

▶ Yes, each servant is responsible to his own master. It's not for us to judge someone else's character because it's none of our business. A growing disciple is someone who is becoming more and more like Jesus in character — no one else can do that for us and we can't do it for someone else.

I'm sure it doesn't happen to you, but I also get tired of having to remind my husband that he should be meeting my needs. Hey, give me some credit; at least I don't expect him to intuitively know what my needs are, like I did in our first years of marriage. I've given him a list!

Don't I have the right to expect this from others?

> Do nothing out of selfish ambition or vain conceit. Rather, in humility value others above yourselves, not looking to your own interests but each of you to the interests of the others. In your relationships with one another, have the same mindset as Christ Jesus. (Philippians 2:3–5)

▶ Ouch! So not only do I have no right to expect my needs to be met by others, I have a responsibility to meet their needs!

So, our responsibilities can be summed up as: developing our own character and meeting the needs of others.

Those of us who are mothers or fathers understand this well. We assume the role of serving and meeting our children's needs selflessly, and we assume it with joy. That is the Christ-like attitude. Can we extend that to all our relationships?

Focus On Responsibilities Rather Than Rights

In every relationship we have rights and we also have responsibilities. Where should we put the emphasis, on our responsibilities or on our rights?

Take a Christian marriage, for example. It's true that the Bible tells wives to submit to their husbands, and a husband might claim that as his right. But he is also given a corresponding responsibility: to love his wife as Christ loved the Church (and just think what that means). Which should he emphasize: his right or his responsibility?

A wife may nag her husband, because she thinks she has a right to expect him to be the spiritual head of the household. It's true that he has been given that calling by God. She on the other hand has been given a responsibility to love and respect her husband. Where should she put the emphasis, on her right or on her responsibility?

What about parents? Should they focus on their right to expect their children to be obedient? Or on their responsibility, to bring them up in the training and instruction of the Lord, and discipline them when they are disobedient?

Does being a member of a local church give you the right to criticize others or to tear apart someone's doctrine? Or does it give you a responsibility to submit to those in authority over you and relate to others with the same love and acceptance Jesus has shown you?

When we stand before Jesus at the end of our earthly lives, where will He put the emphasis? Will He say to me, "Nancy, did those guys give you everything they should have?" Or will He focus on how well I loved those He put in my care?

If we can learn to serve and love other people without expecting anything in return, it's liberating. Instead of being constantly disappointed by others, we will be truly and pleasantly surprised when people serve and love us.

Learning not to focus constantly on the failings of others and choosing to think well of them is so much easier in the long run than always feeling you've been let down and badly treated.

What About When Others Do Wrong?

So, we are to focus on our own character and responsibilities and think well of others and meet their needs.

But, what about when other people go wrong? Do we just ignore it?

▶ Think for a minute about the last time you went wrong yourself. How easy did you find it to apologize to someone you offended? Did you even apologize properly or did you say something like, "I'm sorry if what I said offended you, I didn't know you were so sensitive." What does that actually mean? In effect you're saying, "What I said was perfectly reasonable and you shouldn't have taken offense!" A proper apology takes responsibility for what you did: "I'm really sorry I spoke like that. I was wrong. Will you forgive me?" Most of us do eventually get to the point where we are honest about our failings but it can take a real struggle.

That's a very important thing to bear in mind when we consider alerting other people to their failings.

It's true that we can often see the issues in someone else's life much more clearly than they can. But Biblically, whose responsibility is it to be the conscience of another person and persuade them of their sin, which as we've seen, is no easy task? That's not your role, it's the role of the Holy Spirit (see John 16:8).

You can be sure that the Holy Spirit is on duty, not asleep, and is already gently convicting them. They're already engaged in an internal battle with Him. But the moment we try to intervene and point out the sin, they start to have that struggle with us instead of Him and it's not fun.

What, leave it to the Holy Spirit to tell them their failings? Yes. "But haven't I been given the ministry of condemnation?" No, God has given us the ministry of reconciliation (see 2 Corinthians 5:18).

"But doesn't love expose a multitude of sins?" No, Peter wrote, "Above all, love each other deeply, because love covers over a multitude of sins" (1 Peter 4:8).

We need to understand just how hard it is for most people to own up to sin. Which is harder to say, "I'm sorry," "I did it," or "Will you forgive me?"? It's "I did it."

If I caught my son throwing stones at my car, the conversation might go something like this:
"You just threw a stone at my car!"
"No I didn't."
"Look, I saw you with my own eyes."
"I'm sorry, Dad."

Has he confessed it yet? No.

"What are you sorry for?"
"Oh, you know . . ."
"What is it that you are sorry for?"
"Will you forgive me?"

Has he confessed it now? No.

"Of course I'll forgive you. What for?"
"Well, you know . . ."

Here's another conversation between two church members to illustrate further:

"Things aren't right between you and me at the moment. Will you forgive me?"
"Of course. What for?"
"You know . . . the things going on between you and me at the moment"
"What things?"
"Oh, forget it then!"

PAUSE FOR THOUGHT 2

OBJECTIVE:

TO LOOK IN MORE DEPTH AT WHAT IT MEANS PRACTICALLY TO RELATE TO OTHERS ACCORDING TO BIBLICAL PRINCIPLES THAT WILL FOSTER UNITY.

▶ **QUESTIONS:**

Spend some time discussing the difference between our rights and responsibilities in relation to others. You may like to consider this in relation to specific people in your life, for example, spouse, child, parent, work colleague, church leader, or neighbor.

"If we can learn to serve and love other people without expecting anything in return, it's liberating. Instead of being constantly disappointed by others, we will be truly and pleasantly surprised when people serve and love us." Do you agree with this? Why/why not?

What would it mean practically for you to focus on your own character and on the needs of others?

Discipline Yes, Judgment No

Nancy reminded us that it's the role of the Holy Spirit to convict people of their sin and Jesus was clear that we shouldn't judge others (Matthew 7:1).

However, Paul does talk about disciplining Christians who do wrong, for example:

> Brothers and sisters, if someone is caught in a sin, you who live by the Spirit should restore that person gently. (Galatians 6:1a)

How can we reconcile the fact that we are told not to judge, but we are to carry out discipline? Judgment and discipline are different things. Judgment is always related to **character**. However, discipline is always related to **behavior**.

▶ Discipline has to be based on something we have seen or heard. If we personally observe another Christian sinning, the Bible tells us to confront the person alone — the objective is to win them back to God.

If they don't repent, then we are to take two or three other witnesses who observed the same sin. If they still won't listen, then we are to tell the church (Matthew 18:15–17). The purpose of this process is not to condemn them, but to restore them to Jesus.

If there are no other witnesses, however, it's just your word against theirs. So the best thing to do is to leave it right there. God knows all about it and He will deal with it in His perfect wisdom. It is His job to bring conviction, not ours.

We are so often tempted to judge a person's character. Suppose I catch a fellow Christian telling an obvious lie, and I confront them. I could say, "You're a liar!" but that would be judgment because I have questioned their character. It would be much better to say, "Did you just say something that's not true?" That calls attention to their **behavior** not their **character**. Better still might be, "You're not a liar. So why did you just say something that's not true?" The truth is, they are a child of God who just acted out of character. The first expression implies that they have the character of a liar and indicates that they cannot change. The other two say nothing about their character. They simply call out a behavior issue.

If you point out someone's sinful behavior, you are giving them something they can work with. But calling somebody "a liar," "stupid," "clumsy," "proud," or "evil" is an attack on their character and no one can instantly change their character.

Discipline And Punishment Are Not The Same

There is also a major difference between discipline and punishment.

▶ Punishment is related to the Old Testament concept of paying evil for evil, "an eye for an eye." It looks backward to the past. God does not punish Christians. The punishment we all deserve fell on Christ.

Discipline, however, looks forward to the future. God may discipline us to in order to develop our character and so that we don't continue to make the same mistakes.

▶ A parent who does not discipline their child for refusing to share a cake is not helping that child. Hebrews 12:5–11 tells us that God's discipline is a proof of His love.

> No discipline seems pleasant at the time, but painful. Later on, however, it produces a harvest of righteousness and peace for those who have been trained by it. (Hebrews 12:11)

So the point of discipline is to help produce a harvest of righteousness and peace, to become more like Jesus.

▶ The parent will get their reward when they see that their child has learned to share. And, of course, the child will be a better person for having been disciplined even though it felt painful at the time.

It's wonderful that we don't have a God who punishes us. Instead we have a God who loves us so much, that He sometimes makes the hard choice of allowing us to go through tough circumstances in order to prepare us for the future and to help us become more and more like Jesus in character.

When We Are Attacked

What about when the shoe is on the other foot: how do we respond if someone attacks us? Should we be defensive? We certainly will be tempted to be.

▶ Look how Jesus reacted when people attacked Him:

> When they hurled their insults at him, he did not retaliate; when he suffered, he made no threats. Instead, he entrusted himself to him who judges justly. (1 Peter 2:23)

We have to learn to do the same. We don't need to defend ourselves any more. If you are wrong, you don't have a defense. If you are right, you don't need a defense. Christ is our defense. We need to entrust ourselves to God and leave the outcome with Him.

I remember Neil Anderson telling a story about when he was a pastor. A woman in his church made an appointment to see him. She wanted to discuss a list of the good and bad points about him that she had written. There were just two good points and a whole page of bad ones! When she read each point, he was tempted to defend himself, but he kept quiet. When she was finished, he said to her, "It must have taken a lot of courage to share that list with me. What do you suggest I do?" At that point she started crying and said, "Oh, it's not you, it's me!" That led to a positive discussion that helped her find a new, more suitable role in the church. Now what would have happened if he had defended himself? She would have been even more convinced that she was right.

If you can learn not to be defensive when someone exposes your character flaws or attacks your performance, you may have an opportunity to turn the situation around and minister to that person.

Nobody tears down another person from a position of strength. Those who are critical of others are either hurting or immature. If we're secure in our own identity in Christ, we can learn not to be defensive when people attack us.

Let me read a poem that expresses how we can be the person God created us to be no matter what other people and the world throw at us:

People are unreasonable, illogical, and self-centered.

Love them anyway.

If you do good, people will accuse you of selfish, ulterior motives.

Do good anyway.

If you are successful, you will win false friends and true enemies.

Succeed anyway.

The good you do today will be forgotten tomorrow.

Do good anyway.

Honesty and frankness make you vulnerable.

Be honest and frank anyway.

The biggest people with the biggest ideas can be shot down by the smallest people with the smallest minds.

Think big anyway.

People favor underdogs but follow only top dogs.

Fight for the underdog anyway.

What you spend years building may be destroyed overnight.

Build anyway.

People really need help, but may attack you if you help them.

Help people anyway.

Give the world the best you've got and you'll get kicked in the teeth.

Give the world the best you've got anyway.

▶ Paul says:

If it is possible, as far as it depends on you, live at peace with everyone. (Romans 12:18)

The crucial phrase is, "as far as it depends on you." Conflict is a normal part of life. It's nothing to be feared.

You won't always have happy, harmonious relationships with others. It's how you handle the conflict that matters.

So, are you willing to do the "as far as it depends on you" stuff? Are you ready to lay down your preferences and prejudices and come to others the way God comes to you? Are you willing to commit yourself to the unity of the Body of Christ, so that you can be part of the answer to Jesus' prayer?

If so, let's pray:

Dear Heavenly Father,

Thank You that You do not judge me and that Christ took the punishment that I deserved upon Himself so I would not have to. Thank You for Your love for me and that You discipline me to help me produce a harvest of righteousness and peace. Thank You that You help me learn to love others well even when they have done me wrong or when I have done others wrong. Thank You that in Christ I now have the opportunity to live at peace with everyone. I choose to commit to walk in unity with the body of Christ so that the world may know that You sent Jesus. In Jesus' name. Amen.

We have some homework for you this week!

At the beginning of the next session in your Participant's Guide is a questionnaire entitled "What Do I Believe?" It will be very helpful if you can complete it before next time. ▶

REFLECTION

OBJECTIVE:

TO CONSIDER PRACTICAL WAYS TO RELATE TO OTHERS. THIS SHOULD BE DONE INDIVIDUALLY.

▶ **REFLECTION**

Spend some time asking God for wisdom as to how best to relate to others in your life. First, consider who the main people in your life are. Then ask God for wisdom in how you can best relate to them. Is there a need to stop judging their character and instead offer loving discipline? Or to forgive them? How can you meet their needs?

 WITNESS

How can you be a good neighbor to those who live on your street? How could you get to know them better, so that you would have a better idea of what their needs are?

 IN THE COMING WEEK

Take some time to evaluate your faith by completing the "What Do I Believe?" questionnaire on page 184 of the Participant's Guide (and page 256 of this Leader's Guide).

Give some serious thought as to how you would complete the sentences.

What Do I Believe?

		Low				High
1.	How successful am I?	1	2	3	4	5

I would be more successful if _____

| 2. | How significant am I? | 1 | 2 | 3 | 4 | 5 |

I would be more significant if _____

| 3. | How fulfilled am I? | 1 | 2 | 3 | 4 | 5 |

I would be more fulfilled if _____

| 4. | How satisfied am I? | 1 | 2 | 3 | 4 | 5 |

I would be more satisfied if _____

| 5. | How happy am I? | 1 | 2 | 3 | 4 | 5 |

I would be happier if _____

| 6. | How much fun am I having? | 1 | 2 | 3 | 4 | 5 |

I would have more fun if _____

| 7. | How secure am I? | 1 | 2 | 3 | 4 | 5 |

I would be more secure if _____

| 8. | How peaceful am I? | 1 | 2 | 3 | 4 | 5 |

I would have more peace if _____

Session 10

FREEDOM IN CHRIST

What Next?

Session 10: What Next?

FOCUS VERSE:

1 Timothy 1:5: The goal of this command is love, which comes from a pure heart and a good conscience and a sincere faith.

OBJECTIVE:

To evaluate what we believe in the light of God's Word and make adjustments where necessary so that we can stay on the path of becoming more like Jesus.

FOCUS TRUTH:

Nothing and no one can keep us from being the person God created us to be, but if we want to be truly successful, fulfilled, satisfied, and so on, we need to uncover and throw out false beliefs about what those things mean and commit ourselves to believing the truth in the Bible.

POINTERS FOR LEADERS:

Many Christians are working toward goals that they believe to be God's goals but which are not. In Session 6 we looked at how negative emotions such as anger, anxiety, and depression can highlight that we are working toward a faulty life-goal and we said that we would come back to look at God's goal for our lives. In this session we come back to this topic and see that His goal for our lives is that we should become more and more like Jesus in character.

We will examine what we believe concerning eight aspects of our own personal lives. The purpose is to help participants understand how faith works in the nitty-gritty details of their daily lives.

People don't always believe what they think they believe, or what they say they believe. If, however, participants took the time to complete the eight sentences in the "What Do I Believe?" questionnaire (see previous session), their answers will show them what they really believe about those eight key areas. That is the faith by which they are living right now. This session will challenge them to reconsider what they believe and, where necessary, bring their beliefs into line with what is actually true according to God's Word. Note, if anyone has not completed the "What Do I Believe?" questionnaire, allow a couple of minutes at the start of the session for them to do so.

You will want to help people uncover lies that they can work on using the strategies that they have already learned. Remember to find a space to ask people how their stronghold-busters are going or to encourage them to get started if they have not already done so.

SMALL GROUP TIMINGS:

Welcome	9 minutes	9
Worship	12 minutes	21
Word part 1	11 minutes	32
Pause For Thought 1	20 minutes	52
Word part 2	13 minutes	65
Pause For Thought 2	20 minutes	85
Word part 3	20 minutes	105
Reflection	15 minutes	120

Registered users of the course can download a spreadsheet with these timings. Simply enter your own start time, adjust the length of the various components as desired, and you will have a timed plan of your session.

SONGS:

There are two songs from *Worship In Spirit And Truth* (see page 26) for this final session: *It's A Brave New World* and *My New Name*. See pages 222–223 of the Participant's Guide for the lyrics and background info.

 WELCOME

What would you like to do before the end of your life?

 WORSHIP

Suggested theme: He will be with us always.

Read aloud the following passages:

"God has said, 'Never will I leave you; never will I forsake you.' So we say with confidence, 'The Lord is my helper; I will not be afraid. What can mere mortals do to me?'" (Hebrews 13:5–6)

"The Lord will not reject his people; he will never forsake his inheritance." (Psalm 94:14)

"Jesus said 'I am with you always, to the very end of the age.'" (Matthew 28:20)

Remind people that we can never be alone or go anywhere at all without God being with us.

Suggest each person spends a little time reflecting on the truths of these verses.

WORD

The accompanying material for this session is in the fourth book in the FREEDOM IN CHRIST DISCIPLESHIP SERIES, *The You God Planned*, pages 13–55.

Making Freedom A Way Of Life

▶ Jesus said, "You did not choose me, but I chose you and appointed you so that you might go and produce fruit — fruit that will last." (John 15:16a)

We don't want this to be one of those courses that you enjoy but then as time passes the principles you learned just fade away. Our objective is that these principles become a part of your everyday life so that you will bear fruit that will **last**. What we've taught is very straightforward. There are three main points:

▶ 1. Know Who You Are In Jesus

You are, of course, a holy one who can come boldly into God's presence at any time.

▶ 2. Resolve Your Personal And Spiritual Issues

This is about repenting and getting back on track if you fall into a sin or have some other issue. Hopefully you now know how to go about this. We recommend that you use *The Steps To Freedom In Christ* on a regular basis, like you have a regular service for your car.

▶ 3. Be Transformed By The Renewing Of Your Mind

Stronghold-busting really works. As you keep building your spiritual muscles, remember it will feel like a complete waste of time but you will see progress as long as you keep working.

▶ The Road Ahead

In this session we want to consider where you're heading for the rest of your life. In your Participant's Guide there is a questionnaire entitled "What Do I Believe?" on page 184. If you haven't completed it yet, do it quickly now.

This survey will help you identify what you actually believe right now. Assuming that your basic needs for food, shelter, and safety are met, we're daily motivated by how we can be successful, significant, secure, and so on. How you answered those questions or the way you completed the sentences, "I would be more successful if," "I would be more significant if," reflects what you really believe.

Would it be acceptable, do you think, for a Christian to answer every question with a 5? If you feel uncomfortable about that, the chances are you may not see yourself in the way God does. Does God want you to be successful? Does He want you to feel secure? Well, He certainly hasn't called you to be insecure, insignificant, or a failure!

We're going to look at each of those eight areas.

Success Comes From Having The Right Goals

▶ We looked at life-goals back in Session 6. Success is all about whether you achieve your goals. So if you want to be successful in God's terms it's important to understand what His life-goal is for you.

Before we do that, let me ask you a very important question. If God wants something done, can it be done?

To put it another way, would God ever say, "I have something for you to do. I know you won't be able to do it, but just give it your best shot." That wouldn't be fair! It's like saying to your child, "I want you to mow the lawn. I know the mower doesn't work and there's no fuel. But try your best anyway."

Whatever life-goal God has for you, you can be sure that no circumstance and no person can stop you from achieving it. God loves you too much to give you something you couldn't do.

2 Peter 1:3–8 will show us the life-goal God has for each one of us.

Peter starts by telling us (in verse 3) that we already have "everything we need for life and godliness." Then he reminds us that we share in God's nature — we are holy through and through. That's a great starting point!

The passage goes on to show us God's goal for our lives. Let me read it to you from verse 5:

> For this very reason, make every effort to add to your faith goodness; and to goodness, knowledge; and to knowledge, self-control; and to self-control, perseverance; and to perseverance, godliness; and to godliness, brotherly kindness; and to brotherly kindness, love. For if you possess these qualities in increasing measure, they will keep you from being ineffective and unproductive in your knowledge of our Lord Jesus Christ.

Peter wants us to start with faith. Then we are to make every effort to build on our faith and add to it these characteristics: goodness, knowledge, self-control, perseverance, godliness, brotherly kindness, and love.

What we have here is a list of character qualities. This is where we begin to understand God's goal for our lives.

It's about building our character. His primary concern is not so much what we **do** but what we're **like**. Because what we **do** flows from who we **are**.

Who is the only person who has ever perfectly reflected the character qualities in that list? Jesus, of course.

The life-goal that God has for you could be defined like this: **To become more and more like Jesus in character**.

The great news is nobody and nothing on earth can keep you from being the person God planned. Except . . . **you**!

▶ We looked in Session 6 at how our emotions and specifically anger, anxiety, and depression are like that big red light on the dashboard of your car. Your emotions are a warning that you may have some unhealthy life-goals that depend on people or circumstances that you have no right or ability to control.

Think about the pastor whose life-goal was to reach the community for Christ, which is something that could be blocked by every person in the community. In the light of what we've just said, what if they made their life-goal: "to become the best pastor I can be"? The irony is that, as the pastor learns to adopt God's goal, and gets rid of a lot of anger, anxiety, and depression, they will become more and more like Jesus, and people will follow them and trust them more. Paradoxically they may end up reaching the community for Christ.

Remember the parent whose life-goal was to have a happy, harmonious Christian family? What if they made their goal, "to be the husband and dad or wife and mom that God wants me to be"? Wouldn't that greatly increase the chances of their having a happy, harmonious family?

Perhaps you think you don't have enough talents or intelligence to be the person God wants you to be. Or perhaps you think the circumstances you find yourself in prevent you from being the person God wants you to be. There is no mention in Peter's list of talents, intelligence, or positive circumstances. The fact is all believers are not given the same amount of talents: some have one talent, others have ten. We don't all have the same intelligence and our circumstances can be totally different. You might be thinking, "That's not fair! How can God do that?" Well, God is not

Here's a faith-stretching question: Do you believe you can be successful in business without ever going against the Word of God? Do you think it's possible to get elected to parliament or local government without ever going against the Word of God?

measuring you by those things! He's looking at your **character,** not your talent or your intelligence. It's equally possible for a Christian with one talent and a Christian with a ten talents to see their character grow from here [point somewhere low] to here [point somewhere high] to reach the life-goal God has for each one of us.

PAUSE FOR THOUGHT 1

OBJECTIVE:

HERE WE ARE LOOKING FOR PEOPLE TO SEE THAT ACHIEVING GOD'S GOAL FOR OUR LIVES IS ALL ABOUT OUR CHARACTER AND THAT IT REALLY IS TRUE THAT NOTHING CAN STOP US ACHIEVING IT EXCEPT OURSELVES.

▶ QUESTIONS:

Look at the questionnaire "What Do I Believe?" on page 184 (of the Participant's Guide). If you feel comfortable, share with the group where you put your lowest score and what you wrote for that question.

2 Peter 1:3 states that we have "everything we need for life and godliness." Discuss the idea that, whatever life-goal God has for you, no circumstance or person can prevent you from achieving it — except you.

"There is no mention in Peter's list of talents, intelligence, or positive circumstances." How does that change your thinking?

Significance Comes From Proper Use Of Time

How did you score yourself on significance?

▶ What's forgotten in time is of little significance. What's remembered for eternity is of great significance. Significance is about time.

The tragedy is that often we don't realize our own significance. We read this in Isaiah 49:14–16:

> But Zion said, "The Lᴏʀᴅ has forsaken me, the Lord has forgotten me."

This is how God responded:

> Can a mother forget the baby at her breast and have no compassion on the child she has borne? Though she may forget, I will not forget you! See, I have engraved you on the palms of my hands; your walls are ever before me.

God uses a graphic illustration — engraving them on the palm of His hands. Now, people write things on their hands to make sure they won't forget something. God has placed us somewhere where no matter how much time passes, we will still be there. That's how significant we are!

You may say, "All I do is help with the children at church." No, you are teaching truth to five-year-olds! What they choose to believe will have eternal consequences. That makes it very significant — quite apart from the significant service to their parents, releasing them to worship God and learn about Him.

If you want to increase the significance of what you do, focus your time on things that will make an eternal difference.

Fulfillment Comes From Serving Others

▶ What about fulfillment? You've probably noticed that there is so much self-help advice out there in books, blogs, magazines, and the internet about how to live a fulfilled life. Yet not that many people actually seem to be fulfilled!

Jesus must have been the most fulfilled person that ever walked the earth. Where did He get His sense of fulfillment from? He said, "My food . . . is to do the will of him who sent me and to finish his work" (John 4:34). Interestingly, it didn't come from trying to be fulfilled. It came when He didn't focus on Himself but on serving God the Father.

Peter wrote, "Each one should use whatever gift he has received to serve others, as faithful stewards of God's grace in its various forms" (1 Peter 4:10). God has made each of us unique. And each one of us has different gifts. Yet we are to use them to serve others — and when we do, paradoxically we become fulfilled.

Fulfillment comes when we "grow where we're planted" instead of looking for better soil or a prettier pot by changing the circumstances or people in our lives.

It's not by accident at all that God has sovereignly placed you in your family, on your street, with your friends, at your job, or at your college. [Use whichever of the following examples are applicable to you.] Of the nearly eight billion people in the world, I'm the only one who can be married to [spouse name]. I am parent to [child name] or child of [parent name]. You have a unique role as husband, wife, father, mother, or child in your family — no one can be that person better than you. God has specially planted you to serve Him by serving your family. That's your first and foremost calling.

And you're the only one who knows your neighbors as you do. You have a unique role as an ambassador for Christ where you work. These are your mission fields and you are the worker God has appointed for the harvest there.

God wants Christians who are becoming more and more like Jesus in every area of society. Your calling to business or industry or education or art or the health services, whatever it is, is a high and holy calling where you can make an eternal difference.

Don't try to be someone else. Be the unique person that God has made you to be.

God won't ask me why I wasn't Billy Graham or Mother Theresa. But He might ask me why I wasn't me!

Satisfaction Comes From Living A Quality Life

▶ How did you rate yourself on your level of satisfaction? I wonder what you thought would make you more satisfied — that's a clue to what you've come to believe will bring satisfaction.

Jesus said, "Blessed are those who hunger and thirst for righteousness, for they will be filled [in other words, satisfied]" (Matthew 5:6).

The truth is that nothing else really satisfies except living a righteous life. If you wrote something like, "I would be more satisfied if I worked harder for righteousness in my community," you are on the right path.

Think about something you purchased that left you dissatisfied. What was the issue? It generally has to do with quality. Satisfaction is an issue of quality. We achieve greater satisfaction from doing a few things well than from doing many things in a haphazard or hasty way. The key to personal satisfaction is not found in doing more things but in deepening commitment to quality in the things that we are already doing.

The same is true in relationships. If you are dissatisfied in your relationships, perhaps you have spread yourself too thin. We can learn from Jesus, who taught thousands and equipped 70 for ministry, but invested most of His time in twelve disciples. Out of those twelve, He selected three — Peter, James, and John — to be with Him at crucial times: on the Mount of Transfiguration, on the Mount of Olives, and in the Garden of Gethsemane. We all need the satisfaction that quality relationships bring.

It's interesting to note that rectifying the things which cause people to be dissatisfied does not bring satisfaction. You can see this in churches. People may complain that "It's too cold" or "too hot" or whatever. Fixing the problem does not bring satisfaction. The same people usually find something else to complain about. Satisfaction comes from living a righteous life and having meaningful relationships.

Happiness Comes From Wanting What We Have

▶ What about happiness? The world's concept of happiness is having what we want. Advertisements tell us that we need a flashier car, a better phone, another pair of shoes, or any number of items that are better, faster, or easier to use than what we already have. We become restless (don't we?) and start to want all the latest fashions, fads, and gadgets.

I'm usually content with what I have — until I walk into a shopping mall. Then suddenly it's "I need, I need!" "I want, I want!"

Never has there been a society where people have so many things yet are so unhappy. Why? Because things don't make us happy!

Paul wrote:

> Godliness with contentment is great gain. For we brought nothing into the world, and we can take nothing out of it. But if we have food and clothing, we will be content with that.
> (1 Timothy 6:6–8)

In other words, happiness isn't about having what you want. It's about wanting what you have. As long as you're focusing on what you don't have, or what you can't do, you'll be unhappy. But when you begin to appreciate what you already have, you'll be happy all your life.

Actually, you already have everything you need to make you happy forever. You have Jesus. You have eternal life. You are loved by a heavenly Father who has promised to supply all your needs. No wonder the Bible repeatedly commands us to be thankful (1 Thessalonians 5:18).

God brought the Israelites out of slavery with amazing miracles. He gave them clear guidance as to where to go (a pillar of cloud by day and a pillar of fire by night). He provided bread from heaven and water from rocks. And what did they do? They complained "That's not enough!"

We too are continually tempted to feel like we don't have enough. Christians change churches because the old one "wasn't meeting my needs." And how often do we hear complaints that a sermon or worship time "didn't minister to me."

Church isn't there to meet your needs! You are part of a church so that you can meet the needs of others and glorify God. In God's Kingdom, it's more blessed to give than to

PAUSE FOR THOUGHT 2

OBJECTIVE:

TO CONSIDER SOME OF THE ASPECTS ON THE "WHAT DO I BELIEVE?" QUESTIONNAIRE.

▶ QUESTIONS:

In what ways can we know significance by focusing our time on things that will make an eternal difference?

What causes us to want to be "someone else," rather than growing as the unique person God has made us to be?

Christians can often feel overwhelmed by the many things that demand their time. Discuss the idea that greater satisfaction comes from doing a few things well, rather than from doing many things in a haphazard or hasty way.

receive.

Fun Comes From Enjoying Life Moment-By-Moment

▶ You may think fun is a strange thing to include in this list. Yet of all people, a Christian who has been set free by Christ, and knows who they are and what they have in Him, should be having fun!

Often when you plan for fun, it leads to a let-down because it doesn't turn out as expected. Most fun happens spontaneously. Maybe it was a pillow fight with the kids or a ridiculous conversation with a friend — it just happened. That spontaneous fun comes when we throw off our inhibitions, when we stop worrying what other people will think of us. Paul wrote, "If I were still trying to please men, I would not be a servant of Christ" (Galatians 1:10).

Do you still find yourself thinking, "What will people say?" Those walking in freedom will respond, "Who cares what people say? I'm not playing to the crowd any longer. I'm playing for God alone."

▶ When David got the ark of the covenant back which had been stolen by the Philistines, he was so happy that he leapt and danced before the Lord in celebration. His wife, Michal, was embarrassed by his behavior and told him so in no uncertain terms. David said, "I will celebrate before the LORD. I will become even more undignified than this" (2 Samuel 6:21–22).

I have realized that the same embarrassment that often keeps me from having fun also keeps me from telling others about Jesus if I do not make a constant effort to throw it off.

[You may have your own illustration to replace this one from Steve Goss.]

When my father-in-law died, I had the privilege of doing the address at his funeral service. I started by telling his favorite joke. I was intrigued to see the looks on people's faces, especially those who were not regular churchgoers. They were (not unreasonably) expecting seriousness and "religion." There was quite a pause before they realized it was OK to laugh in church.

How have we managed to give people the impression that our wonderful, loving, creative God is a killjoy? When we are free, we can laugh. We don't need to keep up appearances.

Security Comes From Focusing On Eternal Values

▶ "I would be more secure if . . ." Actually, you can't possibly be more secure than you already are. Jesus said that no one can snatch us out of His hand (John 10:27–29). Paul declared that nothing can separate us from the love of God in Christ (Romans 8:35–39).

We can, however, feel insecure when we depend upon earthly things that we have no right or ability to control. It's all too easy to fall into the trap of working toward a goal of finding our security in money or some other worldly thing.

Every "thing" we now have we shall some day lose. Jim Elliot, a missionary who was murdered, said, "He is no fool to give up that which he cannot keep in order to gain that which he cannot lose."

Jim Elliot (1927 – 1955) wrote these words while still a student, at a time when he prayed for God's direction for his future as a missionary. Writing in his college journal, he also wrote: "Father, if Thou wilt let me go to South America to labor with Thee and to die . . . let me go soon." In 1955 he and four others were killed by Auca Indians on a beach of the Curaray River in Eastern Ecuador, where they were working as missionaries for Missionary Aviation Fellowship.

Peace Comes From Quieting The Inner Storm

▶ How can we have peace? Jesus is the Prince of Peace (Isaiah 9:6) and He said:

> My peace I give you. I do not give as the world gives. Do not let your hearts be troubled and do not be afraid. (John 14:27)

The peace of God is something we need to take hold of every day in our inner person. A lot of things may disrupt our external world because we can't control all of our circumstances and relationships. But we can control the inner world of our thoughts and emotions by allowing the peace of God to rule in our hearts on a daily basis. There may be chaos all around us, but God is bigger than any storm. Nothing will happen to you today that God and you cannot handle.

Difficulties Help Us Toward The Goal

▶ You may think that your past or present circumstances are so difficult that they stop you becoming the person God wants you to be, but actually the opposite is true. Paul says that we can rejoice in our sufferings because "we know that suffering produces perseverance; perseverance, character; and character, hope." (Romans 5:3–4)

James offered similar advice:

> Consider it pure joy, my brothers and sisters, whenever you face trials of many kinds, because you know that the testing of your faith produces perseverance. Let perseverance finish its work so that you may be mature and complete, not lacking anything. (James 1:2–4).

Persevering through difficulties develops our character and helps us fulfill our life-goal to become more and more like Jesus.

Can you share briefly from your own experience how difficult circumstances have helped you grow to become more like Jesus in character?

▶ I remember when my wife was really ill over a period of two years and couldn't really do much apart from sit in a chair. Our children were at a critical stage in their education and the ministry was growing. It was a tough time. One of my friends reminded me recently of something that I apparently said to him during that time: "If I don't come out of this changed for the better then it will have been a wasted opportunity." And I really believe that. It's in the tough times that our characters can really grow to become more like Jesus and in due course we'll see the fruit of that. I don't know anyone with any kind of significant ministry who hasn't persevered through great difficulties.

Defeated spouses say, "My marriage is hopeless," then try to solve the problem by changing partners. Others feel their jobs or churches are hopeless. So they move, only to discover that their new job or church is just as hopeless. What should you do? Can I give it to you straight? Hang in there and grow up! Those difficult situations may be helping you achieve God's goals for your life. There are legitimate times to change jobs or churches, but if we are just running from our own immaturity, it will follow us wherever we go.

We need occasional mountain-top experiences, but the fertile soil for growth is always down in the valleys, not on the mountain tops.

It's The First Day Of The Rest Of Your Life

▶ We're all going to die. One day you will lose everything you have, including your closest relationships, your qualifications, your possessions, and your money. Well, this is the last session of the course so I thought you might need cheering up!

Actually there is just one thing we won't lose: our relationship with Jesus and everything that comes with it.

That is why Paul can say, "For to me, to live is Christ and to die is gain" (Philippians 1:21). If you try putting anything else other than Christ in that verse, it doesn't work. For me to live is my career, to die is . . . loss. For me to live is my family, to die is . . . loss. For me to live is a successful Christian ministry, to die is . . . loss. But when the point of our life here and now is simply Jesus and becoming like Him, when we die it just gets better.

Today is the first day of the rest of your life! You can become everything God wants you to be. Regardless of your current circumstances.

▶ Whether or not you feel you are very far along the path of becoming more like Jesus, you can leave here in the sure knowledge that you are God's holy child and that He delights in you. He is intimately concerned in your life and has plans to give you a hope and a future (Jeremiah 29:11). Amazingly, you can leave here knowing that nothing and no one can prevent you from becoming the person God wants you to be.

Are you ready to adopt God's goal for your life, to become more and more like Jesus in character?

I want to finish by reading something written by someone (of unknown source) who decided to take God at His word:

I am part of the "Fellowship of the unashamed." I have Holy Spirit Power. The die has been cast. I've stepped over the line. The decision has been made. I am a disciple of His. I won't look back, let up, slow down, back away, or be still. My past is redeemed, my present makes sense, and my future is secure. I am finished and done with low living, sight walking, small planning, smooth knees, colorless dreams, tame visions, mundane talking, miserly giving, and dwarfed goals!

I no longer need pre-eminence, prosperity, position, promotions, plaudits, or popularity. I don't have to be right, first, top, recognized, praised, regarded, or rewarded. I now live by presence, lean by faith, love by patience, lift by prayer and labor by power.

My face is set, my gait is fast, my goal is heaven, my road is narrow, my way is rough, my companions few, my guide reliable, my mission clear. I cannot be bought, compromised, detoured, lured away, turned back, diluted, or delayed. I will not flinch in the face of sacrifice, hesitate in the presence of adversity, negotiate at the table of the enemy, ponder at the pool of popularity, or meander in the maze of mediocrity.

I won't give up, shut up, let up, or burn up till I've preached up, prayed up, paid up, stored up, and stayed up for the cause of Christ.

I am a disciple of Jesus. I must go till He comes, give till I drop, preach till all know, and work till He stops.

And when He comes to get His own, He'll have no problems recognizing me. My colors will be clear.

This statement has been circulated widely. Its author is unknown. Some say it was written by a young African pastor who was martyred for his faith. Others claim that it was composed at a Fellowship of Christian Athletes retreat in the USA in 1966. Whoever wrote it, it is a powerful statement of commitment to Christ. Be careful, however, to make sure that people understand that the activity mentioned in the statement comes from internal faith rather than a sense of "having to perform for God."

The rest of your life is ahead of you. It's exciting. You **can** become the person God wants you to be — nothing and no one can get in your way. Let's pray.

Lord God,

Thank You that we are saints, holy ones, because of what Jesus has done. Our goal is to become the people You have created us to be. Thank You that nothing and no one can stand in our way. It is for freedom that Christ has set us free.

We commit ourselves to truth, to being transformed by the renewing of our minds.

Please fill us with Your Holy Spirit and send us out in His power to become more and more like Jesus, to grow as disciples and to bear fruit.

Send us into the world to make disciples too, Lord.

Thank You that nothing can separate us from Your love. Thank You that You will always be with us.

We love You, Lord, and we choose to put You first. For me to live is Christ. To die is gain.

Amen. ▶

You might like to consider whether people might continue to meet together informally from time to time. It may be helpful to some to meet for encouragement, to compare notes on stronghold-busting and for continued fellowship.

FREEDOM IN CHRIST

REFLECTION

OBJECTIVE:

TO MAKE A COMMITMENT TO GOD'S LIFE-GOAL AND WORK OUT NEXT STEPS.

▶ REFLECTION

Discuss the idea that God's goal for your life is that you become more and more like Jesus in character. What would it look like for you to embrace that?

Spend some time in prayer committing to God's goal for your life and thanking Him that you can achieve it in His strength.

Spend some time thanking God for what He has shown and taught you through the course. Ask God what steps He wants you to take next.

 # WITNESS

Pick two or three of the eight areas we have considered. How would not-yet-Christians around you be affected if you were to put the principles into practice?

 # IN THE COMING WEEK

Work out which of the eight areas in the "What Do I Believe?" questionnaire are the most challenging for you. Spend some time reading the relevant passages for those areas in "God's Guidelines for the Walk of Faith" on page 200 of your Participant's Guide. You could use them to develop a stronghold-buster for the ongoing renewing of your mind.

God's Guidelines For The Walk Of Faith

Success comes from having the right goals

Success is accepting God's goal for our lives and by His grace becoming what He has called us to be (Joshua 1:7, 8; 2 Peter 1:3–10; 3 John 2).

Significance comes from proper use of time

What is forgotten in time is of little significance. What is remembered for eternity is of greatest significance (1 Corinthians 3:13; Acts 5:33–40; 1 Timothy 4:7, 8).

Fulfillment comes from serving others

Fulfillment is discovering our own uniqueness in Christ and using our gifts to build others up and glorify the Lord (2 Timothy 4:5; Romans 12:1–18; Matthew 25:14–30).

Satisfaction comes from living a quality life

Satisfaction is living righteously and seeking to raise the quality of our relationships and the things we do (Matthew 5:5; Proverbs 18:24; 2 Timothy 4:7).

Happiness comes from wanting what we have

Happiness is being thankful for what we do have, rather than focusing on what we don't have — because happy are the people who want what they have (Philippians 4:12; 1 Thessalonians 5:18; 1 Timothy 6:6–8)!

Fun comes from enjoying life moment by moment

The secret is to remove unbiblical hindrances such as keeping up appearances (2 Samuel 6:20–23; Galatians 1:10, 5:1; Romans 14:22).

Security comes from focusing on eternal values

Insecurity comes when we depend on things that will pass away rather than things that will last for ever (John 10:27–30; Romans 8:31–39; Ephesians 1:13, 14).

Peace comes from quieting the inner storm

The peace of God is internal, not external (Jeremiah 6:14; John 14:27; Philippians 4:6, 7; Isaiah 32:17).

A Strategy To Impact Your Community And Grow Your Church

Can We Help You Make Fruitful Disciples?

A church with growing, fruitful disciples of Jesus is a growing, fruitful church that is making a real difference in the community where God has placed it. A key question for church leaders is: how can I help our people become mature, fruitful disciples as quickly as possible so that they go out and make a real impact?

A fundamental part of the answer is to help them understand the principles that underlie this course:

1. Know who you are in Christ.

2. Ruthlessly close any doors you've opened to the enemy through past sin and don't open any more.

3. Renew your mind to the truth of God's Word (which is how you will be transformed).

Freedom In Christ Ministries has equipped hundreds of thousands of church leaders around the world to use this "identity-based discipleship" approach. As churches base their discipleship around these principles, they report not only changed individual lives but whole changed churches. When churches start to look less like hospitals full of those who are constantly struggling with their own issues and more like part of the Bride of Christ, they make an increasing impact on their community. People no longer stay at the "baby stage" year after year but quickly move to maturity, become outward-looking, and find the place where they can make a difference.

We encourage you to look at how you can take these principles deep into the life of your church so that you establish a solid foundation for years to come. On the following pages you will find some of our other small group resources that can help you do this. Some of them are based on this course but tailored to the communication styles of different groups such as young people and millennials. Others build on the *Freedom In Christ Course*. If you have a FreedomStream subscription (page 27) you can browse the video component of the courses at your leisure to get a good feel for how they could work in your situation.

But our heart is not to sell you resources. Our heart is to help church leaders develop a long-term whole-church discipleship strategy. We do not offer a "one size fits all" approach but love to help each church team identify their specific calling and gifting and select the tools that are appropriate for their own situation.

We have training courses and people on the ground who like nothing better than to discuss discipleship with church leaders. If you think we can help you in any way as you look to make fruitful disciples, please get in touch (page 285).

Disciple – FIC's Message For The Millennial Generation

Church leaders report that discipling those in their 20s and 30s is one of their biggest challenges. *Disciple* is a powerful tool to help you. It speaks the language of 20s and 30s and invites them to dive into the greatest story ever told: God's story. They will learn how to take hold of their freedom and discover their mandate.

- 10 sessions designed to run for approximately 90 minutes each
- Impactful starter films introduce the theme for each session
- Extra films (via the app) on topics including sex, the occult, and fear
- Chat and Reflect times allow teaching to take root
- App with extra teaching films, daily devotional, daily nuggets of extra teaching, and Stronghold–Buster Builder with reminders

"Thank you so much for caring enough to do this. You have no idea how much it means to us that you have taken the time to understand and help us overcome all the stuff that comes at us."

"You really get us and understand us, you don't just patronize us and talk down to us."

"God is doing incredible things in the young people at our church and I'm just grateful this course has been able to facilitate that."

"*Disciple* is really user-friendly. The young adults really engaged and there were definite lightbulb moments. The Freedom In Christ message really comes across but in a different way to the *Freedom In Christ Course*. It's been three months since we did it and everyone still refers to it."

Freedom In Christ For Young People

"Every young disciple is looking to engage with Jesus in a way that will change lives. This innovative, exciting course will help young people discover the truth of who they are in Christ and be set free to be all that God has made them as a result."

Mike Pilavachi, Founder & Director of Soul Survivor

"*Freedom In Christ* is a creative and relevant course for teenagers with the potential to produce a generation of fruitful young disciples."

Martin Saunders, Editor of *Youthwork* Magazine

The aim of *Freedom In Christ for Young People* is to set young people firmly on the way to becoming fruitful disciples who are sold out for God and will make a radical difference. Watch them change as they connect with the truth about who they are in Christ, become free from pressures that hold them back and learn to renew their thinking — no matter what their circumstances or background.

The course is based on the main *Freedom In Christ Course* and can be run alongside it. The emphasis is on relevant, interactive, multimedia based material tailored to meet the needs of 11–18-year-olds. It is split into two age ranges, 11–14 and 15–18. Each session is packed full of age-appropriate games, activities, discussion-starters, film clip suggestions, and talk slots.

There is also a video teaching component for each session. Presented by Nathan Iles and Kate John from Youth For Christ, the video material was shot entirely on location and is punchy, contemporary, and entertaining. It gets the main points across in segments of just two to four minutes (with around three segments per session).

The Grace Course

"For the first time in the decades that I've been a Christian, I'm suddenly 'getting' grace – it's amazing and it's shocking!"

"I realized that it's not about my performance – He just wants my heart."

"It was AMAZING! During the last session after we had finished nobody moved for what seemed like ages. When the silence eventually did break, people began to spontaneously share all that the course had meant to them. Testimonies to what the Lord had done just flowed out, some were life-changing."

"*The Grace Course* does a marvelous job in introducing the concept of grace in a simple, engaging, and, at times, even humorous way. It is short and to the point, taking an incredibly deep theological issue and making it understandable and practical."

If you don't first know God's love for you in your heart – not just your head – it's impossible for your life to be motivated by love for Him. Instead you are likely to end up motivated more by guilt or shame or fear or pride. You may be doing all the "right" things, believing all the right things, and saying all the right things but there will be precious little fruit.

- 6 sessions plus The Steps to Experiencing God's Grace
- Perfectly complements the *Freedom In Christ Course*
- Ideal for both small groups and Sunday teaching
- Present it yourself or use the DVD presentations
- Video testimonies illustrating the teaching points, practical exercises, times of listening to God and Pause For Thought times
- Works especially well as a course during Lent

Freed To Lead

"The *Freed to Lead* course has been the most amazing leadership development experience of my career, having been called to both marketplace and church leadership for over 20 years. It dispels worldly leadership myths and practices and provides Biblical foundations for Godly leadership. I wholeheartedly recommend this course for anyone who aspires or is currently called to Godly servant-hearted leadership in any arena."

"An outstanding course – inspirational and motivational, affirming and encouraging."

"It has reinforced my conviction that my identity is first and foremost in Christ, whatever leadership role I may hold."

Freed To Lead is a 10-week discipleship course for Christians who are called to leadership — whether in the marketplace, public service, the Church or any other context. It will transform your leadership, free you from drivenness and burnout, enable you to survive personal attacks, use conflict positively, and overcome other barriers to effective leadership.

Church leadership teams will benefit hugely from going through it together and can then roll it out to others in their church who are in leadership in any sphere or think they may be called to leadership in the future.

- 10–session course or retreat plus Steps to Freedom for Leaders
- Excellent follow–up to the *Freedom In Christ Course* and *The Grace Course*, but also stands alone
- Video testimonies and Pause For Thought discussion times
- Ideal for church leadership teams before rolling out across the church

Freedom In Christ In North America

FREEDOM IN CHRIST

Can We Help <u>You</u> Grow Fruitful Disciples?

Freedom In Christ Ministries (FICM) is an international, interdenominational organization that exists to equip the Church to make fruitful disciples so that it can advance Christ's kingdom more effectively. Established by Dr. Neil T. Anderson in the USA in 1989, we are now active in around 40 countries. Our primary emphasis is on equipping and enabling Christian leaders to put in place Biblical principles of discipleship that really work.

How can we help your church? We like nothing more than to come alongside leaders and help them put a discipleship strategy in place that will stand them in good stead for years to come. We have a network of trained people in place across North America ready and waiting to offer advice, guidance, and training. Please feel free to get in touch.

We offer:

- Free half-day events for pastors, church leaders, and ministry leaders to acquaint you with the message, method, and ministry of FICM

- Help to establish a "Community Freedom Ministry" (CFM) in your church

- Teaching and training for transformation via our CFM University, an online institute coupled with a face-to-face Practicum that provides the launching pad for those desiring to start a CFM

FICM-USA

FICM-USA was founded by Dr. Neil T. Anderson in 1989 while he was professor of practical theology at Talbot School of Theology, La Mirada, CA. Its headquarters are in Knoxville, TN, but it has Community Freedom Ministry Associates throughout the nation.

• www.ficm.org • info@ficm.org • 865-342-4000

FICM Canada

Freedom In Christ Canada has been successfully equipping church leaders since 1992. It is based in Regina, SK, but has Community Freedom Ministry Associates throughout the nation.

• www.ficm.ca • freedominchrist@sasktel.net • 306-546-2522

To find out about FICM in other countries, see www.FICMinternational.org

Become A Friend Of Freedom In Christ

Have you seen people's lives transformed through this course? Would you like to be involved in making the impact even greater? If you are excited about the effect this teaching can have on individuals, churches, and communities, you can be involved in making that impact even greater. We'd love to have you in the team!

Join our team of international supporters

Freedom In Christ Ministries International exists to equip the Church worldwide to make fruitful disciples. We rely heavily for financial support on people who have understood how important it is to give leaders the tools that will enable them to help people become fruitful disciples, not just converts, especially when we are opening up an office in a new country.

Typically your support will be used to:
- help us equip church leaders around the world
- help people overseas establish national Freedom In Christ offices
- translate the *Freedom In Christ Course* and our other material into other languages
- partner with other organizations worldwide to equip leaders
- develop further training and equipping resources

Join the team of supporters in your country

We are passionate about working with those who have themselves been touched by the Biblical message of freedom. Financial support enables us to develop new resources and get them into the hands of more church leaders. As a result many, many people are connecting with this life-changing message. There are always new projects — small and large — that don't happen unless there's funding for them.

To find out more about partnering with us please go to:

FICMinternational.org/friends

Thanks!

We are so grateful to the amazing team of people who have contributed to the production of the *Freedom In Christ Course*. We have listed some — but by no means all — below.

Written Material:

Monarch Books	Simon Cox
	Jenny Ward
Bethany House	Andy McGuire
Discussion questions	Matt and Caz Baines
Worship sections	Sue Lindsay
Proofreader	Sam Callard

Design:

Covers	Randy Benbow
Illustrations	Jon Smethurst

Video Material:

Executive Producer	Steve Goss
Presenters	Steve Goss
	Nancy Maldonado
	Daryl Fitzgerald
	Neil T. Anderson
Editors	David Moody
	Chiara Clarke
Post Production Manager	Malcolm Salt
Subtitles	Rob Davies
	Vic Ford

Main filming:

Producer	Leila Bagnall
Director	Mark Minors
Floor Manager	David Moody
Camera Operators	Ben Emery
	Luke Campbell
	Chiara Clarke
	Morgan Griffith
	Ben Thompson
Art Director	Joel Trindale
Set Design	Benn Price

Engineer / Racks	Peter Burch
Audio Engineer	Stephen Roe
Audio Assistant	Juan David Murillo
Lighting	Limelight
Autocue Operators	Emily Martin
	Rebekah Vance
Graphics Operator	Carla Henriet
Audience Manager	Josh Withers
Photographer	Becky Welford

Testimony filming:

UK Testimonies	Andrew Walkington
	David Moody
	Ben Emery
	Rob Davies
USA Testimonies	Alan Cummins
	Rich Miller
	Brian Westphalen
	Stacey Clayshulte
Australia Testimonies	Nathan Younghusband
	Shaun Collins
	Janet Collins
Kenya Testimonies	Henry Wamai
	Howard Ostendorff

Music:

Bumpers, stingers, and bed music composed by Wayne Tester and provided by Testricity Music Group.

Freedom In Christ App:

All-round genius	Daniel Upton
Content	Mike Brewer
	Sarah Brewer